OUTRAGE

ITAMAR MOSES

BACK BACK BACK
CELEBRITY ROW
OUTRAGE

ITAMAR MOSES is the author of *Bach at Leipzig* (Faber, 2005), *Yellowjackets*, *Completeness*, and *The Four of Us* (Faber, 2008); the musicals *Reality!* (with Gaby Alter) and *Fortress of Solitude* (with Michael Friedman and Daniel Aukin); and various short plays and one-acts. His work has appeared Off-Broadway and elsewhere in New York, at regional theaters across the country, and in Canada, and is published by Faber and Faber and Samuel French. He has received new play commissions from the McCarter Theatre, Playwrights Horizons, Berkeley Repertory Theatre, the Wilma Theater, South Coast Rep, Manhattan Theatre Club, and Lincoln Center. Moses holds an MFA in Dramatic Writing from NYU and has taught playwriting at Yale and NYU. He is a member of the Dramatists Guild and MCC Playwrights Coalition, and is a New York Theatre Workshop Usual Suspect. He was born in Berkeley, California, and now lives in Brooklyn.

ALSO BY ITAMAR MOSES

Bach at Leipzig

The Four of Us

BACK BACK BACK

CELEBRITY ROW

OUTRAGE

ITAMAR MOSES

FABER AND FABER, INC · An affiliate of Farrar, Straus and Giroux NEW YORK

FOR CHRIS COLEMAN: "NOT SINCE THE
SEVENTEENTH CENTURY . . ."

FABER AND FABER, INC.
An affiliate of Farrar, Straus and Giroux
18 West 18th Street, New York 10011

Copyright © 2009 by Itamar Moses
All rights reserved
Distributed in Canada by Douglas & McIntyre Ltd.
Printed in the United States of America
First edition, 2009

Library of Congress Cataloging-in-Publication Data
Moses, Itamar, 1977–
    [Plays. Selections]
    Back back back ; Celebrity row ; Outrage / Itamar Moses. — 1st ed.
        p.   cm.
    ISBN-13: 978-0-86547-905-0 (pbk. : alk. paper)
    ISBN-10: 0-86547-905-4 (pbk. : alk. paper)
    I. Moses, Itamar, 1977– Celebrity row.   II. Moses, Itamar, 1977– Outrage.
III. Title.

PS3613.O77889A6 2009
812'.6—dc22
                                                        2008053253

Designed by Gretchen Achilles

www.fsgbooks.com

1   3   5   7   9   10   8   6   4   2

CONTENTS

BACK BACK BACK

Back Back Back had its world premiere on September 19, 2008, at the Old Globe Theater in San Diego. Artistic Director: Darko Tresnjak. Executive Producer: Louis G. Spisto. Director: Davis McCallum. Set Designer: Lee Savage. Lighting Designer: Russell H. Champa. Sound and Music Designer: Paul Peterson. Costume Designer: Christal Weatherly. Production Designer: Shawn Sagady. Stage Managers: Moira Gleason, Tracy Skoczelas.

KENT   Brendan Griffin
RAUL   Joaquin Perez-Campbell
ADAM   Nick Mills

Back Back Back had its New York premiere on October 30, 2008, at the Manhattan Theater Club. Artistic Director: Lynne Meadow. Director: Daniel Aukin. Set and Costume Designer: David Zinn. Lighting Designer: David Weiner. Sound and Music Designers: Ryan Rumery, Daniel Baker.

KENT   Jeremy Davidson
RAUL   James Martinez
ADAM   Michael Mosley

CHARACTERS

KENT   A major-league baseball player, a slugger and an All-American golden-boy type.

RAUL   Another player, also a slugger, Hispanic.

ADAM   A third player, the wiry defensive virtuoso type.

SETTING

California, Texas, New England, the Midwest, Colorado, and Washington, D.C.

A NOTE ABOUT SCENE HEADINGS

The momentum of the play depends partly on the audience's being made aware, at the top of each scene, of how far we've moved in both time and space since the previous scene. What this means is somehow using the headings that appear in the text for each of the nine scenes as an explicit part of the transitions between them. The best way to do this, probably, is to use some type of scoreboard on which the headings can appear, and then remain visible, such that they gradually line up like the recorded outcomes of each of the nine innings of a game. But short of that, some way of conveying up front, at minimum, both what month and year we're in and our geographical location, as a sort of button on each transition, is desirable.

A NOTE ABOUT NUDITY

It is not necessary for the actor playing Raul to be completely naked at any point in Scene 3 or 4. Nudity is, obviously, an option, but is, at that point, needlessly distracting, in the opinion of the author.

SCENE 1

AUGUST 1984, SOUTHERN CALIFORNIA

A press room in the Olympic Village. KENT *is talking to the press. He is wearing a Team USA baseball uniform. Perhaps he is seated at a table, at a microphone.*

KENT: Well, geez. Um, honestly? We're not even thinking about that, we're not even paying attention to that. We're not here to talk about the past, the politics of it, or the behind-the-scenes drama, or the negative, we're just here to play our game. Because, first of all, it's just an honor and a privilege even just to be here, to be playing with this great bunch of guys, in a situation that really is an honor, against all these other countries, who are just being great to us, um, I mean, they're our guests, but you know what I mean, everybody's getting along just great, and we're glad to be playing well, which, I mean, nobody's exactly surprised, this is our sport, and our home turf, so I guess that we, you know, did come in with some expectations that we would do well, but everybody, Thrill, and Larkin, and everyone, we're obviously pretty pumped, pretty psyched, that we were able to meet those, you know, expectations, and we're pretty psyched, pretty pumped, to be out of the elimination rounds, and into the semis where it counts, though then again, it is, you know, we are still a demonstration sport, sure, or, what do they call it, like, an exhibition, or whatever, as opposed to like a full-on medal event, which, okay, they've got guys getting medals for how far they can throw a log, but baseball is somehow this big issue for some reason? I don't get it. (*Beat.*) Oh, but, I don't know, as to a boycott, or whatever, like I said, to be honest, nobody's giving it all that much thought. Definitely not here on the baseball club. That's not even cluttering up our minds, we're just gonna keep doing what we've been doing, keep being positive and try to win this thing. And, uh, not get a medal for it. (*Beat.*) It's South Korea in the semis, right? We're gonna kick their ass.

SCENE 2

OCTOBER 1988, SOUTHERN CALIFORNIA

*A weight room. RAUL is lying on the bench press. He is wearing
the workout clothes of a major league baseball team. He sits up.
Looks at his watch. Lies back down. Moments pass. ADAM enters,
wearing the uniform of the same team.*

ADAM: Hey.

RAUL: The fuck took you so long? (*He sits up. Sees who it is.*) Oh.
    Hey, Adam.

ADAM: Sorry, I, uh . . . Just. I thought there'd be . . .

(*A moment.* ADAM *turns to go.*)

RAUL: Hey, hey, no, it's no problem. I just . . . What's up, rook?

ADAM: Nothing.

RAUL (*with sudden enthusiasm*): Hey! Back to back to back, baby!
    Wooooo!

ADAM: Oh, hey, no—

RAUL: Oh yeah! Back to back to back, baby! Wooooo!

ADAM: They haven't even announced it yet. We don't even know.

RAUL: Yeah, no, you're right, you're right.

(*Beat.*)

ADAM: So—

RAUL: Back to back to back, baby! Wooooo!

ADAM: Stop it, Raul. Seriously.

RAUL: What's the *matter* with you, *Adam*.

ADAM: Nothing! Just. I was actually looking for a place to be alone. Get my head clear for the game.

RAUL: And you came to the weight room?

ADAM: Most of the guys on the team don't lift.

RAUL: That is true.

ADAM: Yeah.

RAUL: Their loss.

ADAM: I guess. (*Pause.*) But so. I just, uh . . . That's all.

RAUL: Okay.

(*Pause.* ADAM *doesn't go anywhere.*)

RAUL: Is there something I can do for you?

ADAM: Uh. No. No, no, no.

RAUL: Okay.

ADAM: Just. I don't feel great.

RAUL: Oh.

ADAM: I mean, it's nerves, it's just nerves, but I do feel kinda antsy. Anxious. But I'm fine. (*Pause.*) It's nerves. I feel a little nervous. And I'm like sweating a lot. And I'm having a hard time keeping my hands still. But I'm cool. (*Pause.*) And I feel maybe like I'm gonna pass out, or throw up, or first one and then the other, but like I don't know in what order. And I don't want Tony to see me like this because then he'll completely lose faith in me as a player.

RAUL: Um. Okay.

ADAM: Yeah. So.

RAUL: You had a great year. You'll be fine.

ADAM: Well, yeah, no, I know. I know. (*Pause.*) I didn't feel this way during the year, though, is the thing.

RAUL: Well, we've got a big game tonight.

ADAM: I know.

RAUL: Game one. And we're in their house. And they've got their ace on the hill. And we've gotta set the tone for the whole series, rook. Tonight.

ADAM: I know. I think that's probably what it is, too.

RAUL: No what I mean is you should get your head straight because we need you.

ADAM: Oh. (*Beat.*) I mean, yeah. I know.

RAUL: Because a big part of this game? Is *mental*. You know?

ADAM: I know that, Raul.

RAUL: I mean you gotta be *in* it. Up *here*.

ADAM: I know what you mean.

RAUL: Yeah, but so my point is, sure, you had a great season, but also you need to deliver when it counts. In the postseason. Which is now. So—

ADAM: Have *you* ever been in the postseason—?

RAUL: Let me answer your question with a question. Am I shaking and sweating and about to hurl like some kind of an amateur pussy? The answer to that question? Is no. I am calm. Fired up, even. How did I do in the ALCS, Adam? I kicked ass. And I cannot wait to step into the box against this guy tonight, this, uh . . . What's his name?

ADAM: Hershiser.

RAUL (*with faux innocence*): Right, but, uh. What Hershiser?

ADAM (*oblivious to the setup*): Orel. Orel Hershiser.

RAUL: Heh heh. I know.

ADAM: What? Oh.

RAUL (*overlapping*): Who names their kid *Orel*? I mean . . . ! That's just cruel! *Orel*.

ADAM: How would you feel if someone made fun of your name, Raul?

RAUL: I would tell them it's the Spanish variant of the Old Norse

Raoulfi, meaning "Counsel of the Wolf." (*Beat.*) As I was saying, I am not afraid of, uh, of Orel . . . Heh. Heh. Sorry. It's just—

ADAM: Please continue.

RAUL: Oh! Hey. That reminds me. And you'll like this. *This* you'll like. After the game? There's this *ridiculous* girl I want you to meet. *Ridiculous.* She's friends with this other chick I'm kind of involved with, or who I get, like, reinvolved with again whenever we come down to L.A.? And actually, I was *kind of* involved with both of them? But not really the second one. But I *can* tell you? That she really likes baseball players. Like. She really *really* likes them. Like. Really a *lot*.

ADAM (*Beat.*): That's fantastic, Raul. Thanks.

RAUL: The fuck is wrong with you?

ADAM: Just . . . ! (*Beat.*) Nothing. Nothing. That will really be great after the game.

RAUL: Yeah. You're right. It will.

ADAM: I . . . ! (*Beat.*) Maybe I should just tell Tony. See if he wants to sit me down.

RAUL: What?

ADAM: If, since, because I don't want to, like, hurt the team!

RAUL: Yeah, but that would be pretty humiliating for you to have to sit one out in a clutch situation. It would be hard to come back from that.

ADAM: Well, you know what? You, like, *riding* me about it? And, like, offering me your leftover *tail*? Isn't helping.

RAUL: Oh! Oh. You, uh . . . You want my help?

ADAM: I, uh . . . ! Why do you think I'm *talking* to you?

RAUL: If you wanted help, why didn't you say so, Adam?

ADAM: I'm a professional athlete. It can be hard for us to just ask.

RAUL: Well, you're in luck. Because I can help you. I mean. I can help you help yourself. In a big way. If, uh. If you're really sure that you want my help.

ADAM: Uh . . . (*Beat.*) Is there something in particular you're trying to say? Because if there is, then I'm not getting it.

(*Pause.*)

RAUL: Come here. Spot me for a minute.

(ADAM *goes over to the bench press.*)

ADAM: It's weird that you and Kent get away with this.
RAUL: Um. With what?
ADAM: Working out with weights.
RAUL: Oh.
ADAM: With lifting. Tony doesn't like it.
RAUL: That's true. He doesn't.
ADAM: He says it's bad for you.
RAUL: That's right. He does.
ADAM: But you guys just go ahead and do it anyway.
RAUL: Sure. I mean, he can make his demands, and yell, but the fuck is Tony gonna do, really? We're his stars. Without us he doesn't—

(KENT *enters, also wearing the team workout clothes.*)

KENT: Sorry. Media. (*Beat.*) Oh. Adam. Hey.
ADAM: Hey, Kent.

(ADAM *moves away from the bench press, clearing space for* KENT *to take up the spotting position.* RAUL *points among the three of them.*)

BACK BACK BACK

RAUL: Hey! Back to back to back, baby! Wooooo!

KENT: Oh, did they announce?

ADAM: No. No. They haven't even *voted*. Not until the season is over.

KENT: Right. That's what I thought.

RAUL: Well, yeah, but come on, Kent, I mean, you sort of get a general sense before that, right? I mean, my year, I pretty much knew a month before. And last year, same for you, right?

KENT: I guess. People are always kind of informally polling each other or whatever so there can be a vague idea of what's going to go down pretty far in advance sometimes, which, um—(*because* RAUL *has been chuckling*)—what is so funny, Raul?

RAUL: Heh. "Polling each other."

KENT: Yeah that's great.

ADAM: Well, whatever, now I'm probably not even gonna get it now and I'll feel extra stupid because you got me all pumped up and then it didn't happen.

RAUL: Not with that attitude it fucking won't.

ADAM: I'm a defensive player. We don't get the awards. I'm not complaining. It's just. That's the way that it is.

RAUL: See? This is what I'm talking about! This mentality you've got going mentally up there is just totally fucking with you!

KENT: Hey, lay off! Rook's trying to get focused.

RAUL: Rook is ready to pass out and vomit.

KENT: What?

RAUL: Tell him.

ADAM: Thanks, Raul, that's awesome.

KENT: You okay?

ADAM: Yeah, I'm fine, I'm fine, it's just nerves, I'm just a little nervous.

RAUL: And?

ADAM: And . . . ! Like sweaty and shaky and nauseous. And light-headed.

KENT: Wow. Maybe you should, uh, maybe you should tell Tony, have him sit you down, if—

RAUL: Great. That's great advice.

KENT: What? I'm just saying if the team—

RAUL: He has an opportunity to play on the big stage and he's spooked and you're instantly telling him to sit it out? Why don't you try for like a half a second to help him get it together?

KENT (*to* ADAM): Um. Okay. Have you tried taking some deep breaths?

RAUL: Deep breaths? That's your advice?

KENT: What.

RAUL: *I* offered to get him laid.

ADAM: Jesus. You guys? I'm *fine*.

KENT: Okay, but, seriously. Just, like, try to slow down your heart rate and get calm and slow your pulse and just take deep even breaths. Okay?

ADAM: Okay.

KENT (*to* RAUL): You ready to lift?

RAUL: Aw, already, really? Yeah, that'd be nice.

KENT: Like I said. Press wanted quotes.

(*During the following,* KENT *spots* RAUL *for a set.* ADAM *attempts to take deep breaths off to one side.*)

RAUL (*lifting*): I hate talking to those guys. It's a total mindfuck. It's like they already know what they want to say about everything, and then they just take whatever you say and make it, like, fit into what they were going to say already.

KENT: Don't talk while you're lifting.

RAUL (*lifting*): Oh, because you're the expert on conditioning now?

KENT: No, just—

RAUL (*lifting*): Because in fact, *Kent,* if I am lifting at a level that is comfortable for me I should be able to talk comfortably while I lift.

(RAUL *is finished with his set. He sits up. He stares at* KENT. *A beat.*)

KENT: You're right.

RAUL: I know I am.

KENT: Well, you are.

RAUL: Good. I know.

(KENT *and* RAUL *switch places.* KENT *does a set.* RAUL *spots him. Meanwhile:*)

RAUL: In fact, this debate about conditioning is not unrelated to what I was talking to you about just a moment ago, Adam.

ADAM: What? What.

RAUL: About how to help you help yourself in a way other than telling you to breathe or to somehow magically slow down your own pulse.

ADAM: Oh.

RAUL: Because you know what the secret to conditioning is? Or what the thing is that gets in people's way the most when they work out?

KENT (*lifting*): Hey—

RAUL (*to* KENT): Don't talk, Kent. (*To* ADAM.) Do you know?

ADAM: No.

RAUL: People think it's how much weight you can lift, or how many reps you can do, or something like that, but it's not, that's not what it is.

ADAM: It's not.

RAUL: No.

(KENT *has finished his set. He sits up.*)

KENT: Raul—

RAUL: Just a second, Kent. The biggest thing that gets in your way? Is recovery time. By which I mean the *time* that it takes you to *recover*.

KENT: He knows what recovery time means.

RAUL (*to* ADAM): Is this helping?

ADAM: Yes.

RAUL: Actual information that's not some Zen bullshit is helpful?

ADAM: Yeah.

RAUL (*to* KENT): So shut up, Kent.

KENT (*gesturing*): Yeah, but just, come on, could we—

(KENT *and* RAUL *switch places. During which:*)

RAUL: Like if you maybe do a set for a particular muscle group and you have to rest awhile before you do the next set? That's way more limiting than amount or reps or anything.

KENT: Are you gonna go or what?

RAUL: In a second. (*To* ADAM.) Or if you do a whole routine for a whole bunch of muscle groups and have to wait a day, two days, before you do that routine again. But if your recovery time was lower, then instead of rotating through, you know, chest, legs, back, arms, whatever, and you could just go arms, arms, arms . . . ! And that's the biggest obstacle. Which is something that not a lot of people know.

ADAM (*feeling unwell*): Ohhh.

RAUL: And the best thing you could do is find a way to eliminate that problem.

ADAM: Oh God, I don't feel good.

RAUL: And it turns out? That there is one.

ADAM: What is wrong with me?

RAUL: Hey. Do what you gotta do. The bathroom's right back there.

ADAM: No, I'm fine. I'm fine. (*Pause.*) Yeah. I think I'm fine. What were you saying? (*Pause.*) I'm fine. Go on.

RAUL: You sure?

ADAM: Yeah, just . . .

RAUL: I was saying—

ADAM: Oh fuck. Oh God.

(ADAM *runs off.*)

RAUL (*calling off, after him*): You do what you gotta do!

(KENT *is staring at* RAUL. RAUL *is oblivious. A moment.*)

RAUL: So it's, uh, is it my turn to—?

KENT: The hell are you doing?

RAUL: What?

KENT: "The best thing you could do is find a way to eliminate that problem"?

RAUL: Oh, come on, relax, okay?

KENT: I'm totally relaxed. I just think that you should leave him alone.

(*Beat.*)

ITAMAR MOSES

RAUL: What?

KENT: You heard what I said.

RAUL: Okay. I see. And . . . is that an order?

KENT: What? No.

RAUL: See, because here I was thinking that you were sitting over there just fucking *telling* me what I could and couldn't do—

KENT: Hey, come on—

RAUL: But now I see that I was wrong—which is good. That's good. Because I'd hate to think that just because you're everybody's can't-do-shit-wrong fucking golden boy over there, Tony in your fucking pocket, that that somehow means you can tell me what to do. I would hate to think *that*.

KENT: You don't have to be a dick about it.

RAUL: *You* don't have to be a fucking dick about it.

KENT: It's just, I think, getting him caught up in it. Might be a little misguided.

RAUL: What does that mean?

KENT: What. (*Beat.*) What "misguided"?

RAUL: Yeah.

KENT: It . . . ! There's risks, there's some risks, and I don't think you should bring him into it. I don't think you should do that to him.

RAUL: I'm not going to do anything *to* him. Kent. He asked me for help. And I'm going to make clear to him some options he may not have thought about.

KENT: Well, you have a way of talking about options that makes a guy feel like if he doesn't take those options, then that means that he's stupid.

RAUL: I think that anyone who doesn't take *this* option *is* stupid.

KENT: Um. Exactly.

RAUL (*with mock concern*): Whoa. Uh-oh. Hey now. Did I make *you* feel stupid?

BACK BACK BACK

KENT: What? Fuck you. No. *You* did not make *me* feel stupid.

RAUL: Oh! Now. What is *that* supposed to mean?

KENT: Nothing. Just. I think you should leave him alone.

RAUL: Huh.

KENT: That's all.

RAUL: Mmm. (*Beat.*) See, it's funny, because when I did the same thing for you, I didn't exactly hear you complain or even really have any doubts.

KENT: Okay, well, first of all, I don't do it like you do it.

RAUL: Uh. *What?*

KENT: Just, I'm just saying, I just do my thing, that I do, but I don't do your whole, like, big regimen, or routine, or whatever, the way *you* do it.

RAUL: Oh, so there's, like, *levels* of it now, that are okay or not okay—?

KENT: But whatever, apart from that, it makes *sense* for me.

RAUL: It does.

KENT: Yeah.

RAUL: But it doesn't for him.

KENT: No.

RAUL: No?

KENT: No. It does not make sense for him.

RAUL: Because you're the expert now.

KENT: No, I just—

RAUL: One year, one year and you're the expert, who should do it, who shouldn't, dispensing it from your locker, with your little lab coat on, hey, everybody come see Doctor K, he knows what amounts are okay and not okay, he knows what makes *sense*.

KENT (*overlapping, on "dispensing"*): No. No. No. Would you . . . ! I'm just saying I don't think that it's necessarily for everybody!

ITAMAR MOSES

And you're a leader and you're a star and he's gonna listen to
you!

RAUL: Well, he should listen to me because I'm the one that
knows what I'm talking about because I've thought about it
and figured it out for years, since I was in the minors, and I'm
not some guy who just got into it like a half a second ago
who's acting now like he invented it!

KENT: I'm not. I'm just . . . saying.

RAUL: Yeah. I heard you.

KENT: Okay. That's all. (*Beat.*) So, go, come on, it's—

RAUL: And what the fuck does that mean, it's not for everybody?

KENT: Uh. I just think that it's not.

RAUL: Why not?

KENT: I think it's pretty obvious.

RAUL: Pretend I'm a fucking moron.

KENT: Uh. Because sure, the extra power is great, and it's not a
problem if you play a position where it's okay to have that
bulk, but . . .

RAUL: But?

KENT: Adam's not camped out in deep right.

RAUL: I know that. He plays third base.

KENT: He . . . What? No he doesn't.

RAUL: Or, I mean—

KENT: Tony moved him.

RAUL: When?

KENT: Like six months ago!

RAUL: You know, it's hard to see who's where from back there, I—

KENT: He's playing second! He's right in front to you!

RAUL: Okay. So?

KENT: So he needs to be fast.

RAUL: Uh-huh.

KENT: And he needs to get the ball off quick. To me.

RAUL: Right.

KENT: And he hits for average. Not for power.

RAUL: Okay.

KENT: So . . .

RAUL: So. Sounds like you just listed a bunch of reasons why he *should* do it.

KENT: Raul—

RAUL: No, I mean, you're talking about he needs to be fast, um, you know what helps people be fast? Strong leg muscles.

KENT: Yeah, but—

RAUL: You know what helps people throw hard? Strong arms.

KENT: Okay, but—

RAUL: And you're talking about he hits for average, not for power, and that just makes me think, like, okay, but what if he could do both?

KENT: I mean, he needs to be nimble.

RAUL: See, now you're just making words *up*.

KENT: He needs to stretch and bend and throw across his body to make plays! He's a fucking defensive player!

RAUL (*overlapping*): No, I see.

KENT (*overlapping*): And he doesn't have the frame in any case, and you know it! You'll ruin his joints! You'll end his career!

RAUL: No, I get it, I see. 'Cause that would really fuck you up, huh? 'Cause you, you don't have to play defense, not really, just put your foot on the bag, stick out your arm, and hope that Adam, or Lance, or Terry, or whoever hits the bull's-eye, and that's good enough, and you're still a potential MVP. because you can park one every now and then. But—

KENT: Are *you* talking to *me* about defense? You can *barely* play right field, Raul.

RAUL: That's not—

ITAMAR MOSES

KENT: Somebody goes the opposite way, you can feel the fans hoping you don't lose it in the sun or give up running before the warning track!

RAUL: That's not the point.

KENT: And don't talk to me about playing first base until you've tried to backhand a short hop from third coming in six feet up the foul line.

RAUL: That's not. My point. Kent.

KENT: What's your point?

RAUL: 'Cause, sure, you can hurt yourself if you do it *wrong*. But if you do it right? Why *not* him? How about a defensive dynamo who's also a slugger? Explosive from a standstill because his calves and thighs are huge. Tossing bullets from wherever the fuck he plays because his arms are jacked. And meanwhile he's hitting balls out, hitting for extra bases, average through the roof because he's getting walked because he's so fucking dangerous in the box, and then whenever he gets on he's a threat to steal, and everybody's just *quaking* at this guy. Why don't you want that for him? "Hey, Adam, sit down for the good of the team!" So concerned. *Fuck* you. That kid scares the *hell* out of you. And you're just worried that if *I* take him on? Suddenly *that's* what everybody's looking for. And that. Was my fucking. Point.

(*There is a silence.* RAUL *stands. And begins to walk off.*)

KENT: Where are you going?

RAUL: I'm going to get our pregame vitamins.

KENT: Oh.

RAUL: Unless. Hm. Do you not want those now?

KENT: No. I mean yes. I do.

RAUL: So I can go get them?

BACK BACK BACK   23

KENT: Yes. But—

RAUL: What.

KENT: I mean, does it ever . . . ?

RAUL: *What.*

KENT: *Bother* you?

RAUL: What? Why.

KENT: I don't know! Um. Ethically?

(*Beat.*)

RAUL: What does that mean?

KENT: *Um.* That it's not exactly. I don't know. Fair? That it's.
    Kind of . . .

RAUL: What? That's it "kind of" what?

KENT: You know.

RAUL: No, I don't know, Kent, why don't you tell me?

KENT: I mean. Isn't it?

RAUL: Well, let me answer your question with a question. Does it
    bother you that you're taller than most guys, so your reach is
    farther and your stride is longer?

KENT: No.

RAUL: Does it bother you that you were born in a town that had
    some money so it had great baseball facilities?

KENT: No.

RAUL: Do you know where *I* was born?

KENT: I mean, not, no, not exactly—

RAUL: Because the way I see it? This is only way to *make* it fair.
    They are watching us *all the time*, guy. Is he hot? Is he
    slumping? We gonna hold on to him or cut him loose? For a
    few healthy years, Kent. And there's two ways it can go. Don't
    pan out and get traded like a chump? Or blow up like a

superstar, go free agent, and get paid. You want to play with a
handicap? You be my guest. But not me.

KENT: That's a great attitude, Raul.

RAUL: I know. I know it is.

KENT: This is not a team sport? Are you *nuts*? Who *cares* about
putting up huge numbers if you're on a losing club, Raul? But
also? You jackass? Free agency has some problems. Because
the owners are colluding. "What does that mean?" It means
they all get together and agree not to sign any free agents so
that we end up back on our old teams with capped salaries, so
I don't care if you *are* a superstar, Raul, because the fact is,
you need the union. Which is full of guys who may or may not
share your personal views on what's fair. So also? Don't call
them our "pregame vitamins." I know in your mind that
counts as being subtle? But it's not subtle. It's fucking stupid.
And anybody who heard you would know exactly what you
were talking about. And who *knows* what happens then.
(*Beat.*) And I am *not* scared of that fucking *kid*.

(*Pause.*)

RAUL: Kent?

KENT: Yeah.

RAUL: I know you're smarter than I am. I know that. Don't think I
don't. But I also think? That you're a little bit of a coward. And
a little bit of a snake. And so you can say whatever the fuck
you want about me. You go ahead and you say it. But I am not
either of those things.

(RAUL *exits. Silence.* KENT *is alone. He fumes for a moment. Then
he does a violent set on the bench press. During this,* ADAM
enters. He watches for a while. KENT *finishes.*)

ADAM: Should you really do that without anybody spotting you?

KENT: Oh. Hey. Feeling better?

ADAM: Yeah, that just . . . What the fuck is wrong with me?

KENT: Hey. Same thing used to happen to me.

ADAM: When you came up?

KENT: Oh, well, no, I mean, not really since like, uh, high school, but—

ADAM: Well, it doesn't happen to me.

KENT: You're a rookie. And this is game one of the World Series. It's okay.

ADAM: No. I mean. It's not the game.

KENT: It's okay if it's the game, Adam.

ADAM: It's not the game. It's a girl.

(*Beat.*)

KENT: What?

ADAM: It's, uh . . . You know what? Never mind.

KENT (*smiling*): You're upset about a girl?

ADAM: Oh, okay, ha-ha, fine, yes, it's hilarious—

KENT: No—!

ADAM: See? This is the exactly the kind of bullshit I figured I'd get from Raul, so I didn't say anything, but I thought that maybe with you, but no, here it is anyway, so that's just—

KENT (*overlapping*): No. No, no. Just. Hey! Just. That's really sweet.

ADAM: Oh yeah? It doesn't *feel* too sweet.

KENT: This is that girl you've been seeing?

ADAM: Yeah.

KENT: What happened, man?

ADAM: I don't . . . ! Nothing. Just. She broke up with me.

KENT: When?

ADAM: Like. The other day.

KENT: Just now?

ADAM: Yeah. Like. Right after we closed out the ALCS.

KENT: Man.

ADAM: Like. Right before I play in the World Series.

KENT: Yeah, no, it's not very considerate.

ADAM: And I don't know. Just. I felt . . . safe? Because like. Why would she break up with a guy who's about to play in the World Series? Like. Isn't it actually really cool to be dating a guy who's doing that? So like. You know. It wasn't really a moment at which I was feeling like that could even happen. And then. It did. And now I'm in really bad shape, like, I always, with this stuff, I go to this place where I'm, like, I'm all up in my head, like, if I try to go out with somebody else, instead I'm just thinking about what she would think about what I'm doing, or I wonder what *she's* doing, which is *worse*, so I'm in this cloud of, like, memories, or all like anxious about if I'm gonna hear about her, or run into her, and this is, yeah, you're right, a really really inconvenient time for that, so fuck, I'm sorry, this is lame and irrelevant, and I am such a loser, I apologize—

KENT (*overlapping*): No, hey, no no, not at all. I'm, hey, I'm glad you feel like you can talk to me about this stuff.

ADAM: I . . . ! (*Beat.*) Really? (*Beat.*) But I mean, what do *you* know? You've been with the same girl since college. You're married. You've got a kid.

KENT: That's true.

ADAM: Yeah. (*Beat.*) No, I mean, come on, tell me, what do you *know*? You've been with same girl since college, you're married, you've—

KENT: Oh! Oh, oh.

ADAM: Yeah.

KENT: Oh, uh. Huh. Well, okay, first of all, forget the athlete thing. Forget it. Because why would you want to be with someone where that was the most important thing to them? Because with anybody worthwhile? I don't get the impression that the things we think are important to them are the same things they think are important. And second of all . . . ? (*Beat.*) No, that's it. That's all I got.

ADAM: Well, thanks, even just . . . Because I couldn't . . . I mean, *you* know Raul.

KENT: Yes I do.

ADAM: On top of which? On top of his own way of dealing with people? It's like the guy's invincible with this stuff, he feels nothing, no matter what any girl ever does, he just bounces back, like, instantly, and then there's two more in line, for which he's always game.

KENT: He feels it. He just . . . handles it in his own way.

ADAM: Great. He'll probably date my ex. (*Beat. He feels unwell.*) Ohhh.

KENT: Hey, whoa—

ADAM: No, I'm cool. I'm cool. Do you want me to spot you?

KENT: Oh. Uh.

ADAM: What.

KENT: I just. I don't know if you're strong enough.

ADAM: Oh.

KENT: I just mean in your present condition.

ADAM: Oh. Yeah. No.

KENT: I just . . . Even just the outside chance of you dropping a barbell on my throat moments before game one—

ADAM: No. You're right. I should . . . (*He looks off.*) There's press out there?

KENT: Um. A, yes, a handful of the most dedicated baseball
writers figured they'd cover the World Series this year, yeah.

ADAM: No. I mean. They scare the hell out of me, anyway. I don't
want to go out there and, like, vomit. On them. On camera.

KENT: You won't.

ADAM: What are they gonna ask me?

KENT: What do they usually ask you?

ADAM: Nothing. They don't usually talk to me at all. Except, you
know. To ask about you or Raul.

KENT: Oh.

ADAM: I'm not good at talking to them like you are.

KENT: I'm not good at talking to them. Tony makes me.

ADAM: Well, you seem good at it.

KENT: All I've got is this one trick that I find helpful.

ADAM: Yeah? What's that?

KENT: Oh. Well. I mean. Um. I could tell you? But this is a very
special technique that is not to be trifled with. Okay?

ADAM: Um. Okay.

KENT: Seriously. If I pass this along to you, you must pledge
always to use your powers for good, instead of evil.

ADAM: Uh. Okay. Sure.

KENT: Okay. Ready? Here it is. Speak? In really complete
sentences.

(*Beat.*)

ADAM: What?

KENT: Speak in sentences that are much much more complete
than necessary.

ADAM: I don't get it.

KENT: Okay. I played for Team USA in '84. *Right* here, actually, all the games were in this park, which, first of all, was a real head trip for a bunch of amateurs, but it was also the first time I really had to do any of that stuff, be on TV, deal with media, any of that, on any kind of big scale, and this was, I don't know if you remember, but there was a *boycott*, like, because we didn't go to Moscow the time before, all the Soviet countries didn't come here, and President *Reagan's* there, and everyone's asking all these questions. And I'm shy. I'm a really shy person when it comes down to it. So that's also when I figured out this trick. Because basically? Anything these guys ask you, you can usually answer it in a word, or like a few words, but you could *also*? Pad that simple answer out to three, four, five times longer. And they think you're just being thorough or complete or something good? But what you're really doing is, you're using your answer as a way of taking the time you need. To get ready. For the next one. "Hey, Adam, how do you hope to play?" "Uhh. I want to play well." No. "What I'd *really* like is, I'd like to be able to contribute *and* to make a real contribution. Here on the ball club." They know what you want to contribute to. You don't have to say "ball club." Say it anyway. "Because I want to be able to give something back to all the great fans who have made me feel so welcome since I came here to play and to all my great teammates because, you know, we've got a great team here." They do know. They are professional sportswriters who cover your team for a living. Say it anyway. "Because, hey, we've got such a great bunch of guys here, Ricky, and Dave, and Big Dave"—see, because they also like it when you refer casually to the other people on the team by their first names, like you're all really tight; for some reason they love that—"and Raul, and of course Kent, it's great to have Kent to look up to, to have a real star and a real hero in the clubhouse to model

ITAMAR MOSES

yourself on." And, by the way, if you listen to Raul talk to them, this is the exact opposite of what he does, but fact is, *you're* the one who gets to set the pace, because they don't get to ask the next question whenever they want, they can only ask it when you stop talking. And you do not stop talking until you're ready. And it's not so you have time to dwell on what you said before, and it's not because you're planning, you *can't*, 'cause you don't know what's coming. It's taking the time. Just to stay in that one question till you are done with it. You hold that fucking moment till it's over. (*Pause.*) Do you understand what I'm saying to you?

ADAM: Yeah. (*Beat.*) Right. You're right. We got this.

KENT: Yes. See? Yes.

ADAM: The Dodgers? Please.

KENT: You read the scouting report on these guys?

ADAM: Yeah. We got this.

KENT: ALCS. Those guys were supposed to be so tough. What happened?

ADAM: We kicked ass.

KENT: So *these* clowns? Come on.

ADAM: No. You're right. We got them on offense. They're playing hurt. Gibson's out of the lineup, so we don't have to worry about that guy.

KENT: But even on pitching! Please. We took out *Clemens*. We *got* these guys.

ADAM: And hey! What kind of a name is *Orel Hershiser*?

KENT: Oh. Um. I don't know. It's, like, Mormon, I think, or—?

ADAM: No, just, it's kind of a ridiculous . . . name I'm . . . saying . . . (*Beat.*) Yeah. (*Beat.*) See, Kent, the thing about you is . . .

KENT: What.

ADAM: I mean, a lot of guys with your ability? They, uh . . . They're fucking pricks? But you, I mean, you've got this . . .

You don't feel like you have to be . . . You're, like. A good player? *And* nice. Which is. It's cool. (*Pause.*) So, wait, how'd you guys do?

KENT: What?

ADAM: At the Games.

KENT: Oh. Lost in the finals to Japan. So silver. Or. Woulda been.

ADAM: Right.

KENT: Hey. Do you want to try to do a set?

ADAM: What?

KENT: Just. Since you're here. Do you—?

(RAUL *enters. He is carrying a small black medical bag. A moment.*)

RAUL: Hey. Adam. Listen, uh—

KENT: We're sort of in the middle of a conversation, Raul.

RAUL: Well, I have something important to discuss with him.

KENT: Dude.

RAUL: What.

KENT: Well, I mean, just . . . I mean, if you . . .

RAUL: What.

(*Pause.* KENT *can't say anything in front of* ADAM.)

ADAM: What is it?

RAUL: I just wanted to tell you. That you got it.

ADAM: What? What. (*Pause.*) Who says.

RAUL: Tony.

ADAM: Tony said that?

RAUL: Well, like you said, they're not gonna announce till after the series, after the season, but the sense he's got, from talking to

the people who vote? Is it's you. You got it. Rookie of the
fucking Year.

ADAM: But I mean, he's just saying, like, the general sense he got.

RAUL: I heard the same way. Kent too.

ADAM: Huh.

RAUL: Back to back to back, baby! Wooooo!

ADAM: Wow. I mean. Wow.

KENT: That's great, Adam. That's really great. (*To* RAUL.) Anything
else?

RAUL: No. That's it.

KENT: Okay.

RAUL: Okay. (*Pause.*) After you.

ADAM: What are you guys doing?

RAUL: Grown-up stuff. You wouldn't understand.

ADAM: What?

KENT: He's joking. It's just. Our pregame . . . thing. It's a ritual. A
ritual thing. Uh. (*Beat.*) Congratulations, Adam. Seriously. I . . .

(*A moment.* KENT *goes.* RAUL *turns back to* ADAM.)

RAUL: Hey. (*Pause.*) Think how stupid. That fucking bitch. Is gonna
feel now.

(*Beat.*)

ADAM: What? (*Beat.*) You, uh . . . How did you . . . ?

(RAUL *goes.* ADAM *is alone. A silence.* ADAM *smiles.*)

ADAM: Man. (*Pause.*) Oh man. (*Pause.*) That feels good.

SCENE 3

APRIL 1994, TEXAS

A locker room. RAUL *is at his locker. He is now wearing a different team's uniform. He is talking to the press. During the following he undresses, and by the end of the speech he is wearing only a towel.*

RAUL: It doesn't look good. It does not look good. Because why? Because the atmosphere is poisoned already by behaviors on the part of ownership that have created a lot of mistrust even going into the thing. Which, it's complicated, so I don't expect everybody here to have total familiarity, but there was a problem with free agency where the owners were doing something called "colluding" that prevented a lot of guys from getting paid, somehow, and honestly, somebody shoulda done something sooner, somebody on the inside who could just be honest and break it open, instead of everybody looking the other way because they want to get their piece, or, if there's some code of silence amongst the owners, then I don't know, somebody else shoulda been in there, the government, somebody should have had someone in there, you know, wearing a wire, like they do. Don't they do that? Like, the FBI? Whatever. 'Cause instead we got robbed. And so the way we're even going in, I mean, when people feel they've been treated that way, you know, cheated, they're that much more likely just to get up and walk. So this is not the time for them to come at us talking about a salary cap, or trying to sneak up on that all subtle by attaching it to revenue sharing. And, whatever, I'm not one of those guys who's gonna tell you that they're a bunch of assholes either, excuse me, but I mean, take my owner, he's a good guy, a personable guy, so there are some good guys on the other side of the table, and maybe they'll come at us with respect. But if they just try to bulldoze 'cause they think we're not gonna strike, well, they're in for a surprise. Not that I'm *hoping* for it. I hope it doesn't happen. Because, just for me, personally, I'm really starting to find my groove here in Texas, you know? 'Cause I was never totally comfortable out West, never really got along too well with Tony, never felt totally appreciated, 'cause, like, no matter what I did, it was always more about some bullshit, or just some irrelevancy, excuse me, that was going on off the field, so I was actually even a little relieved when they traded me. So I've got a really good feeling about this year. I've got some great new kids to play with, Ivan and Raffy, to mentor, or whatnot. And it feels like, finally, it could be my time. To be known. For what I really am. Hold on a second. (*He yells off to one side:*) Do we seriously have to have the lady reporters in the locker room? I'm in a towel here.

SCENE 4

MAY 1995, NEW ENGLAND

Another locker room. RAUL *is at his locker. He is in a towel. He is talking to the press. During the following, he changes into yet another different team's uniform, and by the end of the speech he is fully dressed.*

RAUL: I mean, it's complicated. But what I wish? Is I really wish more of the top guys had been able to see, you know, the link between a salary cap and revenue sharing, by which I mean the practice of *sharing revenue*, which, combined with a *cap* on *salaries*, could have prevented this whole thing. But instead, we cut off the whole season and everybody in the whole country's feelings about the entire game of baseball are jeopardized because of just the greed that everybody exhibited through the whole thing. But you know what, guys? I think? A great player? Who is playing great? Could really help the game to bounce back from all this. But see, instead, with you guys it's, you know, it's Bad Boy Raul is in town, and what kind of trouble is he gonna get into on the club, and what kind of shenanigans is he going to be involved in, and once again that's the story, and frankly, I mean, I just, I find it kinda interesting why a guy like me, or Barry, is the bad guy all the time, while another guy might not be the focus, and why *that* might be, instead of, Oh, let's knock Raul again, because he had some stupid injuries he could have avoided, or got hit on the head by a fly ball one time, or was maybe caught five years ago for speeding, or whatever, crashing, because he was worked up from a fight he had with his wife at the time that, okay, maybe it got a little physical, but which was the whole reason he was speeding in the first place, and we've been divorced four years now, so leave it alone already, or who had a handgun *one time* in his car that the cops only even *found* because he left it on the seat after he accidentally, okay, *accidentally* parked in the handicapped spot at a hospital, which was the only reason they even looked, like it's not like I was even *holding* it! Because if that's the kind of thing that you guys want to write about again this year, instead of something positive? Then you guys go ahead and write about that. And I'll just know? In my heart? That that tells me a hell of a lot more about you guys than it says anything at all about me. Now if you'll excuse me I have a game to play.

SCENE 5

APRIL 1997, NORTHERN CALIFORNIA

A manager's office. KENT *is wearing nice street clothes and the team cap of his original team. He is talking on the phone.*

KENT: It's not what you think . . . it, it just, it's not what you think . . . I understand . . . I understand that . . . I understand that, believe me, I see why you think that, I see why it looks that way from your perspective, but . . . well, okay . . . not, I'm not, look, I'm not denying anything, how can . . . because I don't even know what you're . . . I . . . Of course . . . Of course I do . . . Of course I love you . . . yes . . . I love you too . . . I do . . . that has nothing to, and, and, it's not, in any case, it's not even—!

(The door opens. RAUL *enters. He is back in the workout clothes of his original team.* KENT *makes a "come on in" gesture but then holds up a "just a minute" finger.* RAUL *nods and looks around.* KENT *continues to talk on the phone.)*

KENT *(on the phone)*: Listen, I can't continue this right now . . . I know . . . I know . . . I, look, someone just came in, and I need to deal with it, and I cannot continue to have this conversation right now . . . okay . . . yes . . . I will . . . I will . . . I, listen, I said that I will . . . okay . . . I . . . Hello? . . . Hello?

*(*KENT *hangs up the phone. A moment. Looks up.)*

KENT: Hey!

RAUL: Hey.

KENT: Welcome back!

RAUL: Thanks. Thank you, man.

KENT: How are you doing?

RAUL: Fine. How are *you* doing?

KENT: Oh, uh. Fine. Good. Just. Fine. Feel good to be back?

RAUL: Uh. Sure. Yeah.

KENT: You get to meet everybody?

RAUL: What?

KENT: The new kids. Miguel, Jason—

RAUL: Oh. Uh. Yeah. They seem like good kids.

KENT: Yeah. They are. They are. (*Beat.*) What did you think when you got the call? Could you believe it?

RAUL: I don't know. I just figured Tony took whatever personal grudge he had with him when he left and the new guy just wants to win.

KENT: Oh, is that right?

RAUL: Well, let's see, how many championships since I left, it was, what was it . . . (*He pretends to count to a very high number on his fingers.*) Zero.

KENT: Yeah.

RAUL: How is the new skip?

KENT: Oh, good. He's good. (*Beat.*) I mean, it's a little . . .

RAUL: What.

KENT: No, nothing.

RAUL: He obviously likes you.

KENT: What?

RAUL: He let's you use his office.

KENT: Oh—

RAUL: What the hell are you doing in here?

KENT: Oh. Just. Privacy.

RAUL: For phone calls.

KENT: For instance.

RAUL: I do not have good memories of this room.

KENT: No?

RAUL: No. I was only ever in here for Tony to yell. Or, you know, trade me.

KENT: Well, let's put an end to that. I mean, hey, if you're lucky, this is where you end up, right?

RAUL: What?

KENT: You know, managing. Or upstairs even, front office, instead of, whatever. Broke. Or in the hospital. (*Pause.*) Close the door.

(*A moment.* RAUL *closes the door.*)

RAUL: Uh. "You cutting me from the team already, coach?"

KENT: Heh. Yeah, right.

RAUL: Right? The "close the door" conversation—

KENT: Yeah, no, uh, "This isn't easy for me to say, kid. You've been a great asset to the team. But—"

RAUL: "Oh, come on, coach, just gimme another chance!"

KENT: "You had plenty of chances. Plenty!"

(RAUL *chuckles.* KENT *joins in. They chuckle for a moment. Then, silence.*)

RAUL: Uh. What's up?

KENT: What did you notice about the new guys?

RAUL: What do you mean?

KENT: Anything that . . . caught your eye.

RAUL: Caught my eye? Uh. I don't think so.

KENT: You don't think so?

RAUL: Why do you ask?

KENT: You tell me.

RAUL: I don't even know what the fuck we're talking about, Kent.

KENT: You don't?

RAUL: No.

(*A moment.* KENT *lifts his shirt.* RAUL *looks him over and pats him down a little.*)

KENT: Okay?

RAUL: Just, you know—

KENT: Yeah, I do know, I know that you think you live in a movie. Okay?

RAUL: Okay. (*Pause.*) All right. So what have you been doing to those kids?

KENT: What am I *doing* to them?

RAUL: Yeah, because, and I assume this is what you're getting at, because, for example, Jason? Looks like he's filled with water.

KENT: Okay—

RAUL: So, yeah, man, what are you *doing* to them?

KENT: Okay, first of all, I haven't been doing anything *to* them. Second of all, whatever it is that's been *happening,* it's been according to a very specific regimen that is not something that I myself pioneered or developed.

RAUL: Oh, I see, so it's *my* fault.

KENT: It's your system.

RAUL: Whoa, okay—

KENT: No, I'm just, I'm saying now that you're *back*—

RAUL (*overlapping*): No, hold on, because if somebody, hell *yes,* it's mine, no *doubt,* but if a certain someone who doesn't really know exactly what he's doing is the one that's passing it along, without direct supervision, then that person is the one that is fucking it up.

KENT: I am not fucking anything up.

RAUL: Oh? Huh. See, because after I left here? Didn't you spend, like, the next *two seasons* hurt?

KENT: What?

RAUL: Once I was no longer watching over you, Kent. In '93. You barely played 'cause you were hurt. And '94.

KENT: There was a strike in '94.

RAUL: There was a strike and you were hurt.

KENT: I hurt my *foot*, it wasn't . . . What's your *point*?

RAUL: Just—

KENT: And weren't *you* hurt *all the time*? In Texas?

RAUL: Hey, okay—

KENT: *And* back East? *And* here? Aren't you just like a nonstop festival of time on the DL?

RAUL: That has nothing to do with anything. I've been that way since I was a kid.

KENT: Oh, so some injuries have to do with something, and some don't have to do with anything, and you're the expert on which is which?

RAUL: You don't have to . . . (*Beat.*) Look, I just want to hear you say it.

KENT: What. Say what.

RAUL: The words, the specific words, I want to hear you say the words.

KENT: What are you talking about?

RAUL: Here. I'll help you get started. "Raul, I need you . . . to . . ."

KENT: What.

RAUL: Say it. Out loud. Specifically. "Raul, I need you to . . ."

(*A moment.* KENT *looks at* RAUL *curiously. Then suspiciously. Then he grabs* RAUL *and pats him down, during which:*)

RAUL: Hey! What the fuck, man, the fuck are you doing—?

KENT (*overlapping*): Just, let me, just let me, come on—

RAUL (*overlapping*): Who the fuck is being paranoid now? Jesus.

(KENT *backs off. A moment.*)

KENT: Sorry.

RAUL: Yeah.

(*A moment.*)

KENT: I just—

RAUL: *What.*

KENT: I don't know! Just—

RAUL: There's a code, bitch. What do you think I am? There's a
   fucking code.

KENT: Oh, but you thought *I* was wired.

RAUL: Yeah. I did.

KENT: I see. Cool. (*Beat.*) Okay, so then what were you trying to
   get me to say?

RAUL: What do you think, man? That you need me. Because I
   know best. Because I'm the king. (*Beat.*) Dude, if I wanted to
   dime you out, I wouldn't be all stupid and blatant about it,
   come on! I'd sneak up on it

KENT: I, uh—

RAUL: I'd be subtle as a motherfucker.

KENT: I'm sure you would.

(*Pause.*)

RAUL: So?

KENT: So? What. (*Pause.*) Seriously? (*Pause.*) Um. Okay. Raul?

RAUL: Yeah.

KENT: I need you. Because you know best. Because you're the
king.

(*Beat.*)

RAUL: See, now I don't know—

KENT: Jesus Christ—

RAUL: No, because, I mean, doesn't it *bother* you? Isn't it a little,
uh—?

KENT (*overlapping*): Oh, I see. Okay. Yes. Ha-ha. It's hilarious.

RAUL: What was that? I couldn't hear you from up here on my
high horse.

KENT: See, I thought maybe we could just, but no, here we go—

RAUL: Well, come on, I mean, when I left, you were kind of on the
fence about it. Now you're Johnny Appleseed? What gives?

KENT: I don't know. Jason hits a ton. We haven't had a prospect in
the infield like Miguel since we traded Adam in '92, *before*
that, really, since Adam wasn't even Adam anymore by '92.
We've got some pitching. I don't know. This club could go all
the way.

(*Beat.*)

RAUL: Well, but it's even tougher now, you know that, right?

KENT: What do you mean? Testing's a joke, which, if that isn't the
tacit approval of management I don't know *what* is, so—

RAUL: No, I mean but *now* it's even against the *law*.

KENT: Oh, why, because Congress *said* so, like a half a second
ago? That's politics. *We're* the ones who actually have to go
out there every day, while they sit up there in Washington, and
it's all over the league now, *pitchers* even, so I'm gonna send

my boys, fucking *defenseless*, into *that*? No, sir. (*Pause.*) *What*, Raul, *what*, what *is* it?

(*Beat.*)

RAUL: "Since Adam wasn't even Adam anymore by '92."
KENT: What.
RAUL: What does that *mean*?
KENT: I don't know, just—
RAUL: You had a pretty shitty year yourself in '91 if you remember.
KENT: Okay.
RAUL: You hit .201. The only reason you didn't drop below the Mendoza Line is Tony sat you down the last game. To protect your *average*. To *protect* you.
KENT: Yes. I remember. So?
RAUL: So a lot of different factors go into trades.
KENT: Well, you ought to know.
RAUL: Heh. *Zing.* Okay. But what I mean is, *anybody* can slump, but *certain* guys get another chance, and then another chance, and so I just find it kind of interesting to hear you, of all people, knocking Adam like that, when maybe, if *somebody* had protected him when they had the chance, we wouldn't need Miguel *or* Jason, or whoever else, filling up his spot.
KENT: Adam is doing fine—
RAUL: Oh, *now* he's *fine*—
KENT: He is a major league baseball player.
RAUL: Yeah? Where.
KENT: I don't know. *Some*where. What do you—?
RAUL (*overlapping*): Somewhere?
KENT: What, now it's my job to keep *tabs*? He's not my *responsibility*.

RAUL: Oh, now he's *not* your responsibility.

KENT: Adam got *married*, he had a *kid*—

RAUL (*overlapping*): The, *what*? The fuck does *that* have to do with anything?

(*Beat.*)

KENT: I don't know what you want me to say. Are you gonna help me out or not?

(*The phone on the desk rings. It rings a second time.* KENT *picks up the receiver and hangs it up immediately. A moment.*)

RAUL: You want me running this, I'll run it, but you gotta follow my lead. I mean, I see how it is. You've been here nine years, Tony's gone, new guy's nice enough to let you kick him out of his office, but I don't want any prima donna crap. Not only are we gonna correct whatever you're doing, but I've picked up a thing or two. In my years. In the wilderness. We're gonna take this to a whole 'nother level. Okay?

KENT: Okay.

(RAUL *turns to go. Then hesitates.*)

RAUL: Did you *ask* for me?

KENT: What?

RAUL: Did you tell the new skip. To go for me.

KENT: I'm not management, Raul. I just go out and play.

(*A moment. Then* RAUL *opens the door.*)

RAUL: You want to work out? I'm going to do a back routine.

KENT: I did back already today.

RAUL: Want to do it again?

KENT: I already did three.

RAUL: Wanna spot me?

KENT: You don't need a spotter to do back.

RAUL: Hey. Uhhh. Okay.

(*A moment.* RAUL *goes. Leaves the door open.* KENT *goes to the door. Closes it. Goes back to the phone. Picks up the phone.*)

SCENE 6

JULY 1997, THE MIDWEST

A general manager's office. KENT *is wearing nice street clothes.*
He is talking to the press. During the following, he puts on the
cap, and perhaps also holds up the jersey, of a different team.

KENT: Geez. Well. I'm not really thinking about it, is the truth. And
   I honestly don't know how to account for it. I mean, first of all
   everybody's saying that there's different balls now, that the
   league's using these new ones which are more juiced, and,
   I don't know, it does seem like guys are getting a little more
   pop. And people are saying it maybe has to do with the
   expansion clubs, diluting the talent, on top of which the umps
   are calling a smaller zone, they've been tightening up the
   zone, harder to hit the corners. And also the league's building
   all these new parks, you know, these nostalgia, throwback
   parks, and the dimensions are different, a little smaller, and
   for me personally, it's, you know, it's, I've been around longer,
   you get better at reading pitchers, psyching guys out, getting
   ahead in the count, you refine your swing, everything. So I
   don't know, you know, it's all of that, mixed together, and
   who's to say what the key factor is. All I know is, I'm having a
   good year, hitting real well, hitting a lot of balls out, the fans
   are real excited again, and the hope now is that switching
   teams won't have any kind of a negative impact on my
   performance. But then I'm playing for Tony again, so, and, you
   know, it was always a little weird for me out West after he left.
   So if anything, I think it might help me. To, you know, to go

ahead, do the job I came here to do, and make the contribution I'm expected to make for all my great teammates and the great fans who've made me feel so welcome. Here on the ballclub. Otherwise, other than that, I'm just not giving the subject a whole lot of thought.

SCENE 7

JULY 1998, COLORADO

The steps of a dugout. KENT *is looking out at the field. He is wearing a National League All-Star uniform and the cap from the previous scene.*

KENT: Okay. Come on now. Swing away. Let's see what you got. (*A moment. He applauds.*) That's it. That's what I'm talking about. Yeah. Now. One more. One more just like that. Come on. (*A moment. He applauds again.*) There it is. There it is. Yeah.

(ADAM *has walked up behind* KENT. *He also wears a National League All-Star uniform and the cap of his new team.*)

ADAM: "You hold that moment till it's over."

(KENT *turns.*)

KENT: What's up, rook!
ADAM: Hey, man!

(ADAM *goes for the handshake.* KENT *goes for the hug. They hug awkwardly.*)

KENT: *Gosh* it's good to see you.
ADAM: I know, right? Too long, too long. Look at *you*, man! Damn!

KENT: What.

ADAM: You're friggin' huge, man! "Superman" indeed.

KENT: Oh God, yeah. I was fine with "Kent"? But I guess journalists get bored easy. (*The cap.*) That's right! You're down South now!

ADAM: Yeah.

KENT: You like it there?

ADAM (*shrugging*): Great team.

KENT: Yeah, man. Great club. *Great* pitching.

ADAM: Our rotation is indeed fierce.

KENT: Seriously, every time you face those guys, you're happy it's not one guy, turns out it's another guy, Glavine, Maddux, Smoltz—

ADAM: Some of them are here.

KENT: What?

ADAM: Greg and Tommy, they're here. You want to meet them?

KENT: I, uh . . . (*Beat.*) I've met them, Adam. I've been in this thing before.

ADAM: Oh yeah, no. Right. That's right.

KENT: Yeah. (*Beat.*) That's right! This is your first All-Star game!

ADAM: Yeah.

KENT: Congratulations, Adam. That is really awesome.

ADAM: Yeah, no, thanks, yeah. He comes up, he breaks in, and ten short years later he makes the National League All-Star team. It's a really overwhelming story.

KENT: Hey, knock that crap off. You're an All-Star second baseman.

ADAM: Actually, they play me in center.

KENT: I, really? (*Beat.*) Point is, I never doubted it would happen for you.

ADAM: You don't have to say that.

KENT: Don't listen to me. You're the one got the votes.

ADAM: I, um, I didn't actually, no.

KENT: What?

ADAM: My manager's the National League team manager, so—

KENT: Right.

ADAM: So he just put me on the team.

KENT: Right, yeah, no, right. (*Beat.*) But! The support of your manager. Who sees you play every day. Over the opinion of some fans who may or may not be even watching, I mean, *that's*—

ADAM: No. Yes. It's nice to have a manager who believes in me.

KENT: Ahh, fuck Tony. You ever look at his stats from when he played?

ADAM: Well, okay, but managing is a different skill, and that one he's got, I mean, he'll get into the Hall of Fame for managing, so that's not exactly—

KENT: Well, no, I mean, you're right, you're probably right. I'm just saying. (*Beat.*) Or, hey, then maybe look at it that way.

ADAM: What? What.

KENT: That there's a way to have a whole second career. If it doesn't pan out for a guy. As a player.

ADAM: Oh.

KENT: But no, I mean, hey, don't sell yourself short. Here you are.

ADAM: Here I am. (*Beat. Then, pointing:*) You taking batting practice?

KENT: Did already. Just sticking around to watch. You?

ADAM: Yeah. I'm . . . coming up.

(*A moment.*)

KENT: Okay. Bring it on home now. Come on. Bring it on home.

ADAM (*simultaneously*): Swing away. Show it to me. Show me what you got.

(*A moment. They applaud together.*)

KENT: That's what I'm talking about. Nice. Now keep it up.

ADAM (*simultaneously*): Righteous. Cannot argue with that. One more like it.

(*A moment.*)

ADAM: Yeah, I always sort of badmouthed it? Meaningless game, empty spectacle, home run derby, souvenir T-shirts. But I gotta say, actually being here? Pretty much kicks ass. Especially after such a rough year.

KENT: Right. (*Beat.*) Oh! Hey. My God. Yes. How's your wife?

ADAM: Oh, thanks, she's fine. Thank you. She's doing good.

KENT: Great.

ADAM: She's here, actually. She's here to watch the game.

KENT: So she's all recovered.

ADAM: Oh well, I mean, recovery means different things? The issue now is what impact the whole thing had on her immune system. Like if it's gonna be easier for her to get sick in the future? But yes, we're okay now as far as the initial scare is concerned, yeah.

KENT: Well, you guys seemed to handle it well. I mean, from what I read and saw.

ADAM: Yeah, suddenly the press wanted to talk to me again.

KENT: No, just, I mean—

ADAM: No, yeah, you're right, we hung in there. I mean, we also totally collapsed. Like, after it was over? I don't know. Something like that, you sort of put your feelings aside for the duration. But then, as soon as there was time, we both just lost it. (*Pause.*) At least out here you know when you're up, right?

Out there nobody tells you when those moments are gonna
be.

KENT: Well. It's really good that you guys have each other.

ADAM: Definitely. Definitely. (*Beat.*) Oh God, Kent, yeah. I was
really sorry to hear that you split up.

KENT: Oh yeah. Thanks.

ADAM: No, I always liked you guys together.

KENT: Uh, me too.

ADAM: I mean. You don't have to talk about it. I'm just saying I'm
sorry.

KENT: Yeah, no, thanks. It's okay. (*Beat.*) I mean, whatever, I had
some . . . I wasn't totally . . . (*Beat.*) I'm a professional athlete.
It can be hard for us to stick those out. You know?

ADAM: Can be.

(*A moment.*)

KENT: Okay! Park this one. Just park it. All the way.

ADAM (*simultaneously*): Okay, now swing down, make sure
you're down on it.

(*A moment. They applaud together.*)

KENT: What did I tell you. What. Did. I. Tell. You.

ADAM (*simultaneously*): If not now, when. If not now, then tell me
when.

(*A moment.*)

KENT: So! Any tips?

ADAM: What?

KENT: About this park. You played here for a while, right?

ADAM: Oh, no, yeah, I was here. After Florida.

KENT: That's right. You hit *all* the expansion clubs.

ADAM: Uh. Yeah.

KENT: So?

ADAM: You'll do fine. New park. Hitter friendly. Also something about the Colorado altitude. Thin. Air. Something. (*Beat.*) Whatever, who am I talking to? The year you're having. (*Beat.*) I mean, you're on pace, Kent. You're on *the* pace.

KENT: That's what they tell me. I'm not really thinking about it.

ADAM: Well, you've got, what, thirty-five, *now*, thirty-six, at the break? So—

KENT: Thirty-seven.

ADAM: Thirty-seven home runs at the break? You've never put up numbers like this. Not this fast.

KENT: If you say so. Like I said, I'm not really—

ADAM: Sure. No. Sure. (*Beat.*) But I mean, come *on.*

KENT: Hey. One game at a time. One at bat at a time. Anything else, you've gotta just get control of it in your mind and put a cap on it, otherwise—

ADAM: Okay. But. I mean, come *on.* It's me, Kent. It's Adam.

KENT: So . . . ?

ADAM: So talk to me for real.

KENT: Hey, give me a break, okay? We're only halfway through the season, so don't talk to me like it's definitely gonna happen, because then I'm gonna feel extra stupid when it doesn't. It could easily not.

ADAM: No. I know.

KENT: So okay.

ADAM: That's not what I'm saying.

KENT: Well, good. (*Beat.*) Wait, what are you saying?

ADAM: Just. What do you think it is?

KENT: What do I think what is.

ADAM: Come on. This is me.

KENT: Yeah. You said that already.

ADAM: So what do you think is going on?

KENT: Okay. Well. First of all. It's happening all over the league.

ADAM: What's happening.

KENT: Uh. The numbers, the huge numbers getting put up.

ADAM: Well, okay, but so then—

KENT: And? It's not like this is some sudden jump for me, either. I hit fifty-eight last year.

ADAM: Yes. You were also pretty exceptional last season. Oh, hey, you know who else is having a pretty good year?

KENT: Who.

ADAM: Raul.

KENT: Is he?

ADAM: Up in Toronto.

KENT: That where he is now?

ADAM: Yeah. He's charging back this year. Really on a tear.

KENT: Good for him.

ADAM: Man. I haven't seen that guy in a long time. How's he doing?

KENT: Your guess is as good as mine.

ADAM: Oh. Uh. Okay. (*Beat.*) Okay! No pitcher. No pitcher. Drill this one. (*A moment. He does an announcer voice and applauds. Alone.*) "He got all of that one . . . long fly ball to deep left field . . . he's gonna run out of room . . . to the wall . . . ! Gone!"

(*A moment.*)

KENT: Is there something you're trying to ask me, Adam?

ADAM: What? What.

KENT: Because if there's something you want to ask me, then I

wish that you would go ahead and just fucking ask me instead
of roping me into what I thought was going to be like a
pleasant conversation about catching up with an old friend
that at this point I am no longer enjoying at all.

(*Beat.*)

ADAM: Well, okay, Kent. I mean, I'm not real slow. When we
played together, I knew what was going on. I knew. And we
were just coming up, and we were young, we were kids,
Jesus, I look at these rooks now . . . And also I can't say what
happened after I left. Of course not. All I know are the stats.
But what I'd like to think? Is that you stopped. That maybe you
felt bad about it, mentally, and that's why you started to
struggle. And that maybe you tried to push yourself too hard
without them and so that's how you hurt your foot. Maybe
that's not what happened, but that is what I'd like to think. But
this? Nothing explains this. And so I guess what I'm asking is
for you to tell me to my face. 'Cause I'm not a reporter. I'm not
Tony. I'm not the fans and I'm not your son. This is just me
here. This is just Adam. Asking why you cheated, Kent. Why
are you still cheating?

(*A silence.* ADAM *waits. Then can't anymore.*)

ADAM: Um . . .
KENT (*He points.*) Shh, hey, hold on. Barry's coming up to take his
cuts.
ADAM: Oh. Hey.

(*They watch. A silence.*)

BACK BACK BACK

KENT: I love that little batting practice net that the batting practice pitcher has to stand behind? I love that thing. It's pure fear. It's like, "Please don't hurt me Mr. Awesome Batter. Please don't strike me down with your mighty power." I love that. Look how this guy is throwing. It's like he thinks Barry's gonna kill him. (*Beat.*) You talk to that guy yet today?

ADAM: Who, Barry?

KENT: Oh my God. What a prick, right?

ADAM: Oh. Yeah. I guess.

KENT: What a total prick.

ADAM: Yeah. No. He is. (*Beat.*) Although. I mean. You know.

KENT: What.

ADAM: Just. It's possible that he maybe had to face some things that you and me didn't have to face.

KENT: Like what. What things. (*Beat.*) Oh.

(*A moment. They watch. They react.*)

KENT: Damn.

ADAM: Yeah. That is a sweet swing.

KENT: You're not kidding.

(*A moment.*)

KENT: So okay. Do you remember 1919?

ADAM: What?

KENT: Just—

ADAM: No, Kent, I do not remember 1919, as I was not exactly around.

KENT: Do you remember what *happened*.

ADAM: I think so. Yeah.

KENT: Black Sox. A handful of gangsters bribes the best team in

the game to throw the World Series. So there everybody is.
After the biggest thing in American sports just got *bought*.
And the game is dead. Except. The thing back then that almost
nobody could do? Was hit one out. Guys were parking fifteen
a year, twenty, tops. And *that* made you a slugger. Not even.
Those were flukes. You hit a fly ball and it happens to catch
the wind and carry. Nobody's thinking about clearing the wall.
It almost never happens. But then who comes along?

(*Beat.*)

ADAM: So okay, you're just not gonna—
KENT: Who comes along, Adam?
ADAM: Babe Ruth.
KENT: Until 1919 he's a pitcher, basically. Most homers he's ever
    hit in a season is twenty-nine. Second most is eleven. After
    1919, he gets traded to the Yankees, and instead of putting
    him in the rotation, which would be wise since the guy is a
    great pitcher, they put him in the outfield so he can focus on
    hitting. In 1920, he hits fifty-four home runs. In 1921? He hits
    fifty-nine. Nobody had ever done anything close to that. Black
    Sox broke everybody's heart and people thought it was going
    to take the game years to recover from that. A decade. If ever.
    Two seasons later, all anybody's talking about is Babe Ruth.
    Who by the way? Was no angel. And when he hits sixty in
    1927 everybody knows *that's* the best team ever. Fuck the
    Black Sox. It's murderer's row. Gehrig, Combs, Dugan. Ruth.
ADAM: Okay, but—

(KENT *puts a hand on* ADAM's *shoulder, silencing him. A moment.*
KENT *looks at* ADAM *earnestly, as though he's going to say*
something else. Then, instead, slides his other hand up ADAM's

shirt. ADAM *allows it, not resisting.* KENT *brings his hand back out after a moment. Clutching a wire and a tiny microphone, a length of duct tape still dangling from it. A moment. Then* KENT *brings the microphone deliberately near his mouth and speaks directly into it.)*

KENT: And yeah, I got shook up a little, with pressure to perform, and I had some injuries, because this game is hard, but I came back from that, and that is one of the things I've done I'm *proudest* of, and, yeah, *you* weren't there, because *you* got traded, because *you* weren't living up to your potential, because *you cracked* like a *little bitch*, even though a guy like you doesn't have *half* of what I do resting on his shoulders for the survival of the fucking sport, and now you're gonna get in my face with this melodramatic and accusatory horseshit like you can talk from some place of moral superiority when all you really did was fail? *Fuck* you. Now is there anything else? Because if not, I think we're done.

(KENT *drops the microphone and turns back out to the audience. A moment.* KENT *claps.)*

KENT: Okay. That's right. We've got a team here. We have got a team.

(*During this,* ADAM *tears the microphone the rest of the way off, and shoves it into his pocket. A long silence. When at last they do speak, it is without looking at each other.)*

ADAM: Well, that is a great attitude, Kent.
KENT: *What?*

ITAMAR MOSES

ADAM: The Black Sox threw the series because their owners treated them like slaves. We went on strike because ours *asked* our *union* if they could attach revenue sharing to a salary cap. Babe Ruth? Sure, he lived on whiskey and cigars and he was really fat and he had a ton of women and he was kind of a cocky bastard, but he *played* straight, Kent. He played it straight. Man, those guys played the *game*. Work the count, draw the walk, steal second, take third on the hit and run, score on the sac fly, the actual *game—*

KENT: *This* is the game, Adam. *I'm* playing the game.

ADAM: Yeah, everybody's on board. Ownership on down. Why not? The fans are back. So, hey, forget leveling the field, let's all watch rich teams from big cities beat up poor teams from small cities with nothing but home runs. So I don't care if you are the savior of the sport, Kent, because the fact is, the sport is fucked. So you know what I think? I think it *should* have been years. A decade. If ever. I think when something like that happens? It's supposed to hurt. Real bad. For a long long time. I think that's how you learn enough so that next time? You approach the thing with a little bit more fucking respect.

(*Pause.*)

KENT: So, what, you got caught?

ADAM: I . . . What? Caught at what.

KENT: I mean, they caught you and flipped you, right? You cut a deal?

ADAM: This isn't a movie, Kent. And I never did anything to get caught *at.*

KENT: Okay, so then what do you want? A fucking medal?

ADAM: I'm up.

(ADAM *starts up the steps.*)

KENT: Rook.

(*A moment.* ADAM *goes.* KENT *remains, alone. A moment. Then* KENT *applauds.*)

KENT: That's it, rook. Keep your head down. (*Pause. Then he applauds again.*) Nice. Don't force it. (*Pause. He applauds.*) There it is. On the screws. (*Pause. Then, to himself:*) On the screws.

SCENE 8

FEBRUARY 2005, COLORADO

A batting cage. ADAM *is by a pitcher's mound. He is now wearing yet another different team's cap and starter jacket. He is talking to the press.*

ADAM: Well, first of all, no. I haven't read it. I have not. I mean, from my understanding, it hasn't even been published, right? But, um, the way it's been described to me is, basically, he talks about his experiences, and things he did, and also things he says all kinds of other guys all did, and goes so far, is my understanding, as to, like, advocate this stuff? To say this is a good thing, and everybody should try this, and do this, and if you're an athlete and you don't do this, you're just being stupid, which . . . (*Pause.*) I'd hope he would find better things to do with his time, better ways to contribute, and to make a contribution, than by writing a book where he's using the names of all these guys, Sammy, and Jason, and Ivan, and Barry, and Miguel, and Raffy . . . and Kent . . . to advocate something like that. (*Pause.*) Because, on top of which, on top of just the unsavoriness, to my mind, of the whole enterprise, is the fact that it's not even true. I mean, this is a long time ago now, but I never witnessed anything, nothing, that would indicate that that was the case. I mean, weights weren't even a part of the game back then. Most guys in the game wouldn't even lift. And it's not hard to imagine various motivations Raul might have for writing those things now, like, if he's just mad with how his own career turned out and the kind of attention he got, as opposed to Kent and all the attention that he got, and feeling excluded from that, you know, them having come up together . . . (*Beat.*) But look, I mean, obviously, it's not even particularly or really relevant to me, which is I guess one small thing to be grateful for, or at least my understanding is, is that I myself am not mentioned in it at all. Or, like, barely mentioned. In one sentence. Like, literally, that my name comes up once, and he doesn't seem to have any idea what position I even played, and he basically just sort of acknowledges he knew me. And that I was there.

SCENE 9

MARCH 2005, WASHINGTON, D.C.

A side room in the United States Capitol. RAUL *is sitting in a chair. He is wearing a suit. A long silence.* RAUL *takes out a bottle of pills and a bottle of water. Takes a pill with a swig of water.* KENT *enters. He is also wearing a suit. And glasses. A moment.*

RAUL: Oh! Oh. Hey.
KENT: Hi.
RAUL: Uh. Hey.
KENT: Hey.

(RAUL *puts the bottle of pills and the bottle of water away.*)

RAUL: Um. This, uh, they told me, uh . . . (*Pause.*) I'm supposed to, I'm just, you know, waiting. In this room. Until, uh . . .

(*A silence.* KENT *just stares at* RAUL.)

RAUL: How is everybody? Is everybody here? Are they nervous? I'm nervous. A little shaky, a . . . Just, talking in public, you know? And I hear they got all these weird little rituals and things you're supposed to follow? So that was just, I was just, to calm me *down*, just taking some . . .

(*A silence.* RAUL *waits for* KENT *to speak.* KENT *just stares.*)

RAUL: You found me, okay? They hid me and you found me. Good job. I guess they just figured it would be better for everybody if I was separate from, you know, until we were actually *in* the thing. But if you, I mean, there's not, I don't have a, just, okay, look, Kent, I wrote a book, okay? I wrote a book. Just to talk about my life and some of my thoughts and feelings and beliefs and things that happened to me which I have the right to talk about because they *happened* to me, okay?

KENT: Okay.

RAUL: And I definitely didn't know that there would be congressional fucking *hearings*. Okay? I never paid attention to politics in my *life*. I didn't have any idea that guys like this even watch sports. But apparently they do. And here we are now, and this was the result, and we have to deal with the reality of that. Right?

KENT: Right.

RAUL: And if you think about it, just bear with me here, if you really kind of think about it, it's not really such a bad thing, overall, from the biggest, like, point of view, because the point here is to educate people, right? Because, you know, we're role models, and so this is an opportunity to make sure some young kid who maybe looks up to me, or to you, or to whoever, who's in there, doesn't try to emulate a behavior that we know to have certain risks. And which also? Is questionable ethically.

(*Beat.*)

KENT: *What?*

RAUL: What? What.

KENT: In your book you say that everyone should do it in order for us to reach the full limits of human potential and kind of

dismiss the health risks as not relevant under proper
supervision.

RAUL: Right, well—

KENT: And you don't really seem interested in the ethics at all.

RAUL: Well, right, but yeah, but—

KENT: But?

RAUL: Well, you know, things change. The book came out a while
ago.

KENT: It came out a month ago.

RAUL: And I have since then backed away from the positions you
just mentioned.

KENT: Oh, I see. And you did that on the advice of a lawyer, or—?

RAUL: Look, is there something you want to say to me?

KENT: Well, I—

RAUL: Because if there is, then I wish that you just say it, okay?

KENT: Okay. Well—

RAUL: But wait, wait, so wait, hold on. You, uh, you read it?

KENT: What?

RAUL: The, you know—

KENT: Oh. Yeah, Raul. I, um. I did read parts of it. Yes.

RAUL: So, uh . . . What'd you think?

KENT: *What?*

RAUL: No, just—

KENT: Um. I thought the description of taking me into a bathroom
stall and injecting fluid into my buttocks with a syringe was
not totally necessary.

(*Beat.*)

RAUL: Right, well, the thing with that is—

KENT: Um, okay, look, I'm not mainly concerned with what you
tried to do to me or what you said about me, okay? That

doesn't really bother me, because I can rise above personal attacks and slander and whatever you want to call it because that isn't the kind of thing that I like to clutter up my mind with. That's not even what this is about for me as far as I'm concerned, because unlike *some* people I am not always all the time just about me and how things are going to affect me personally. What I want to say to you is. Do you even realize what you have done to the game of baseball? To this thing that gave you everything you have in your life? To everybody that plays it, and to all the fans that love it, with this toxic bullshit of yours? Do you even realize?

(*Beat.*)

RAUL: I'm sorry. Bullshit?

KENT: What.

RAUL: Well, we can talk about what I did or I didn't realize if you want, Kent, but first off I'm gonna have to hold you up there from calling it bullshit.

KENT: What else would you like me to call it.

RAUL: Well, it's the truth, Kent. However else you feel like you want to react to it, that's fine, but what I put in that book is the truth, so I'm confused, maybe because, as you like to remind me, maybe 'cause I'm not exactly the brightest penny in the fountain over here, but isn't that the exact *opposite* of bullshit? Kent? (*Beat.*) Wait, what are you planning to say?

KENT: What?

RAUL: When they ask you. What are you gonna say?

(*Beat.*)

KENT: I'm—

RAUL: Holy shit. You're gonna lie.

KENT: No—

RAUL: You're gonna lie. You're gonna lie to fucking Congress.

KENT (*overlapping*): I'm, no, I'm not—

RAUL: They make you take an oath in there. You know that, right?

KENT: Yes. I know that.

RAUL: Well, so then—

KENT: I'm not going to lie under oath, Raul.

RAUL: Okay. Good. But so . . . (*Beat.*) Oh. Right. So you've, uh, you've got one of those vague answers, right? That's not a lie but that doesn't so much answer the question either. Right? I'm right, right?

KENT: Everybody thinks you're full of shit.

RAUL: See? You're doing it already. That's not an answer to my question.

KENT: *Everybody.* Thinks you're full of shit.

RAUL: Everybody *wants* to think I'm full of shit. That's not the same.

KENT: Well, they're *saying* it.

RAUL: I don't care.

KENT: Tony says you're full of shit.

RAUL: I don't care.

KENT: Even Adam says you're full of shit.

RAUL: What? Who?

KENT: Um. Adam?

RAUL: Rook said that?

KENT: To the press. In Colorado.

(*Beat.*)

RAUL: Why did he say it to the press in Colorado?

KENT: Because he lives in Colorado.

(Beat.)

RAUL: Why does he live in Colorado?

KENT: That's . . . ! Because he's their batting coach! That's—

RAUL: Whoa. Rook's coaching now? *Man.* That really—

KENT: That's not my—!

RAUL: I know. I know it's not—

KENT: That's not my point.

RAUL *(overlapping)*: It's not your point. I know that.

KENT: My *point*—

RAUL: You're point seems to be that everybody's afraid to tell the
   truth but me.

KENT: No—

RAUL: Well, that is what it seemed to be.

KENT: Well, it wasn't.

RAUL: Well, then I missed it.

KENT: Would you let me—!

RAUL: No. Because I don't give a shit *what* that little backstabbing
   faggot said to the press because, just like everybody else in
   the whole entire world, that kid always *worshipped* you, for
   absolutely no reason at all that I could understand, and so of
   course he's gonna have your back, and so I don't give a shit.
   Come on! The fuck *is* this, Kent? You start to believe your own
   hype? You even fooling *yourself* now? I mean, you want to try
   to duck and weave once you're inside there on the spot, then
   that's your call, but can you even *say* it?

KENT: What.

RAUL: To me, here in this room, can you even say it out loud?

KENT: *What.*

RAUL: That you did it! That it happened!

KENT: Keep your voice down.

RAUL: Who the fuck are you *talking* to, Kent? I was there! I did it with you! I already know! Just say it! Say it! Say it, motherfucker!

(KENT *grabs* RAUL. *Slams him up against the wall. A moment.*)

RAUL: Go ahead. What are you waiting for? Take a swing. I'll *let* you. I'll even let you. Take it. Free shot. (*Pause.*) The fuck are you *waiting* for? Bring it, brother. Bring it, Superman. Fucking bring it.

(*Pause.*)

KENT: *Fuck!*

(KENT *lets* RAUL *drop to the ground. Turns. Walks a few steps away.* RAUL *brushes off his suit, straightens his tie. A moment.*)

KENT: Do you have any more of those?
RAUL: What? (*Beat.*) Oh. Yeah. Sure.

(RAUL *hands* KENT *the bottle of pills and the water.* KENT *takes a pill. Hands the bottles back. Takes a deep breath. A moment.*)

KENT: It is fucked up that you did this to me. It is so totally fucked up.
RAUL: Okay, I didn't do anything *to* you—
KENT (*overlapping*): Because it's not my fault that you squandered your talent. It's not my fault that I worked harder. It's not my fault you got hurt over and over and over again. None of those things are my fault.
RAUL: That's not it.
KENT: Then what is it?

RAUL: It's what I said, it's for the game, for, you know, the *kids*—

KENT (*overlapping*): That's, don't give me that, that is crap, why, *really*?

RAUL (*overlapping*): No, because it's, I—!

KENT: Why the *fuck*?

RAUL: I don't know! I, uhhh . . . ! (*Pause.*) I don't know. I don't.

KENT: Well, that's . . . even worse.

RAUL: I mean. I'm a professional athlete . . .

(*Beat.*)

KENT: Is that supposed to be some kind of explanation?

RAUL: Just. We don't—

KENT: And, I mean, you couldn't have *waited*?

RAUL: What?

KENT: You couldn't at least have *waited*, oh, I don't know, three more years?

RAUL: Why?

KENT: You couldn't have fucking *waited* until after 2007.

RAUL: Oh! Oh. Yeah, I guess not.

KENT: Well. That's just great.

RAUL: Come on. You think it's gonna make a *difference*? You think your eligibility's gonna come up, *you*, and anybody's gonna say a goddamn thing? No. They're gonna look the other way, and talk about the benefit of the doubt, and vote you right into the Hall, they—

KENT: But . . . ! Don't you . . . ! (*Pause.*) Of *course* everybody's afraid but you.

(*Pause. KENT looks at the door. He hesitates.*)

RAUL: What do you think they're gonna do?

ITAMAR MOSES

KENT: To me?

RAUL: To *you*? Listen to this guy. Once he gets going . . . No, not to you, you fuck. To baseball.

KENT: Oh. Um. Nothing, probably. I mean, they'll make some recommendations, some demands, whatever, more testing, stiffer penalties, but what's the government really gonna do? Stop the season? Shut us down? Without baseball . . . Okay, what, Raul, what is so funny?

(*Because* RAUL *has started chuckling.*)

RAUL: No, no, nothing, just . . . "Stiffer penalties." Sorry.

KENT: Yeah, that's great.

RAUL: Sorry. (*Pause.*) Hey, so what's it gonna be?

KENT: What? What.

RAUL: Your vague answer.

KENT: Oh. It's, uh. It's, "I'm not here to talk about the past."

RAUL: Good. That's good.

KENT: And sometimes, "I'm not here to talk about the past. I'm here to be positive about this subject."

RAUL: Lawyers, man. (*Beat.*) Mine told me? With my book? That I should, like, change some names, leave some things vague, but, I was like: Fuck *that*. This is America. Sue me, bitches. (*Pause.*) Look. This'll be done quick, I bet. They got other work to do, these guys, some other committee, agriculture . . . whatnot. Something about . . . endangered species, or . . . farms . . . (*Beat.*) Hey! After this whole thing is over, you want to maybe grab a game?

KENT: *What?*

RAUL: Just. D.C.'s got a team now. Ever since the Expos folded and came down from Montreal? I've never seen them play.

KENT: Um. I don't think so, Raul.

RAUL: Hey, okay. (*Pause.*) George W. Bush said to me once, he said to me one time, "What does Canada need with baseball teams, anyway? It's ours. They've got hockey."

(*Beat.*)

KENT: What?

RAUL: Yeah. Funny. He's right, though. I played in Toronto for a while? They don't know what to do with baseball up there. They sing the wrong national anthem before the game. I mean. Not the *wrong* one. Theirs. But it's weird.

KENT: You know the President?

RAUL: I played for him, Kent. When I was in Texas? He owned the team.

KENT: Oh yeah. (*Beat.*) Bill Clinton called me once.

RAUL: Yeah?

KENT: Yeah. When I hit sixty-two. When I broke the record. Just to say hey.

RAUL: Huh. (*Beat.*) What a couple of pricks, right?

KENT: Seriously. What a pair of fucking pricks.

RAUL: Two total douchebags.

KENT: Just this duo of ridiculous unrepentant sacks of crap.

RAUL: Yeah. (*Pause.*) Hey, I heard you got married again.

KENT: Oh. Um. Yeah. Yes. I did.

RAUL: That's nice.

KENT: Yeah, it is. She's great.

RAUL: What does she do?

KENT: She, uh. She's, um. (*Beat.*) She's a pharmaceuticals representative.

RAUL: Nice.

KENT: I heard you got divorced. Again.

RAUL: Yeah. Can't really. Can't seem to stick one of those out.

KENT: Looks that way.

RAUL: What can I say? I love women.

KENT: Raul, you hate women. It's a subtle difference.

RAUL: Look, I'm just trying to—

KENT: What.

RAUL: I don't know. (*Pause.*) Adam's *coaching*?

KENT: Adam's been retired five years. Some new kid came up on his club. Took Rookie of the Year at his position. He was done.

(*Pause.*)

RAUL: Okay, see, when I met you? You were this hot prospect, California all-American, six foot a thousand, but you're coming up for the first time, so you've got that look all the rooks have, that wild-eyed look, are they gonna find me out, *that* look, and I—

KENT: What. You what. You "took me under your *wing*"—?

RAUL: No.

KENT: You *made* me, is *that* it?

RAUL: No—

KENT: Are you giving me *that* speech now? Because that is bullshit.

RAUL: No. Yes. It is.

KENT: Because I broke the rookie record for home runs.

RAUL: I know.

KENT: I walked onto the field with that. I didn't need you.

RAUL: Yeah. No. (*Pause.*) Yeah. Exactly.

KENT: What. (*Pause.*) *What?*

RAUL: You didn't need me. You never did. And you used me anyway.

KENT: I "used" you?

RAUL: And then I came back a few years later, when I was the one

in real trouble, I was the one everybody was giving up on, and
you used me again!

KENT: Oh *come on!* You *loved* being that guy! You *loved* that! You
loved it!

RAUL: Maybe. Maybe I did. I don't care. All I know is? That after
that? Every time I saw you, or heard your name, or read it in
print? I wanted to take an aluminum bat? And beat you to
death with it. And then I did the book? And I felt better. So
look, I know what everybody's saying and what they think, and
they can go ahead and they can do that. But all this really
happened. And you *know* it. And Tony knows it. And fucking
Adam knows it. And when you go talk to Congress? You
hypocrite? Oh, yeah, I picked that one up along the way. When
you go in there, you ingrate? You spoiled brat? You pathetic
fucking crybaby? When you lean into the mic and tell them
you're not here to talk about the past because you're just here
to be positive about this subject, when you say that, over and
over and over again? Everybody else will know it too.

(*Long pause.*)

(KENT *goes to the door. Stops. Perhaps* ADAM *is already visible
now, beginning the next transition.*)

(KENT *goes.* RAUL *remains alone. Long pause. Then* RAUL *follows*
KENT *off.*)

ADAM: Ready? Here comes the next one.

(*And suddenly the space opens and for the first time we are
actually on a baseball diamond. In the center. On the mound.*

ADAM *is here. He is dressed as before. There is a bucket of balls by his feet and he is holding a ball in his hand.*)

(ADAM *pitches. Watches a grounder.*)

ADAM: Come on. The fuck is that? You gotta get down on it, swing down, you're coming over the top, hitting it on the ground. Don't get me wrong, you've got good speed, but we don't want you having to leg it out all the time. Okay? Okay. Here we go.

(ADAM *grabs another ball and pitches. Watches a pop-up.*)

ADAM: Great. Now you're under it. Now you're under it too far and you popped it up and the inning is over and we lost. Come on. Show it to me.

(ADAM *grabs another ball and pitches. The batter misses entirely.*)

ADAM: Hey! Okay. Who are you? Are you the right guy? Are you the same guy I read the scouting report on? 'Cause I gotta tell you that this doesn't seem like the same guy to me. First of all, you're watching yourself. I am watching you watch yourself. You're up in your head, thinking, Here I am, this is it, I'm in the majors, let me put on a big show, let me put on a show for Coach Adam, and you gotta forget that, and just take your time. Take your own time. Step out of the box, knock dirt off your cleats, spin the bat, and then step back in, to *your* rhythm, because you're only as good as this game, you're only as good as this at-bat, what you do right now, forget everything before, forget about that last pitch, even if you missed it, like you did, like some kind of bush league chump, forget it, and just step in for the next one, like it's the first. Okay?

(ADAM *pitches. Watches one lined past him to one side.*)

ADAM: There it is, rook. Now you're down on it. That's a base hit. I mean, not if *I'm* in the infield, but mostly, you're on, you moved somebody over, you drove somebody in. Now forget that one. Step in for this. This one is the only one there is.

(ADAM *pitches. Ducks as one is ripped back up the middle.*)

ADAM: Whoa! Don't hurt me now, rook. Don't hurt me. Okay. One more.

(ADAM *pitches. Spins around as a long drive is launched over him.*)

ADAM: There it is! There it is! On the screws! Now we're talking! Woo! (*He claps.*) Back . . . back . . . back . . . !

(ADAM *spins to face the batter. His expression is melancholy as all hell. A moment.*)

(*Blackout.*)

CELEBRITY ROW

Celebrity Row had its world premiere on March 21, 2006, at Portland Center Stage in Portland, Oregon (Chris Coleman, Artistic Director). Director: Chris Coleman. Set Designer: Daniel Ostling. Lighting Designer: Daniel Ordower. Sound Designer: Casi Pacilio. Costume Designer: Jeff Cone. Dramaturg: Mead Hunter. Stage Manager: Mark Tynan.

MAZE CARROLL and others	Leslie Kalarchian
LUIS and others	Jesse J. Perez
TIMOTHY and others	Daniel Thomas May
RAMZI and others	Ariel Shafir
TED and others	Ebbe Roe Smith

A revised version of *Celebrity Row* had its premiere on October 16, 2008, at the American Theater Company in Chicago (PJ Paparelli, Artistic Director). Director: David Cromer. Set Designer: Andre LaSalle. Lighting Designer: Keith Parham. Sound and Music Designer: Josh Schmidt. Costume Designer: Alison Siple. Stage Manager: Helen Lattyak.

MAZE CARROLL and others	Kelli Simpkins
LUIS and others	Joe Minoso
TIMOTHY and others	Christopher McLinden
RAMZI and others	Usman Ally
TED and others	Larry Neumann Jr.

CHARACTERS

MAZE CARROLL   Forty, white, Southern.

LUIS   Thirties, Cuban.

TIMOTHY   Thirties, white.

RAMZI   Thirties, Saudi.

TED   Fifties, white.

SETTING

ADX Florence Federal Prison, in Colorado. And elsewhere.

A NOTE ABOUT QUICK CHANGES

Actors often have to change characters quickly and before our eyes. This is only possible if a few relatively simple costume pieces are associated with each character: a camouflage cap, a tweed jacket, a beard, glasses, a turban, and so on. Perhaps the basic costume for the four men, over which these other pieces are worn, is a prison jumpsuit.

A NOTE ABOUT THE FACTS

Most of the characters in this play, and all of the play's major events, are fictional. But ADX Florence is a real prison and Luis Felipe, Ted Kaczynski, Timothy McVeigh, and Ramzi Yousef did in fact occupy neighboring cells there and exercised together for an hour a day. And while McVeigh has since been executed, the other three are presumably still there.

WHO PLAYS WHO

The actor playing TIMOTHY also plays EARL, ANGEL, DAVID, PETER

The actor playing RAMZI also plays NORMAN, MOM

The actor playing TED also plays FENDELL, DJINN, EVAN, DAD

The actor playing MAZE also plays JENNIFER

The actor playing LUIS also plays HELLER, SCUBAMAN

ACT 1

In near darkness. Voices.

DJINN: First Surah.

ANGEL: *Al-Fatihah.* "The Opening."

RAMZI: In the name of God, the merciful, the compassionate.

DJINN: First Ayah.

RAMZI: Praise belongs to God, the lord of all being,

ANGEL: Second Ayah.

RAMZI: The merciful, the compassionate,

DJINN: Third Ayah.

RAMZI: Lord of judgment day.

ANGEL: Fourth Ayah.

RAMZI: I serve You; I pray to You alone for comfort

DJINN: Fifth Ayah.

RAMZI: Lead me on a righteous path

ANGEL: Sixth Ayah.

RAMZI: The path of those You bless.

DJINN: Seventh Ayah.

RAMZI: Not the path of those who incur Your wrath.

ANGEL: Eighth Ayah.

RAMZI: Nor the path of those who have gone astray.

(*By now perhaps we can see that the source of the voices is* RAMZI, *kneeling, flanked on one side by an* ANGEL *and the other by a* DJINN. *A moment. They all vanish.*)

(LUIS, *alone.*)

(*He sits in a cell, unmoving. The image is stark, and bleak, and simple. A man alone in a cell. A silence. Long enough to feel it.*)

(*A phone rings.*)

(MAZE *and* FENDELL, *on the phone.* LUIS *has vanished.*)

FENDELL: If you're a journalist I have no comment. And I frankly resent your calling me at home.

MAZE: No—

FENDELL: If you want to know how I sleep at night while representing a ruthless killer, I have no comment. Or if you seek to explain the kinship between the Cuban gangster and the Jewish lawyer by charting an analogy or equivalence between inner-city Chicago and the shtetls of Eastern Europe wherefrom hails my ancestry? I have no comment on that either.

MAZE: I am not a journalist. (*Beat.*) Though at some point I'd love for you to unpack that analogy for me—

FENDELL (*overlapping*): Who are you?

MAZE: My name is Maze Carroll. I'm an attorney with Justice Nation, a small civil liberties outfit in D.C., and we're preparing a class action suit against BOP officials in their individual capacities, under *Bivens*, on an Eighth Amendment violation, with the eventual aim of getting the entire ADX, or colloquially "supermax," model of incarceration declared unconstitutional, and *I* was wondering if I could interview your client so that we might include a sworn sealed affidavit from him in our case.

(*Pause.*)

FENDELL: Yeah. No.

MAZE: Perhaps you would consider extending the offer to Mr. Felipe before you turn it down, sir.

FENDELL: Luis isn't a lawyer. And what I'd advise him is? The bigger the case, the slower it moves.

MAZE: Well, okay, but—

FENDELL: Ms. Carroll, as you of all people surely know? There are hundreds of prisoners in supermax facilities. Maybe thousands. Make some more calls. Now good night.

MAZE: I need Luis! (*Pause.*) Hello?

FENDELL: Go on.

MAZE (*carefully*): The details of your client's case are particularly compelling.

FENDELL: You mean that the extremity of his suffering is good news for your cause.

MAZE: I'm not gonna bullshit you, Mr. Fendell. He's the one I've been waiting for. He's a criminal, but not some crazed random killer. He's gang affiliated, but not with an ideology of hatred like the Aryan Brotherhood. In fact, the Latin Kings' manifesto, which he *wrote*, is pretty lucid, I mean, the guy writes poetry, for God's sake—

FENDELL: You think I didn't argue all this at trial?

MAZE: Due respect, sir, the key is the *effect, on* him, of the terms of his sentence, which you couldn't argue because it hadn't *happened* yet, but *now*, and please correct me? He is on lockdown twenty-three hours a day. He exercises for an hour a day with the three other men on his block, but otherwise he is allowed no human contact of any kind, his meals are passed through a slot in the cell door, and he has under these conditions not surprisingly deteriorated to the point where he barely eats, has stopped speaking virtually altogether, and will sometimes throw himself against the walls of his cell all night, such that in the morning it looks as though he's been severely beaten, and since, as his isolation order covers even letters and phone calls, he has no outlet for these feelings, save his official correspondence with his lawyer, which is to say, you?

FENDELL: Well, I'm appealing.

MAZE: Oh I don't know. You're all right.

FENDELL: What?

MAZE: Little joke. Lighten the mood. It's not just the federal facility, sir. Twenty-five states have these things now. Even if *you* save *him*, how long before this happens to some other guy? Hundreds? Maybe thousands?

FENDELL: You're too late. The district court is about to rule on my appeal. It's not in Luis's interest for me to derail that now. I'm sorry. This way's just faster.

MAZE: For you.

FENDELL: Of course for me.

MAZE: What if you lose?

FENDELL: If I lose I'm going to appeal higher up. That's the beauty of the system.

MAZE: What if you lose twice? (*Beat.*) I mean, would you call me? 'Cause the failure of your appeals would really help me to establish exhaustion of administrative remedies—

FENDELL (*overlapping*): I'm not going to call you. (*Pause.*) I'm not going to lose.

(MAZE, *walking with a prison administrator,* CARL NORMAN, *and a guard,* EARL.)

NORMAN: ADX Florence is, in fact, part of a complex of five federal prisons, ascending in security, and we've now passed the work camp, the minimum, the medium, and the regular max we're passing now. (*Pointing up.*) Smile. You're on camera. Now, Ms. Carroll, I'm going to assume that in your line of work you've been on the inside of a prison before?

MAZE: On occasion.

NORMAN: Perhaps even as an inmate?

MAZE: No, sir.

NORMAN: In any case, you no doubt have some experience with minimum security, probably medium, but please understand that this facility, and the special wing in particular, requires a different level of stricture for the prisoners, and, likewise, a different level of stricture for us.

MAZE: Mr. Norman, that is why I'm here.

NORMAN: Yeah. Nevertheless? I'll be goddamned if anything's gonna happen to you on my watch. The infrared, the remote-controlled gates, the pressurized areas of the floor, this is all here for your protection. (*Guiding her by the elbow.*) Whoa, watch out, that wire'll cut you right open! Okay. Having passed between these towers, you are now standing inside ADX Florence, a.k.a. Colorado Supermax, a.k.a. the Alcatraz of the Rockies. Welcome to the most secure prison in the United States.

MAZE: I, yes, I *feel* welcome.

NORMAN: This entrance hallway is an underground tunnel full of armed human guards, and also attack dogs, who have been rendered silent through the removal of their vocal cords.

MAZE: The guards?

NORMAN: No. The dogs. That's funny.

MAZE: Not for the dogs.

NORMAN: Which reminds me. Earl here is gonna be assigned to you whenever you have call to be inside Celeb— the, uh, the block that houses Mr. Felipe, in the further interest of ensuring your safety. You've met Earl, yeah?

MAZE: We've howdied but not been officially introduced.

EARL: Hi there.

MAZE: So you *can* speak. (*Because he has offered his hand.*) Hey! *And* shake. That was a joke. I'm sorry. When I'm anxious, I make jokes, it's annoying—

NORMAN: But let me emphasize finally, Ms. Carroll, that it is most important of all for you be in charge of your *own* safety. Do you understand?

MAZE: Yes. Guarding me, there'll be just me, the towers, the razor wire, the checkpoints, the laser eyes, the pressure pads, the video monitors, the voiceless attack dogs, and Earl.

(*Beat.*)

NORMAN: That's correct.

(MAZE, *being guided by* EARL *through the prison. Which is to say, throughout the following, he leads her "deeper" and "deeper" into the complex.* EARL *pauses at "doors" to punch in codes, or to have his fingerprints scanned, or to swipe an ID card, all accompanied by appropriate sounds: beeps, clicks, gates sliding, doors slamming, etc.*)

EARL: Don't let him get you.

MAZE: Don't let him get me to what?

EARL: He's just proud of all his gadgets. We got full-time guys watching the video, right? He's got his own bank of monitors. Gives him the illusion of control in a world otherwise run amok.

MAZE: The "illusion" of control?

EARL: Let's just say that, despite all the closed-circuits, I'm not sure Carl Norman has a particularly good view of things from where he's sitting.

MAZE: Isn't he listening to us right now?

EARL (*matter-of-factly*): Probably. (*Beat.*) Okay! We are now entering the Special Wing. Do not ever lose sight of me while we are inside this area. The hallways curve in ways designed to increase disorientation. You may also notice that the walls are painted in alternating shades of maroon and green.

MAZE: It's a nice touch, yeah.

EARL: It's to frustrate depth perception. In addition, as you can see, the windows reveal only slivers of sky so that it is never possible to know exactly where inside of the prison you are. Don't get lost in here, ma'am.

MAZE: Don't you lose me, soldier.

EARL: This wing houses sixty-four prisoners. Their cells are staggered with geometric precision such that the prisoners can never see each other's eyes. They are soundproofed so that they cannot communicate by tapping on walls or furniture or floors. When I am forced to enter a cell, my key ring is equipped with an aluminum shield that hides it from view to prevent prisoners from memorizing the configuration of teeth and fashioning duplicates. Do you understand what I'm saying? This guy Felipe? Don't fuck around with him.

MAZE: What?

EARL: You know what I mean.

MAZE: I'm sure I don't.

EARL: I mean that he is not to be fucked with. He is not your friend.

MAZE: I was not under the impression that he was, Earl. I've not met him.

EARL: Well, you're about to. So. Do not tell him anything about your life. Do not tell him where you live. Do not give him the impression, Ms. Carroll, that you continue to exist beyond the walls of this room.

MAZE: What room?

EARL: This one. We're here.

MAZE: Well. All right, then.

(*One final, booming door closure.*)

(MAZE *and* LUIS. *Across a table. Separated by glass.* EARL *outside.* MAZE *smiles at* LUIS. LUIS *stares at* MAZE.)

MAZE: Okay! Let's get started!

(RAMZI, *alone.*)

RAMZI: In the name of God, the merciful, the compassionate:

(RAMZI *is flanked by his* DJINN *and his* ANGEL.)

DJINN: Second Surah.

ANGEL *Al-Dubb.* "The Great Bear."

DJINN: First Ayah.

RAMZI: This is the truth about which there can be no doubt.

ANGEL: Second Ayah.

RAMZI: Those who believe it, they are righteous, and good, and
    for them there will be great rewards. They are the believers
    and they say:

ANGEL: "We believe."

DJINN: Fifth Ayah.

RAMZI: For those who do not believe it, they are evildoers, and
    fire awaits them. They are the unbelievers and they do say:

DJINN: "We do not believe."

RAMZI: And worst of all are the hypocrites. Those whose belief is
    idle, or who only pretend to believe, who say:

ANGEL: "We believe! We are with you!"

RAMZI: But who then say:

DJINN: "We were only mocking. We do not believe. We are not with you."

ANGEL: Twentieth Ayah.

RAMZI: O believers! Remember when we allied with the Americans in the West, who said:

ANGEL (*as an American*): "We are with you."

RAMZI: And opposed the Soviets in the East, who said:

DJINN (*as a Russian*): "We are not with you."

RAMZI: Remember when, in the one-thousand nine-hundred seventy-ninth year, the Great Bear did invade the holy soil of Afghanistan. And said:

DJINN (*Russian*): "Cower before our Communist war machine. For it is pitiless and extremely efficient."

RAMZI: And the people did cower before this Goliath, for his might seemed insurmountable, until an angel descended, saying:

ANGEL (*American*): "We will provide you with weapons, and training, and intelligence. But we cannot intervene directly or it will cause an international incident."

DJINN: Fifty-third Ayah.

RAMZI: O believers! Remember, then, how a David emerged in the form of the holy warriors of the mujahedeen, and how they did fight for nine and one years, and the West was awed by our fearsome resistance, saying:

ANGEL (*American*): "They can resist the Soviets because they are pure of heart, and are on the side of good, whereas Communism is a dark force, a corrupt system, and lo, is weak, therefore, at its core."

RAMZI: But the Eastern bloc was skeptical, saying:

DJINN (*Russian*): "These so-called freedom fighters are awfully

well funded and trained and equipped. We find it suspect but
cannot know for sure."

ANGEL: Eighty-fourth Ayah.

RAMZI: O believers! Remember! How, as the tide of battle turned,
young men flocked to the cause, Daniels to the den, and lo,
remember that among these was one called: Ramzi Yousef.

ANGEL, DJINN: O believers! Remember!

RAMZI: Born of Palestinian mother and Pakistani father, adherent
to the Sunni form of Wahhabi Islam, he did seek his glory.

DJINN: One-hundred-fifth Ayah.

RAMZI: And lo, in the one-thousand-nine-hundred-and-eighty-
ninth year, the Great Bear was defeated. And the Red Army
fled, crying:

DJINN (*Russian*): "They know the land as we do not. They are
willing to sacrifice themselves as we are not. These
motherfuckers are crazy."

RAMZI: And the angels rejoiced, saying:

ANGEL (*American*): "This is a huge embarrassment for the
Russians. Communism now teeters on the brink of total
collapse."

RAMZI: And with the Soviets defeated, only the Afghan army
remained opposed to the mujahedeen, and lo, we did
surround the city of Kabul.

ANGEL: One-hundred-twenty-ninth Ayah.

RAMZI: And yet: victory was denied. For our angel proved to be a
djinn in disguise, saying:

DJINN (*American*): "Lo, though you served us well all this time,
Moses, though you led your people through the hardships of
the desert, you must die here, on the mountainside, in sight of
the promised land, but forbidden to enter."

ANGEL: One-hundred-sixty-first Ayah.

RAMZI: And it was then that a new angel emerged, surrounded by men full with the loyalty forged among those who stand together in battle, and he said:

ANGEL (*Saudi*): "Come, mujahedeen! You will be reborn! And renamed!"

RAMZI: Thus: believers are strong. Unbelievers are weak.

DJINN: Two-hundredth Ayah.

RAMZI: But believers must be wary of the hypocrite, and his hidden unbelief.

(MAZE *and* LUIS, *with* EARL *outside, as before.*)

MAZE: Luis? (*Pause.*) Luis? (*Pause.*) Luis? (*Pause.*) Okay. I'll just . . . go ahead. My name is Maze Carroll. And you are . . . Luis Felipe? Just, you know, important to make sure I didn't wander into the wrong room. And you're not a whole *different* Latin gangster in the special wing of the supermax prison. So: that's you, yeah? Luis? (*Pause.*) Luis? Please talk to me. (*Pause.*) Luis? (*Pause.*) Or, not, you don't have to, we can just, you know . . . sit here. I'm not going anywhere, I'm going to stay here the whole time, okay? You just . . . You do what you need to do.

(*Pause.* LUIS *doesn't do anything.*)

MAZE: Um. (*Beat.*) I was born in 1960. In Wilmington. In the great state of North Carolina. (*Pause.*) That's the South as far as most people are concerned but we're Yankees according to the folks in South Carolina. (*Pause.*) "First in Flight!" (*Beat.*) That's uh. That's our motto.

(EARL *has entered. He stares at* MAZE.)

MAZE: What? (*Pause.*) Oh. Yes. You may go.

(EARL *goes. A moment.*)

MAZE: Earl thinks it's probably best if you don't know a great deal
     about my life. He's probably right, yeah? I mean, uh . . .
     (*Pause.*) *So*, uh, you're a member of the Latin Kings, is that
     right? Sort of a big shot there. (*Pause.*) I've been dealing
     with prisoners for a while, so you get to learn a lot of things
     about gangs, you know, because there's a whole hell of a lot
     of you guys in these places. Affiliated, I mean, with various
     gangs, so—
LUIS: Nation.
MAZE: What? (*Pause.*) Luis? What did you say?
LUIS: The Latin Kings nation.
MAZE: That's your gang, yes.
LUIS: Um. It's *not*. A gang. (*Pause.*) The Latin Kings is a nation.
MAZE: Oh, I see. (*Beat.*) In fact, I don't. Um: what do you mean?
LUIS: It's not a gang.
MAZE: Right, but, so, uh: what would you say is the difference?
LUIS: You heard of the Latin Lords?
MAZE: Yes I have.
LUIS: The Imperial Gangsters? The Latin Disciples?
MAZE: They all ring a bell, yes.
LUIS: All those bitches is gangs. The Latin Kings is a nation.
     (*Pause.*) That's the difference.
MAZE: I see. (*Pause.*) So the distinction in some way defies
     articulation.
LUIS: What?
MAZE: It just "is."
LUIS: That's right. It just is. (*Beat.*) Like *you*.
MAZE: Me?

LUIS: That place you from.

MAZE: Oh, you mean Justice Nation?

LUIS: Yeah.

MAZE: That's just a name. We're basically five people in an office.

LUIS: So?

MAZE: So . . . (*Beat.*) So, *hey*, how 'bout that? We got you talking. (*Pause.*) So, Luis. Is there anything that Gary didn't explain about how this process will differ from his failed appeals? How you'll be part of a suit on behalf of many prisoners so that it's no longer just about Gary arguing to change the terms of your individual sentence but actually about demonstrating that this entire category of sentencing is unconstitutional?

LUIS: Uh-huh. And then what. You gonna get me out?

MAZE: Um, *out*? Uhhh, no. Um, no, Luis, you won't be getting *out*, no, it's more about you're the, uh, the quality of your treatment as a—

LUIS (*overlapping*): Fuck this shit.

MAZE (*warning him*): Language.

LUIS: What?

MAZE: Watch your language.

LUIS: Or?

MAZE: Or they might try to use it as an excuse to drag you back to your cell.

LUIS: So?

MAZE: Well, so neither of us want that.

LUIS: I'm cool.

MAZE: That's not what I hear. (*Pause.*) Where'd you get those bruises?

LUIS: Guards.

MAZE: Really?

LUIS: Yeah.

MAZE: Okay. Because, um, from what *I've* heard, you don't eat, and you don't really sleep, and you've even injured *yourself*, from what I hear. (*Pause.*) Luis? Is that true? (*Pause.*) Luis? (*Pause.*) Okay. (*Pause.*) I know what you think. That I'm just another part of the system that put you here. And that's right. You're right about that. Because I got to you through your lawyer, and he was court appointed in the first place, and the only reason you correspond with *him* is because it's court ordered, and that makes me two or three degrees of separation away from someone you might choose to associate with given your free choice, right?

LUIS: Yeah.

MAZE: So. That's fine. But I'm what's available.

LUIS: Heh-heh.

MAZE: What.

LUIS: Uh . . . Not *really.*

MAZE: Excuse me? (*Beat.*) Oh. I get it. That's not really appropriate. (*Pause.*) You think you should be able to handle it, right? Because no one is hurting you, not really, not *physically.* But they *are* Luis, they *are* hurting you, because isolation? Total isolation? Is one of the worst forms of torture that there is.

LUIS: Yeah? The fuck you care?

MAZE: Why do I *care*?

LUIS: It's bad in here, okay. What's that to you?

MAZE: Well—

LUIS: How I'm treated, that makes you sad for me?

MAZE: No, Luis. It makes me sad for us. That we as a society cannot deal with people like you without violating our own laws.

(*Beat.*)

LUIS: Heh. Okay. But Gary? He tried, and then he tried again, and it didn't do shit, so I don't really see why my case gonna be any different with you.

MAZE: Maybe not. But *my* case is going to be different with *you*.

(MAZE *opens a folder on the table in front of her.*)

MAZE: Chicago. 1940. The Latin Kings, um, nation is established when Puerto Rican immigrants, arriving to find white police on one side, black gangs on the other, no work, and no housing, decide they need an organization to ensure social justice for themselves. So yeah. Maybe a little like what I do after all. (*Beat.*) 1979. Castro opens up the port of Mariel, refugees from Cuban Communism flood on in, and here comes *you*, at which point, pull back to big picture, Jimmy Carter, partly for being so welcoming to y'all, gets tagged a liberal dupe, gets the boot, and Ronnie Reagan's in, slams the door to any more, cuts minimum wage, cuts public housing, cuts funds for schools, and suddenly here's not so friendly either, and you join the Kings. Get in some trouble. End up East, in Attica. And there you find black gangs on one side, white guards on the other, and you say to yourself, Hey . . . what is it that we need . . .?

(*A moment.*)

LUIS: What else you got in there?

MAZE: Your manifesto.

LUIS: You read that?

MAZE: Yeah.

LUIS: Huh. (*Pause.*) What you think?

MAZE: It's the reason I'm here. Luis, you've got two things that are too common on their own but extremely rare in combination. The ability to articulate experiences? And experiences worth articulating. And so I was hoping that you would write something for me, or, not *just* for me or, I mean, obviously, for you, but not just for you either, because there are so many like you whose suffering is unnecessary, but who lack your voice. And so I was hoping you could join us. I was hoping that you'd join.

(*Pause.*)

LUIS: What I write. It would get out of here, you saying?
MAZE: Uh. In a manner of speaking. Yeah.
LUIS: And also you would come visit me some more times?
MAZE: Oh. Well, under the terms of your sentence you're not allowed any visitors, Luis. I can only come back so long as I'm representing you. I mean. That's why I'm appealing.
LUIS: Oh, I don't know. You all right.

(*A classroom.* TED KACZYNSKI, *flanked by his brother,* DAVID. *A chalkboard reads "Continuous Maps of Boundary Functions in the Complex Plane," under which is an insanely complex-looking math problem.* DAVID *has a pointer and a table of mathematical and scientific models that he uses to highlight* TED's *remarks throughout.*)

TED: "Continuous Maps of Boundary Functions in the Complex Plane." (*He points to the problem.*) What happens to the boundary of the unit disk, D, of radius less than, or equal to, one from the origin of the complex plane, when a continuous complex-valued function, f, is applied? (*Pause.*) Anyone? (*Pause.*) David?

DAVID: This problem remains open.

TED: What is meant here by the term *boundary*?

(DAVID *underlines the word* boundary.)

TED: 1942. I am born.

(DAVID *points, with the pointer, to* TED.)

TED: Consider, then, the unit disk to be me. I am inside the disk. There is nothing outside the disk. The disk, as we say, goes to infinity. (*Pause.*) 1948. My brother, David, is born.

(DAVID *points, with the pointer, to himself.*)

TED: Where there are two objects. A boundary is formed. David?

DAVID: We're not the same person. But we are brothers. Open parenthesis.

(TED *is suddenly alone, in a searchlight.*)

TED: " 'Industrial Society and Its Future.' Paragraph one. The Industrial Revolution and its consequences have been a disaster for the human race. They have destabilized society, made life unfulfilling, subjected human beings to indignities, led to widespread psychological and physical suffering, and inflicted severe damage on the natural world." Close parenthesis.

(DAVID*, and the classroom, reappear.*)

TED: Secondly: What is meant here by the term *continuous map*?

(DAVID *underlines this term.*)

TED: Consider the unit disk, now, to be the incorporated township
    of Chicago. The Chicago unit disk grows to include more
    elements. African. Puerto Rican. Eastern European. And so
    on. When a *map* is applied to the unit disk, the individual
    points . . . *move*. In a *non*continuous map, this movement may
    completely sever the prior relationships among the points. But
    in a *continuous* map, the relationships are retained, even as
    the disk is twisted, bent, folded, stretched. David?

(DAVID *is by now manipulating a large, bendable disk. He peeks
over it.*)

DAVID: As Chicago grows, its neighborhoods remain divided by
    race.
TED: And where the boundary is seemingly stretched to the point
    of rupture—
DAVID: May 1954. The United States Supreme Court finds for the
    plaintiff in Brown *v.* Board of Education.
TED: —its integrity is always somehow nevertheless retained.
DAVID: White flight.
TED: Thus forms the unit disk of urban Chicago with suburban
    Chicago outside. In sum: Where there is a fixed relationship
    among the points, the map is continuous. David?
DAVID: We moved to Evergreen Park. Our parents supported the
    cause. They did not support actually staying in town once it
    succeeded. Open parenthesis.

(TED *alone in a searchlight again.*)

TED: "Paragraph fifteen. Leftists hate America. They say they hate the West because it is warlike, imperialistic, sexist, ethnocentric, but where these same faults appear in socialist countries or in primitive cultures, the leftist finds excuses for them. He hates America and the West *because* they are strong and successful. (*Beat.*) Paragraph fifty. Conservatives are fools. They whine about the decay of traditional values, yet enthusiastically support technological progress and economic growth. Apparently it never occurs to them that you can't make changes in those areas of society without also causing changes in all others." Close parenthesis.

(*Back in the classroom. But* DAVID *is gone.*)

TED: Third, and finally: What is meant here by the term *complex plane*? David? David? (*Pause.*) David?

(NORMAN*'s office.* NORMAN *sits before a large bank of video monitors, a wall of screens each showing a different cell, or hallway, or turret, or what have you, of the prison. And, when he speaks into the intercom, all of the images change.* MAZE *is here.*)

NORMAN (*into intercom*): Next! (*To* MAZE.) Okay, first of all? I don't care for your tone. Secondly? Why don't you back up. (*Into intercom.*) Next.
MAZE: Okay. *You* said—
NORMAN: I meant physically.

(*Beat.*)

MAZE: Oh.

(MAZE *steps back.*)

NORMAN: Thank you. Now. I said that you could meet with
 Mr. Felipe and you have. I said that he could then produce a
 written statement and he did.

MAZE: Yes, but I was under the impression? That I might then feel
 free to go ahead and *use* his statement in my case.

NORMAN: I never said that. I'm sorry if you misunderstood.

MAZE: I believe you deliberately misled me, sir. I believe you've
 intentionally wasted my time.

NORMAN: Oh is *that* what I did? As one of the people *personally
 named* in your lawsuit, I'm *so sorry* if I've inconvenienced you!

(*Beat.*)

MAZE: So are you now modeling for me the *appropriate* tone,
 or—?

NORMAN: Do you even know why Luis Felipe is here?

MAZE: He was the leader of East Coast Latin Kings.

NORMAN: You make it sound like he was fronting a salsa band. He
 was overseeing a crime syndicate steeped in drug dealing,
 robbery, and murder, under the pseudonym King Blood.

MAZE: I know that.

NORMAN: Do you know where from?

MAZE: From . . . Chicago, initially, but then Luis brought it—

NORMAN: Do you know where from he was *running* it.

MAZE: I—

NORMAN: His cell. In Attica. Do you know *how?*

MAZE: These are rhetorical apparently, so why don't you tell me.

NORMAN: Through the mail. Using secret codes. In his
 correspondence. (*Into intercom.*) Next please. Next.

MAZE (*the monitors*): Are you looking for something in particular?

NORMAN: Nope. That's why it's effective. (*Back to her.*) People were shot. People were set on fire. Enemy people, his own people, didn't matter, anybody who became a problem. One guy was strangled and found in a bathtub, decapitated, missing his hands and feet, with his tattoos sliced off.

MAZE: And he was indicted on seven counts of racketeering. You already got him.

NORMAN: And I am not about to let him do it again. Because *now,* Ms. Carroll, at your urging, he has composed his entire life story, in which he conveniently fails to mention that he wasn't actually so much a refugee but rather one of the incarcerated murderers Castro booted as undesirable, and continuing this whitewashed account through the eighties and nineties, playing down the drive-bys and cocaine, and focused more on a so-called struggle for social justice, capped off by what seems to be a poem describing his state of mind here in the prison. Why a poem? I'm not sure. But apparently somebody told him that he had a voice.

MAZE: I do not believe this.

NORMAN: I was a little taken aback myself.

MAZE: My communications with Mr. Felipe are privileged! You *read* it?

NORMAN: His words are too dangerous to leave unread.

MAZE *I* won't be *using* his words! I'll be drafting an affidavit!

NORMAN: Which he would then review and adjust.

MAZE: Well, it isn't *sworn* until he *signs* it, which I won't ask him to do without *looking* at it, if that's what you mean.

NORMAN: So he'll wield some control over the final text. Which is not acceptable. Unless I get to review it thereafter. After which, since who knows *what* new codes or methods he's worked out, I'll have to exclude it regardless.

MAZE: *Pardon?*

NORMAN: Whoa, hey, now you're *really* reaching.

MAZE: *What?*

NORMAN: Little joke. Lighten the mood.

MAZE: *Why* are you even *doing* this? *Nobody* on the outside's gonna *see* it! It'll be judge's eyes only!

NORMAN: Right, because in the entire history of the legal system *no* sealed document has *ever* been leaked to the press or posted on the goddamn Internet—

MAZE: So I can't argue that the conditions in your prison are too extreme *because* of the extremity of your prison's conditions.

NORMAN: No, ma'am. *I* can't allow a bunch more traitors and rivals and bystanders to turn up dead while we're putting together another two-year-long RICO prosecution so that *I* don't have to look at those people's families and say: "What was *I* supposed to do? Take precautions?"

MAZE: You're wrong. You're actually just wrong. Because if that's the choice? Then yes, I will, yes, take my chances with a poem, and with a little revisionist history, though, by the way? Saying something in a sarcastic tone of voice doesn't actually make it untrue. So I will take my chances. If the alternative is pissing on the Constitution? Yes. I will.

NORMAN: Look, let's cut the crap. Do you know why you have the freedom to sit inside the safety of your home, spending all day dreaming up ways to get the supermax shut down? Because the supermax exists. Bad people are *real*, Ms. Carroll. People who don't belong in society. Prison is where we put those people. And some of them are so bad they don't even belong in regular prison! So let's say you win. You win! Hooray! Then what? What then? Where do they go? The forest? Your house? You find yourself in a room with these guys and a gun I bet you start to see my side. So humor me and consider for a moment the possibility that this may be after all *not* such a terrible place. Most prisons? You're in some dirty hellhole and you can't see shit, it's noisy as hell, everybody's gotta worry about getting stabbed, raped, but here? Here it's clean and it's safe, the air is temperate and there is silence. *Silence.* And on top of all that? People often compliment Florence for how she looks. From a distance, I mean. How she glitters in the sun. Because, Ms. Carroll, a prison? Need not be ugly. To be secure. (*A moment. Then:*) Next!

(MAZE *and* LUIS. *Table and glass between them.* EARL *outside.* LUIS *is holding his handwritten statement and is pacing and ranting.*)

MAZE: I understand your anger.
LUIS: *Fuck* you! Coming in here, talking about I can help you, if you help me, I can help you, but I knew it was just the same shit!
MAZE: No, no, it's just that it seems like it might be smarter and faster for me to find other clients—
LUIS (*overlapping*): Oh, I see, okay—
MAZE: So that I can help you *all*, by starting with inmates who aren't so—
LUIS: *What.*
MAZE: Who aren't so . . . so . . . You know.
LUIS: Oh. (*Pause.*) Okay, but see, before, I was thinking, Win, lose, whatever, at least some part of me gets out of here, because you told me, you said, but—
MAZE: Well, it, okay, I mean, *that*, specifically—
LUIS: What.

(EARL *has entered. A moment.*)

MAZE: That was never . . . I was, yes, I was going to use your
    statement as the basis for . . . (*Pause.*) I wasn't going to use
    your actual words.

LUIS: No?

MAZE: No. I, um. I'm sorry if you misunderstood.

(EARL *goes.*)

LUIS: I mean, that's cool. I mean, you always *knew* you was
    gonna lose. Anyway. Right?

MAZE: What?

LUIS: Right? Because, with things like this, people like you? All
    you can do is make *yourself* feel better. Like you tried. Because
    then you can have it *both* ways, right? Say they being unfair to
    me. But keep me locked up too. (*Beat.*) I mean, like you said,
    you a part of the system. But see, you not just a part. You the
    worst part. The part that *pretend* you don't like it. So
    everybody else can feel okay about how nothing ever gonna
    change.

MAZE: That's not true.

LUIS: Funniest thing is? Nobody on the outside even listening.

MAZE: What? What do you mean?

LUIS: 'Cause I'm out.

MAZE: You're out of what?

LUIS: The Kings.

MAZE: What?

LUIS: Indicted. Put on trial. Excommunicated.

MAZE: The Latin Kings indicted you?

LUIS: They got a new leader now and everything.

MAZE: But you mean they actually wrote up an indictment.

LUIS: Eleven counts. My federal indictment only had seven.

MAZE: I didn't know that.

LUIS: Uh. Wasn't exactly in the papers.

MAZE: The Latin Kings actually wrote an *indictment* and had a
trial.

LUIS: Maze. That's how the nation do.

(*Long pause.*)

MAZE (*carefully*): Luis, I have to go now. So I want to tell you one
more thing. I want you to always remember? That whatever
they can monitor, or control, or take away? That there's one
thing they can't touch.

LUIS: Oh yeah? What's that.

MAZE (*pointing to her head*): They can't touch what's up here.

(*Beat.*)

LUIS: Okay, um, that's really, like, inspiring and whatnot? But
come on—

MAZE: Luis. They can't touch. What's up here.

LUIS: No. (*Pause.*) No they can't. (*Pause.*) I guess that's true.

MAZE: So I'll tell you what, Luis. Just as the last thing. Before we
say goodbye. Why don't you tell me your poem? Why don't
you just recite your poem to me? So that I can hear it. So that
someone will at least have heard it. Okay? (*Pause.*) Luis? What
do you say.

(TIMOTHY, *alone. He wears a Burger King crown and is holding a
gun. During the following, he lines up five cans on a fence, walks
to a slight distance, and aims.*)

TIMOTHY: "First Amendment: Congress shall make no law
   respecting an establishment of religion. Or prohibiting the free
   exercise thereof."

(*His sister* JENNIFER *appears, following him.*)

JENNIFER: Timothy?
TIMOTHY: "Or abridging the freedom of speech. Or of the press."
JENNIFER: Timothy?
TIMOTHY: "Or the right of the people peaceably to assemble. And
   to petition the Government. For a redress of grievances."
JENNIFER: Tim?

(TIMOTHY *shoots the cans off the fence one by one.* JENNIFER
vanishes.)

(*The exercise yard.* TIMOTHY, RAMZI, TED, *and* LUIS. *In separate
spaces. Separated by a metal mesh. Exercising or chatting, as the
case may be.*)

TIMOTHY: Morning, boys.
TED: Hello, Tim.
RAMZI: Hello, Timothy.
TIMOTHY: Everybody sleep okay?
TED: Yes.
RAMZI: Yes.
TIMOTHY: Yeah, me too.

(*Pause. They work out.*)

RAMZI: I have a question for all of you.
TIMOTHY: It better not be what I think it is.

RAMZI: Have either of you considered partaking in the glory of
Islam?

TIMOTHY: Are you going to ask us that every *day*? Because: Jesus
Christ.

RAMZI: It is my duty to make attempts to convert you.

TIMOTHY: Well, cut it out.

RAMZI: But—

TIMOTHY: Hey! (*Pause.*) Anybody see any good movies lately?

(*Beat.*)

RAMZI: Yes.

TED: Yes.

TIMOTHY: Anybody catch *Unforgiven* last night? Hoo! That is my
hands-down, all-time favorite movie.

RAMZI: I'll see anything with Morgan Freeman.

TIMOTHY: I know, right? That guy is like incapable of delivering a
false line reading.

TED: He's very skilled, yes.

TIMOTHY: You watched it?

TED: On and off. Not all the way through.

TIMOTHY: I'd watch that thing every *day* if it were on. Something
about it.

RAMZI: Is it because the sheriff is the villain and the outlaw is the
hero?

TIMOTHY: Maybe. I also think the soundtrack is really evocative.

(*Beat.*)

TED: I find the frontier whores unrealistically attractive.

TIMOTHY: Well. Hollywood.

TED: But, Timothy, what concerns me, really, is that you don't use your time more productively. Ramzi, myself, we have the rest of our natural lives, but you actually have an approaching date of execution—

TIMOTHY: Thanks, thank you, Teddy, I had managed to forget for one sweet sweet minute, but thank you so much for reminding me—

TED: But to *use* that time for reading, for writing, writing especially—

TIMOTHY: I'm a lover, not a writer.

TED: Well, that probably won't do you a lot of good in here.

TIMOTHY: No, sir. Good stock going to waste. The continuation of the line is all up to Jenny now.

TED: Jenny?

TIMOTHY: My little sister. (*Beat.*) Either way, it's the end of the name.

TED: This is my point. Maybe not. Not if you *write*.

TIMOTHY: And what is it that you suggest I write, Teddy? My life story?

TED: I don't know.

TIMOTHY: I don't care to. But I'll give you the highlights in ten seconds so *you* can.

TED: That really isn't—

TIMOTHY (*overlapping*): Born April 1968. Mom left when I was ten. Dad stuck around. Granddad taught me how to shoot. Cans on a fence. Heh. (*Beat.*) Finished high school, worked at Burger King, that *sucked*, except for I had sex with this girl. Then I drove an armored car, worked security, you know, jobs where I could use my real skills. Joined the army. Went to the Gulf—

(*A searchlight hits* TIMOTHY.)

TIMOTHY: Which, but hey, there's absolutely no reason to talk too much about what went on over there, so why don't I just move on.

(*The searchlight goes out.*)

TIMOTHY: Came home. Saw Waco. On TV? Packed a bag, went down to protest, lot of good *that* did, selling *bumper* stickers, so I hooked up with my old army buddy, Terry, and me and him—

(*The searchlight hits* TIMOTHY. *A moment.*)

TIMOTHY: Well. You know.

(*The searchlight goes out.*)

TIMOTHY: That's it. Here I am. Oh, and died. August 2001. If all goes according to plan. So there it is. Write it down, Teddy. Knock yourself out.

(*Pause.*)

RAMZI: Timothy.
TIMOTHY: What.
RAMZI: You were born, you said, in April of 1968?
TIMOTHY: Is that the beginning of a segue towards converting me to Islam?
RAMZI: No.
TIMOTHY: Good.
RAMZI: Only, I too was born in April of 1968.
TIMOTHY: Seriously?

RAMZI: Yes.

TIMOTHY: Dude!

RAMZI: I know!

TIMOTHY: Wow. Huh. Wow.

(*Pause.*)

TED: I was never around women. Harvard was all male. They'd
    bring girls, on buses, literally, trains. Like cargo. I couldn't . . .
    And then, Michigan, graduate school, everyone in the
    department . . . Mathematics. After all. Likewise with most of
    my students at Berkeley. And then Montana. The woods. There
    was no one.

(*Beat.*)

TIMOTHY: What the fuck are you talking about?

TED: Nothing. Never mind.

RAMZI: At Harvard you studied only mathematics?

TED: Oh, no. There was a core curriculum. Built around logical
    positivism. Do you know what logical positivism is?

TIMOTHY: Nobody. Cares.

TED: Actually that about sums it up.

(*Pause.*)

TIMOTHY: Hey, Felipe. You ready to talk to us today? (*Pause.*)
    Felipe? (*Pause.*) Felipe? (*Pause.*) Luis? (*Pause.*) See now, that's
    just inconsiderate.

RAMZI: Perhaps he simply does not want to talk to you, Timothy.

TIMOTHY: Why not? I'm extremely personable.

TED: You can be a little grating, Tim.

TIMOTHY: Excuse me?

RAMZI: It's true, Tim, you can. A little forward, a little . . . what's
the word.

TED: Overeager?

RAMZI: Yes! Yes, that's it.

TIMOTHY: Huh. I had no idea you guys felt this way.

RAMZI: Oh, no, no: we like you, Tim.

TED: Very much.

RAMZI: Yes, very much. In fact, I was surprised by your
friendliness. In the videos you always appeared angry, sullen.
But in fact you are talkative, ehhh, how do you say it: upbeat?

TED: Yes. But. Some people might take a little while to get used to
your manner. It's nothing to be ashamed of.

TIMOTHY: Well, he's not exactly chatting you guys up either, so I
don't know what the hell you're so smug about.

TED: Tim—

TIMOTHY: Yeah, no, let's just have some quiet.

(*Pause.*)

RAMZI: Mr. Felipe? May I ask you a question?

TIMOTHY: Oh, you want to talk about over*eager*—

RAMZI: I'm not talking to you, Timothy.

TED (*looking up*): Hey, be careful, you're—

TIMOTHY: Right, but *that's* not *grating* or *forward*, right, what *he's*
about to do?

RAMZI: You have no idea what I am about to do. So please.
(*Beat.*) Mr. Felipe, have you ever considered partaking in the
glory of Islam?

TIMOTHY: Aha!

RAMZI: Because I would be more than willing to discuss it with
you, or, if it's something you'd rather consider quietly, on your

own, you can arrange to have Earl procure for you the text of
the Holy Qu'ran.

TIMOTHY (*simultaneously*): Meanwhile, Mr. Devout Holy Man,
you're laying there in your cell watching *movies*, which, and
please correct me, but isn't that technically not even *allowed*
by your religion?

(*Searchlights hit* TIMOTHY *and* RAMZI.)

TED: I warned you, gentlemen.

(*Searchlights out. Pause.*)

RAMZI: In the desert, it was dark in the caves. We told stories to
keep from losing our minds. Technically? Yes. I am not allowed
movies. But. Likewise here. The caves are dark.

TIMOTHY: You know why no one wants to read your book,
Ramzi?

RAMZI: No. Why don't you enlighten me.

TIMOTHY: Because it sucks. I mean as a *story*. It is boring,
repetitive, and impossible to understand.

(*A moment.* RAMZI *chuckles.*)

TIMOTHY: You find that funny in some way?

RAMZI: No, only, this is the typical reaction of the Western reader.

TIMOTHY: Oh, now it's supposed to be a Western?

RAMZI: Because it is *your* expectation that the text will proceed as
though wrought for your *amusement*. But the Qu'ran is not
constructed this way. After the brief opening incantation, the
Surahs are arranged not in narrative sequence, but simply
from longest to shortest, two hundred lines or more, then one

hundred, then fifty. Furthermore, in the Qu'ran, ideas, laws, morality, these things are not derived *from* events, and subordinate *to* them, but quite the opposite. Events are cited only when needed in support of ideas. The structure of the Qu'ran is entirely coherent with regard to its *lessons*. *Story* emerges only fragmentally. Like rays of the sun through a wood-lattice window. Slivers of light! But most of all, the Qu'ran is, finally, untranslatable. Its meaning is not simply in the words or in their order but in the rhymes and rhythms of the Arabic itself. And as the final Surahs unfold, fifteen lines, ten lines, five, what we are left with is poetry. The most exquisite poetry in the history of mankind. Why poetry?

LUIS: Because poetry's the easiest to memorize.

(*Beat.*)

RAMZI: Yes. That's right.

LUIS: Black Muslim that I knew in Attica had it in his cell. Old guy. He was reading it all the time, quoting things, and all the young black guys, they was listening to him all the time, like, they really followed him, and respected him, and, you know, I was trying to learn how to do that a little bit. So I asked him about it.

RAMZI: And was it helpful for you?

LUIS: In a manner of speaking.

(*Pause.*)

TIMOTHY: You know that's just my game face.

RAMZI: What?

TIMOTHY: The angry, sullen thing? That's just my game face. I use it around feds. I mean, around you guys, or even state guys, I

can just be myself, but the feds, I mean, they're the *enemy*,
so . . . Oh, wait, crap—

(*The searchlight hits* TIMOTHY. *He waves in acknowledgment. It goes out.*)

TIMOTHY: Does anybody else just totally hate that fucking searchlight?
TED: Actually, gentlemen, I've been paying close attention, trying to discern a pattern? And it seems that if we adhere to a few fairly simple guidelines it should be possible to converse uninterrupted. Um. Obviously, plans for disruption of or escape from the prison are off-limits. Also, fighting amongst ourselves, as we've just seen. Also, explicit reference to your crimes, or to the events to which you were responding when you committed your crimes, or discussion of, or reference to, the key ideological positions you hold that justified your crimes. Simply confine yourself to the mundane and the abstract and you should be able to speak. Freely.
TIMOTHY: "Sometimes the tree of liberty must be refreshed with the blood of patriots."

(*Searchlight on.*)

TIMOTHY: "Go ahead. Make my day."

(*Searchlight off.*)

TIMOTHY: So. Clint Eastwood, okay. Thomas Jefferson, not okay.

(*Pause.*)

ITAMAR MOSES

LUIS: Colorado. 2001. Four guys in a exercise yard. Guards on one
    side. Murderers on the other. And nothing for themselves.
    Except each other. If they could only find a way. To really talk.
TIMOTHY: "This spring. The only way to get out . . . is to look
    within." You guys ever notice that? With those taglines, how
    it's always opposites, like, some opposite that makes no
    sense? "The only way to stand up . . . is to fall down." "The
    only way to win . . . is to lose." Right, guys?

(*Beat.*)

RAMZI: I think I take your point, Mr. Felipe. The Western listener,
    you see, cannot comprehend ideas communicated entirely by
    means of metaphor.
LUIS: Like you said. It's untranslatable.
TED: "Gentlemen! You can't fight in here! This is the war room!"
    (*Beat.*) *Doctor Strangelove.* 1964. Before your time.

(MAZE, *alone.*)

MAZE: *En la prision de las sombras, solo oigo voces*
    Temo pensar, porque lo único que me viene a la mente es
        agonía
    Y así, un muro me protege de mis propios pensamientos
    Y así, solo hay muros, por un poco más esperare unas buenas
        noticias
    Buenas noticias de Dios

(*During this, a man appears. Wearing black. Sunglasses. This is*
EVAN.)

(NORMAN's office. MAZE is seated across from EVAN; NORMAN
stands off to one side of him, deferentially. EARL stands behind
MAZE. On one of the monitors a tape is playing of the last
meeting between MAZE and LUIS. There is no audio, but NORMAN
is reading from a transcript.)

NORMAN: MAZE CARROLL: "There's one thing they can't touch."
  LUIS FELIPE: "Oh yeah? What's that." MAZE CARROLL: "They
  can't touch what's up here."
MAZE: This is all a misunderstanding.
NORMAN: I see. So you accidentally smuggled volatile materials
  that I specifically forbade you to transport—
MAZE: The document remained on the other side of the glass. You
  cannot prove that anything Luis wrote ever left that room.
NORMAN: And you cannot be permitted to leave this complex
  unless you leave behind what you're carrying.
MAZE: I'm not carrying anything!
NORMAN: Inside your head.
MAZE: So I can go if I leave behind my head?
NORMAN: Don't tempt me.
EVAN: Whoa, hey, gee whiz, Carl, relax, would ya? (To MAZE.)
  Sorry about that. Hi there. Do you know who I am?
MAZE: No. But under the circumstances I'm guessing that you're
  FBI.

(Beat.)

EVAN: My name is Evan.
MAZE: Okay.

(A moment.)

EVAN (*he peers at her*): So okay, here's what I can't figure out. Is whether you actually think you did a nice thing for a suffering man. Or if you know that you were just a mule for transmitting orders to the outside.

MAZE: Whoa, whoa. What?

EVAN: Oh, it took us a while. He's changed up some of the encryption since the Attica days. But we cracked the sucker in the end.

MAZE: What are you talking about?

EVAN: This so-called poem. It's a code. And if past is prologue, then the thing is likely some kind of assassination order, directed against an emboldened opposition, or recalcitrant underlings, or both.

MAZE: I don't believe you.

EVAN: Uh. *You* don't believe *me*?

MAZE: Why would he do that? He has nothing to gain.

NORMAN: He has nothing to lose.

MAZE: Yeah, thanks to you, you moron!

EVAN: Hey, calm down! Both of you!

MAZE: Luis isn't even running the nation anymore. He was excommunicated.

EVAN: Oh yeah? Who told you that? (*Beat.*) And of course you vetted this intelligence with several unbiased independent sources? (*Pause.*) Yeah.

MAZE: I want to see a lawyer.

EVAN: Actually, that won't be necessary. 'Cause luckily for you? Something new's come up. Something urgent. Something you can help us with.

MAZE: What.

EVAN: Luis exercises for an hour a day. With the three other men on his cellblock. Do you know who those men are?

MAZE: Um. Unabomber Theodore Kaczynski; Ramzi Yousef, who did the World Trade Center in '93; and Oklahoma City bomber Timothy McVeigh—which, by the way? Whose frickin' genius idea was *that?*

NORMAN: Okay, that's not really our focus here?

EVAN: See, suddenly? There's a lot of suspicious chatter in the yard. About movies, mostly. Rehashing plots. Quoting lines. Having entire conversations this way. And we think? They're planning something. Because also? They've all started writing. Yousef's doing what looks like some kind of religious text, chapter and verse, but the narrative elements are all about Afghanistan and the Gulf. Kaczynski's doing math, but for some reason all his examples are about urban planning in Chicago and Harvard and the Cuban missile crisis. And McVeigh? He's writing out, verbatim, articles of the Bill of Rights. We believe Luis's experience with you has inspired the rest of them. To try to convey instructions to allies on the outside.

(MAZE *looks unwell.*)

EVAN: Yes. But. This is also an opportunity. To round up who knows who else, militias, ecoterrorists, Islamo-Fascists, anybody they try to contact. And meanwhile Luis still thinks he can trust you. Or use you. Whichever. Do you see?

MAZE: No.

EVAN: You've got to get him to do it again.

MAZE: (*Beat.*): No.

EVAN: What you're gonna do is, you're gonna go back in, escorted by Earl, and you're gonna tell Mr. Felipe that you've got good news, that Norman here caved and you can represent him after all. But this time you're not his mule. This time you're our mole.

MAZE: I said no.

NORMAN: Maze, this could be your only shot at immunity. I don't think you want to go to prison. You of all people know what that means.

(*Beat.*)

MAZE (*to* EARL): Don't make me do this.

EVAN: Hey. Whoa. It's not exactly up to him.

MAZE (*still to* EARL): You don't want to do this. Don't do this.

EVAN: And even if he won't, I'll just find someone who will.

MAZE (*still to* EARL): You agree with me, Earl, I know you do, I heard you say it, they don't have a good view, I heard you—!

EARL: Hey! (*Pause.*) Do you know why the supermax prison exists?

(*Beat.*)

MAZE (*sheepishly*): Um. So that I have the freedom to sit in my house all day, dreaming up ways to get the supermax shut down?

EARL: I mean literally. The specific event that led to its creation.

MAZE: Oh. Um. 1987. Federal pen. Marion, Illinois. A member of the Aryan Brotherhood killed a guard.

EARL: You make it sound . . . (*Beat.*) Guy was walking down the hall, escorted, hands cuffed in front of him, and, when they passed the cell of another Aryan brother, the first guy shoved his hands through the bars, where his friend in the cell, who had a stolen key, unlocked the cuffs, gave the first guy a knife, inmate turned around and stabbed the guard forty times in less that sixty seconds. Nobody. Could fucking. Believe it. Nobody in the entire prison system could believe it had happened. We couldn't believe it. We simply could not. Later that day? It happened again. (*Beat.*) Guys like this? There are no defenses. There are no deterrents. And they simply do not give a fuck. So sure, Carl Norman has his party line: "Blah blah *society* blah *silence* and blah blah *it glitters in the sun.*" All *I* meant is? I'm the one in trenches. And I have no intention of getting stabbed for sport. Because if that's the choice? Then you're wrong. You're just wrong.

(*A moment.* MAZE *turns back to* EVAN.)

EVAN: Don't worry if he catches on. Don't worry if he gets upset. Just keep him talking. The more he says? The more likely he'll give something away. And if you get in any real trouble? Say my name.

(RAMZI, *alone.*)

RAMZI: In the name of God, the merciful, the compassionate:

(TIMOTHY, *alone.*)

TIMOTHY: "Second Amendment."

(TED, *alone.*)

TED: Third, and finally, what is meant here by the term *complex plane*?

(TIMOTHY *puts on a United States Army uniform, stands at attention.*)

TIMOTHY: "A well regulated Militia. Being necessary to the security of a free State. The right of the people. To keep and bear Arms. Shall not be infringed."

RAMZI: Third Surah. *Al-Zumar.* "The troops."

TED: A plane is an infinite two-dimensional space created by the intersection of two number lines, each stretching from the origin, in either direction, to infinity and to negative infinity. Each point in a plane is a coordinate containing two pieces of information. If, for instance, we assign a coordinate to every undergraduate who attended Harvard between, for instance, 1958 and 1962: Open parenthesis: Student Ted. Comma. Public school graduate. Or: Of Foreign Descent. Or: On Financial Aid. Close Parenthesis. Or: Open Parenthesis:

RAMZI: O believers! Remember! When the nation of Kuwait was invaded by the nation of Iraq and the American president declared war, saying:

TED (*as George H. W. Bush*): "Just two hours ago, allied air forces began an attack on military targets in Iraq and Kuwait. These attacks continue as I speak."

RAMZI: And lo, he spoke on, saying:

TED: "The troops know why they're there. And listen to what they say, because they've said better than any president or prime minister ever could."

RAMZI: And he did not say, but might have said:

TED: Listen to Private Timothy James McVeigh, who says:

(TIMOTHY *is in a tank. He is the gunner. During the following, he spots a target and aims.* RAMZI *is the target.*)

TIMOTHY: "Third Amendment: No Soldier shall, in time of peace be quartered in any house, without the consent of the Owner,

nor in time of war, but in a manner to be prescribed by law."
Forty-ninth Ayah.

TED: "May God bless each and every one of them and the
coalition forces at our side in the Gulf, and may He continue to
bless our nation, the United States of America."

(TIMOTHY *fires the gun.* TED *tracks the path of the projectile with
his pointer until it strikes* RAMZI.)

TED: The *complex* plane is the infinite, two-dimensional space
created by the intersection of the real number line and the
imaginary number line. Each coordinate in the complex plane
is thus half real and half imagined. If, for instance, we assign a
coordinate to the events of October 1962. Open parenthesis.
Satellite photos reveal Soviet nuclear missiles in Cuba.
Comma. Millions lost to fallout radiation. Close Parenthesis.
Or: Open parenthesis:

TIMOTHY: Fourth Surah. *Al-Vizier.* "The Viceroy."

RAMZI: O Believers! Remember! How the presence of these
troops in the Kingdom of Saudi Arabia angered the new angel
of the mujahedeen, and he too declared War, saying:

TIMOTHY (*as Osama Bin Laden*): "The Muslims' blood has
become the cheapest, and their wealth loot in the hands of
their enemies."

RAMZI: And he went on, saying:

TIMOTHY: "The latest and greatest of all these aggressions is the
occupation of the land of the two holy places by the American
crusaders and their allies."

RAMZI: And did not say, but might have said:

(TIMOTHY *watches TV, horrified, and packs a bag.*)

TIMOTHY: "Fourth Amendment: The right of the people to be secure in their persons, houses, papers, and effects, against unreasonable searches and seizures, shall not be violated, and no Warrants shall issue, but upon probable cause, supported by Oath or affirmation, and particularly describing the place to be searched, and the persons or things to be seized."

TED: "Paragraph Two Hundred Thirty-One. Throughout this article we've made imprecise statements that ought to have qualifications attached. And some of our statements may be flatly false. And, of course, in a discussion of this kind one must rely heavily on intuitive judgment and that can sometimes be wrong. All the same, we are reasonably confident that the general outlines of the picture we have painted here are roughly correct."

(MAZE *and* LUIS. *Table and glass.* EARL *outside.*)

MAZE: I have some good news. Turns out I was . . . It, uh, it looks like I can maybe represent you. After all.

LUIS: Oh good. That's good. So what you need? You need, like, a statement? Because I still have the one from before. Or no. Why don't I just go ahead and give you the rest of my orders for the Latin Kings on the outside?

(*Beat.*)

MAZE: What did you just say?

LUIS: Yeah, because you not very good at this, so let's not pretend we don't know why you back in here, okay?

MAZE: So you did it. So it's true.

LUIS: I did what. What did I do.

MAZE: Do you even realize that I was trying to help you? And that you've *ruined* it? And not just for *you*, for *everybody*?

LUIS: Oh, is that what I did?

MAZE: Maybe I should have seen it coming. You did it before, right? In Attica? Before *that*, even. The Marielitos. Noble refugees, seeking a better life, with murderers like you hiding in the crowd. So this is actually kind of a theme for you, huh? Something beautiful. With your poison stowed away inside. So congratulations. You win! Hooray! You proved them right! You killed my case! So maybe, this time, *I'm* the dupe. But I'm *also* the one who's gonna slam the door. Because I don't like being used.

LUIS: Who used who first, Maze? Who tried to use who first? "Poor baby, you suffering, oh, but if you join us we can help you." You think I don't know a recruitment speech I hear one? You think I ain't *said* that shit a hundred times, some kid shows up in Chicago, New York? You just mad 'cause now you see that, really? It was *you* that was getting recruited. It was *you* was joining *me*. But you should be grateful. 'Cause you helped a good cause.

MAZE: What, social justice? *Bullshit*. You're a frigging crime boss. And you do what *you* have to do to keep *your* power and *your* money.

LUIS: Why it can't be both?

MAZE: You can't run social programs *and* kill people, Luis! You have to pick one!

LUIS: No. *You* do. You *get* to pick one. But see, a drug dealer? He got short flexible hours, cash in hand, tax free, and, meanwhile, half Chicago PD keeps the other half off your back, for kickbacks, so *we* have to pick *both*. *You* the ones started a war.

MAZE: What?

LUIS: War on Drugs. Put away junkies, right? Or maybe the guy selling two ounces of coke, which meanwhile got here from South America with the fucking CIA, I'm just saying, and putting those nobodies away for a long time, people who if you could maybe *help* them instead of putting them in *jail*, but no, *you* lock 'em up, which is how we *got* so many recruits in prison *anyway*, because five hundred nobodies come in every day and they want to feel like *somebody*, and there *I* am, and I can *do* that, and that's the whole reason there even is the Latin Kings on the East Coast in the *first* fucking place, okay? And, meanwhile, these *gangs* come along, Latin Lords, Latin Disciples, who don't have the *legitimacy* we got, don't have the founding *documents*, don't know the history, *they* come along, and *they* just see the money, and *they* think it's cool to just deal coke, and kill people, and who you want in control? Those *gangs*, who just be evil and crazy? Or the *nation*, who *use* that money to do some good? 'Cause whoever controls the most *blocks sells* the most, has the most *cash*, and can *do* the most. So when the Lords do a drive-by, what are we supposed to do? Nothing? Just stand by and encourage more of that shit? So that next time they maybe taking out a bunch of, like, little kids that's just hanging out on our *block*? No. You strike *back*. And sometimes, yeah, you strike *first*. And if you *don't*? Then that's just you being *stupid*.

MAZE: And so then *you* accidentally kill a bunch of little kids that are just hanging out on *their* block.

LUIS: Maybe. And that's too bad. Then we sad about that. But when *they* do it, see, they not sad. They be like *celebrating*. They be like, "Well, if those kids was growing up in Latin Kings territory, then in about five years they gonna be Latin Kings, so we just got those bitches early, and there's plenty more where they come from." Which is fucked *up*. And that just shows you.

MAZE: It shows me *what*.

LUIS: The difference!

MAZE: That when *they* do it it's a senseless, murderous act that must be avenged, but when *you* do it it's collateral damage?

LUIS: No. That we a nation. And they a gang.

MAZE: Repeating something over and over doesn't make it true, Luis! Oh my God, it's like arguing with an addict! This great founding document? The manifesto? How many people have actually *read* it? Anybody? Or is it just this *thing* that people *know* about, just *looming* there, its only purpose anymore is to grant *legitimacy* to whatever *you* happen to decide. So you can all just make *reference* to it. "We've got our manifesto!" This big *idea* nobody even believes in. Just a big *excuse*. Because let me tell you what *I* see. *I* see a bunch of scared immigrants establishing something they call a nation, but that *became* a corrupt organization exploiting its *own* youth, its *own* disenfranchised, sending them out to make money through the illegal sale of addictive goods, using them as foot soldiers in suicide missions against rivals in order to expand the territory in which they can *make* that money, suppressing individuality with slogans and uniforms, spurring them on with rhetoric about wrongs committed against them by dehumanized enemies, and all of a sudden, you're *not* a nation. Not anymore. You've soiled the name. And you're a fucking *gang*.

(*Beat.*)

LUIS: Is Earl even *out* there today?

MAZE: He's out there to protect *me* from *you*.

LUIS: Well, maybe he should broaden his mandate, you know?

MAZE: Are you afraid I'm gonna *hurt* you?

LUIS: You definitely starting to hurt my *feelings.*

MAZE: Oh? Well, then maybe you can just lean on your new friends. (*Pause.*) Yeah. Maybe we should talk about *those* guys.

(*Suddenly the lights dim as if the electrical grid has failed. A moment. Then the lights return. Another moment. Then, very slowly, during the following,* LUIS *stands and walks around the table to the door that separates them.*)

LUIS: See. Your biggest mistake is? You can only see me in a certain way.

MAZE: What are you doing?

LUIS: Ignorant inmate breaks down, finds his goodness inside, that's the kind I can be, not the *genius* kind, right, pulling all the strings, get inside your head, make you *do* shit, oh, that can't be *me*, right, that guy's got to be *white*, got to have a British *accent* and shit, but my *dark* skin, that just means I got to be, like, *rescued*, or, like, *understood*, right? 'Cause I can be *dangerous.* But not *powerful.* 'Cause I gotta be dealt with from above. Not face-to-face like an equal.

MAZE: Evan? Are you watching this?

LUIS: But then again, maybe not. Maybe while you thought you was keeping me talking? Maybe really I was keeping you talking. Maybe I was just waiting you out. Until it was time.

(LUIS *pushes the door between them. It swings open.* MAZE *freezes. Then bolts.*)

MAZE: Earl!

(*The outer door opens. For a moment it looks like* EARL. *But it's* TIMOTHY.)

TIMOTHY: Earl's not in at the moment, but if you leave a message, he'll get back to you as soon as he can.

(TIMOTHY *grabs* MAZE *and propels her back into her chair.*)

LUIS: Hey.
TIMOTHY: Here.

(TIMOTHY *has a gun. He tosses it to* LUIS.)

LUIS: You keep it.

(LUIS *tosses the gun back. Meanwhile, perhaps a ceiling panel has opened, and* RAMZI *has dropped into the room from above.*)

RAMZI: Hello. Have you ever considered partaking in the—
TIMOTHY: Oh my God!
LUIS: If she moves? Shoot her in the leg. She moves again? Shoot her in the face.

(TED *has entered, perhaps through the floor.*)

TED: Nobody is shooting anybody.
TIMOTHY: Relax.
TED: Oh yes, I'm extremely relaxed about the prospect of bullets ricocheting throughout an enclosed space.
TIMOTHY: They only ricochet if you miss.
LUIS: Okay, shut up a second, everybody. Guys? This is Maze Carroll. Maze? This is Timothy, Ramzi, and Ted. And we hereby welcome you. To the sovereign nation. Of Celebrity Row.

(*Blackout.*)

ACT 2

A porch in Wilmington, North Carolina. A sunset dinner. MAZE, HELLER, *and* DAD *around the table.*

MOM (*from off*): I'm sorry I don't have any iced tea to offer the two of you.

HELLER: That's all right.

MOM: No, you have no idea how mortifying that is, to be a Southern woman and not to have any iced tea.

DAD: Dammit! He said it's all right!

MOM (*entering*): Well, what else is he gonna say? "I am deeply disappointed in you, Mrs. Carroll"? Of course he's gonna be polite. But for all I know, on the inside? He's crushed.

DAD: It's a day for beer. That right, Heller? We gonna throw back a few beers?

HELLER: Yes, sir.

MAZE: Dad, please don't bully my husband.

DAD: Who's a bully? You feel bullied, son?

HELLER: Constantly. It's nice to get it from somebody else.

DAD: Ha-ha! I like your Yankee husband, Maze. You hold on to him.

MAZE: Don't do that. Don't gang up on me to endear yourself to my father.

MOM: You know who I saw at the pier today, Mazie, was your old high school friend, whatsername, with the red hair, went steady with Peter for a while? She has two children now! One in the stroller, one by her side, and she was just aglow, I tell you. Just glowing. (*Pause.*) Glowing.

MAZE: Oh for God's sake, Mother, we're not even sure if we want kids.

MOM: Who said anything about you having kids? I was simply
telling a story.

MAZE: Yes. You're very subtle. You're a master in the art of
subtlety.

MOM: But if you were to have a child, Mazie, you could raise her
just however you want, tell her every day that she could grow
up to be anything, a doctor, or a lawyer, or even a president.

DAD: Don't fill my grandson's head with that nonsense.

MAZE: Oh, okay, it's a son.

DAD: And you tell him that some people grow up to be failures
and that that's just the way it is. The constant looming
possibility of failure is what's made our country great. And if
your kid goes belly up? Tell him not to come back lookin' for
handouts.

MAZE: Heller and I will be there to support the hypothetical child
that we don't have, no matter what.

DAD: Oh, that's great. So you're just a big bank, and supermarket,
and hotel, all rolled into one.

MAZE: This conversation is baffling.

DAD: No, who can blame you? A bunch of pothead Democrats in
the White House treating it like a bachelor pad while the whole
country goes batshit crazy. Ever since Kennedy!

MOM: Kennedy was a great man.

DAD: Not until he got shot in the head he wasn't.

MOM: You will not speak blithely of the Kennedy assassination in
front of company! (*To* HELLER.) Don't you listen to him. We did
the same for Mazie, told her she could be whatever she
wanted, an acupuncturist, or a puppeteer, or a president or
anything.

MAZE: Why do you always say *a* president?

MOM: What?

MAZE: Like I could be the president of Brazil?

MOM: Well, I swear I don't know, dear. That is up to the Brazilians.

HELLER: Actually, Brazil is a federative republic. (*Beat.*) Though its government does in fact have . . . an executive . . . branch . . .

(*Pause.*)

MOM: So! Anybody want to go for a walk along the river?

HELLER: That sounds great.

DAD: Lotta history down there, son.

MAZE: Oh yes. Cape Fear was a key strategic port for Confederate blockade runners during what some still call the War of Northern Aggression.

DAD: Hey—

MAZE: Then? Postabolition? The black community here thrived until a riot by their white neighbors drove them out. They burned the black newspaper. That day the river was full of floating bodies.

DAD: Those accounts are sketchy and disputed!

MAZE: There is some disagreement about how many bodies, yes.

DAD: Why must you insist on being so inflammatory all the damn time?

HELLER: Don't worry. She's just engaging in the time-honored liberal practice of paying relatively meaningless lip service to the crimes of our nation so that we might feel superficially exonerated while carrying on exactly as before.

DAD: Well, okay.

MAZE: Of course, the river is *so* important that in the seventies it was abandoned for the fast money of urban sprawl such that a neon rainbow of gas stations and chain stores even now sprouts like kudzu in all directions!

DAD: That waterfront is, as we speak, being revitalized and restored.

MAZE: Yes. Due to the presence in town of the television show
Dawson's Creek.

DAD: So you are also, I take it, opposed to prosperity.

MAZE: No. But the sight of a strip mall doth cleave my very heart
in two.

DAD: You are so melodramatic.

MAZE: Dad, the natural beauty of North Carolina—

DAD: The goddamn planet Earth is not going anywhere! It was
here long before us and will remain here long after we are
gone, and I do not need my tree-hugging daughter to tell me
that I cannot enjoy conveniently located gasoline during the
brief time that I do walk upon it!

MAZE: They want to put a landfill in the Green Swamp.

DAD: Heller, do you know what she's talking about?

HELLER: Yes, sir.

MAZE: The Green Swamp contains endangered flytrap colonies, a
protected Indian burial ground, *and* it is located in a
floodplain!

DAD: Well, maybe there's a factor in play more important than
carnivorous plant life. If you can imagine such a thing.

MAZE (*to* MOM): Did he just not *hear* me say *burial ground* and
floodplain?

MOM: You know perfectly well that your father hears only what he
can refute.

MAZE: Yeah, Dad, the "factor in play" is that accepting garbage
from elsewhere is supposed to be a big economic boon for the
state, but actually we're poisoning ourselves in exchange for,
once again, a windfall for the wealthiest one percent—

DAD: You will not continue to bad-mouth Reaganomics at this
table, young lady! I had to hear that from you your entire
twenties, and the man's been out of office nine years! For
God's sake leave him alone! (*Beat. Then, quickly:*) Anyhow,

that was like an incentive to encourage people to work harder so they could get *into* that bracket.

MAZE: I see. So if everyone had just *applied* themselves, then one hundred percent of Americans could have been in the wealthiest one percent.

DAD: Okay, answer me this, smarty-pants. All the other lawyers at your office over there at Tree Huggers Incorporated—

MAZE: That's not what it's called.

DAD: They win as much as you?

MAZE: What?

DAD: Just answer the question.

MAZE: It's not a competition, Dad. And we mostly work together. And it usually isn't even about winning, it's more—

DAD: But when you're the one doing the arguing out front, you get your way more often than the rest of 'em, isn't that right?

MAZE: I guess.

DAD: Because you prepare better and fight harder.

MAZE: I don't know.

DAD: Well, how about this. How about we take all your victories and just sort of spread 'em around, make it so you actually lost more of your cases and somebody else actually won some more so you've all got the same number of victories, would you think that's fair?

MAZE: No, Daddy, I wouldn't.

DAD: Welcome to the Republican Party.

MAZE: *Dad!*

MOM: Your father doesn't really mean it.

MAZE: I *know* that. *That's* what infuriates me.

MOM: Yes, well, you getting angry only spurs him on more. Just remain placid in the face of his outrageous remarks. That is what I do.

MAZE: To what end?

MOM: Well, I swear I don't know, darlin'. To what end do you fly off the handle? Look at Heller. He seems perfectly capable of participating in a conversation without losing his mind every forty-five seconds.

MAZE: You're not his parents. Anyway, Heller's a few years younger than I am.

MOM: So?

MAZE: So the Vietnam War was over and Carter was president by the time his bunch had reached the age of cogency, and as a result his entire generation is particularly vapid.

DAD: You gonna take that, son?

HELLER: We're also remarkably easygoing.

DAD: Oh yeah?

HELLER: Well, our marijuana was stronger.

DAD: I see.

MOM: You know, I didn't care for that war at all.

(*Beat.*)

MAZE: What?

MOM: The way they'd just ambush a group of soldiers like that from the trees not even as part of a prearranged battle? Who would do that?

DAD: The Vietcong.

MOM: Well, I didn't like it one bit.

DAD: That's what a guerrilla war is, dear.

MAZE: Mom? *What* are you *talking* about?

MOM: And for gosh sakes, Mazie Carroll, what *exactly* is your problem with *Dawson's Creek*?

MAZE: Oh my God, I don't have a problem with the *show*—

MOM: Because that Katie Holmes is a sweet sweet girl.

MAZE: I'm certain that she is.

MOM: I saw her down there at the café? And she smiled at me, you know, with half her mouth like she does? Just like a regular person!

MAZE: Imagine that.

MOM: You are so irritable, I don't know what's gotten into you, I really don't.

(*Pause.*)

MAZE: Where is Peter tonight?

MOM: He, uh. He said he'd try to make it. You know how he is. (*Pause.*) He's, uh. He's actually been talking about moving. To New York City.

MAZE: How on earth can he afford to move to New York City? (*Pause.*) Mom? You didn't. (*Pause.*) Mom!

MOM: He's doing real well, Mazie,—

MAZE: Dad! You allowed this?

DAD: You try telling this woman not to help her son.

MOM: He promised me that he would stop, Maze, he—

MAZE: He will say whatever he thinks you want to hear!

DAD: Can we please. Talk about. Something else.

(*Pause.*)

HELLER: Actually, Maze has left the environmental firm.

MAZE: Oh, Heller, no—

HELLER: No it's great! She's going to be working with a small civil liberties outfit that goes into prisons and helps inmates file lawsuits.

(*Pause.*)

MOM: Are you completely out of your goddamn mind?

MAZE (*to* HELLER): Thanks. Thank you.

MOM: Do they even *hire* women for that sort of thing?

MAZE: Of course they do, Mom.

MOM: But prisons are such terrible places!

MAZE: Which fact serves as the foundation for the bulk of our lawsuits.

DAD: Let me handle this, dear.

MOM: You go right ahead. I am at a *loss.*

DAD: Mazie. Baby. You gonna get to carry a gun?

MAZE: No, Dad.

DAD: They teach you hand-to-hand combat?

MAZE: Not really.

DAD: I bet they would if you asked. I bet you'll be able to show me a thing or two, some choke holds or takedowns or leg locks?

MAZE: I don't know. But I really don't think so.

DAD: Be a good girl and show your old man some choke holds.

MAZE: I just might.

DAD: You know what? Take my knife.

(DAD *pulls out a knife and stabs it into the table. A moment.*)

MOM: *You are not helping!*

MAZE: Mom! If anybody should be supporting my desire to do this, it's you!

MOM: I *do* support your desire, Mazie. I do not support you actually *going.*

DAD: Your mother's just worried for your safety, dear.

MOM (*to* DAD): And you're not?

MAZE: That's how he expresses concern. By citing your concern.

MOM: Heller? You're okay with this?

MAZE: I can take care of myself!

MOM: Gee. Now where did she get *that* attitude.

DAD: Right. She got *my* attitude and *your* politics. I will trade you any day.

MOM: Mazie. Think of your child.

MAZE: I don't have a child!

MOM: But you might. And the last thing that little one will need is the stigma of having a mother in prison.

MAZE: Having her there *working* as an *attorney*?

MOM: He is an infant! He will not differentiate! And nor will the other children. You know what children are like. They are so cruel!

DAD: Here's what you really oughta think about. Talk about poisoning yourself with garbage. You oughta think about who it is you'll be helping in those places. And if it's even possible to change people like that.

MAZE: I'm not trying to change them. I'm trying to improve their conditions such that their incarceration will be rehabilitative rather than punitive.

DAD: Right. And then they get out. Then what. You think they're still your friend? Seriously, Maze. Whatever you might say or do, you know what the one thing is you can't touch? You know what that is? (*He points to his head.*) You can't touch what's up here.

(*A moment.* MAZE *pulls the knife out of the table. She tries to hand it back to her* DAD *but he won't take it. Meanwhile, a young man,* PETER, *is at the edge of the space. One by one they notice him.* MAZE *puts the knife away. A silence.*)

HELLER: Hey, brother.

(*A moment. Then* PETER *walks onto the porch, past the table, and into the house.*)

DAD: Jesus Christ. What in the hell is it now.

(DAD *throws down his napkin and follows* PETER *inside.*)

MOM: Dear? Go easy on him!
MAZE: Heller? Can you go keep an eye on this? Make sure it
    doesn't get too—?
HELLER: Yeah. Yes. Of course.

(HELLER *follows* DAD *inside. A silence.*)

MAZE: We went to the aquarium today.
MOM: What? Oh.

(*During the following,* SCUBAMAN *appears, floating in a tank.*)

MAZE: And you know how my favorite thing there's always been
    the supertank? The really big one? When we were over by
    there today, there was, like, a field trip, of a bunch of kids from
    some school? And there was this *guy*, this guy who I guess
    works for the aquarium, and he was *inside the tank*, he was in
    scuba gear, floating in there, and he had some infrared
    earphone microphone doodad or something hooked up,
    because the kids were asking him questions through the glass,
    and he was answering them, and we could hear the answers
    over loudspeakers, and then there was a lull in the questions
    coming from the people actually on the tour, and, you know, I
    was like, what the hey, and so I piped up. And I asked the

scubaman why the sharks in the pool don't eat the other fish. And the man said:

SCUBAMAN: Well, we don't want the fish to be in a predatory environment, as they are in the ocean. So they're fed twice a week. And, as this is plenty to keep them satisfied, they have no need to eat one another. As they do in nature.

MAZE: I mean . . . ! (*Pause.*) Doesn't that just break your heart?

(EVAN *and* CARLSON. *Facing the bank of monitors. All are filled with static. There is a long silence.*)

EVAN: Interesting.
NORMAN: Mmm.

(*Pause.*)

NORMAN: How did they—?
EVAN: Hard to say.

(*Pause.*)

EVAN: Earl?
NORMAN: Nothing.
EVAN: Mmm. (*Pause. He paces.*) Geez. Okay. I'm gonna talk this out. Interrupt me if you disagree. They've got the hallway with their four cells, each of which is twelve by seven, and the interrogation room across the hall. And the distance from the door into the hallway to the back wall past the last cell. Assets-wise, worst case, they've got one guard, so they've got one gun. Three clips, maybe four. That's it for weapons, since all their furniture is bolted to the floor. There's two hostages. One

of whom is female. And no food or water. (*Beat.*) Kaczynski
can make a bomb out of basically anything. McVeigh's an ex-
marine. Which means we trained him. Also, he can make a
bomb out of basically anything. Yousef was a desert guerrilla
in a war the CIA was running. Which means we trained him
too. (*Beat.*) You know, after WTC in '93, he evaded every law
enforcement agency in the world for two years *while* sneaking
in and out of countries to blow things up and shoot people? It
was hard not to be proud of the kid.

NORMAN: What did you, train him yourself?

EVAN: (*Beat.*) All right. Let's get started.

(EVAN *exits.* NORMAN *remains, staring at the monitors.*)

NORMAN: Next!

(*The sovereign nation of Celebrity Row.* MAZE *is handcuffed to a
chair.* LUIS *stands, and* TED *is also here. A silence.*)

TED: Luis?

LUIS: Yeah.

TED: There's something I always wanted to ask you? But never
    could before.

LUIS: What?

TED: I understand you wrote a manifesto for your gang.

LUIS: Nation.

TED: What?

LUIS: You know what? Never mind. Yeah. I did that.

TED: And that, while the Kings predated your writing, you
    reinvigorated the organization, drew many new followers—

LUIS: How you know so much about the Kings?

TED: I grew up in Chicago.

LUIS: No shit.

TED: No, um. None at all. But, uh, *my* manifesto, or more just an *essay*, really, two hundred thirty-two numbered paragraphs, likewise, tried to galvanize an extant movement, the environmentalists, not, uh, not because I sympathize particularly with their cause myself but because I felt they represented a convenient force that could potentially be mobilized.

LUIS: But it didn't work.

TED: No. Why is that?

LUIS: Probably they could tell.

TED: Tell what.

LUIS: That you didn't really believe.

(TIMOTHY *enters.*)

LUIS: We good?

TIMOTHY: Earl's tied to the inside of the door. And they know it.

(RAMZI *has entered from the other direction.*)

LUIS: Ready?

RAMZI: Ready.

LUIS: What time is it?

RAMZI: Difficult to say. Slivers of sky.

LUIS: But so we got like a few minutes maybe before somebody coming in?

TIMOTHY: Yeah.

LUIS: Okay. Let's deal with her.

(*They all look at* MAZE. *A moment.*)

MAZE: Please let me go.

LUIS: Oh we would love to, Maze. But it's more complicated than that.

MAZE: Just, you're mistaken if you think that hurting me will make them more likely to cave in to your demands.

TIMOTHY: No, it's more, you'd have to apply for a visa, pass through customs—

RAMZI: Yes, also? Criminals who have illegally seized *hostages* make *demands*. Nations who are hosting foreign ambassadors on their home soil and within recognized borders? Issue declarations.

MAZE: What? What are you talking about?

TED: Didn't you hear us, Ms. Carroll? We have declared ourselves. Sovereign.

LUIS: Like the Kings.

RAMZI: Well, the invocation of monarchy is unhelpful—

TIMOTHY: Yeah, how about an authoritarian caliphate, right, Ramzi?

RAMZI (*still on his own track*): Unless we're talking about a constitutional monarchy operating under a parliamentary system in which royalty serves a purely symbolic function.

TIMOTHY: We're an oligarchy, jackass. A parliament would require a prime minister and some sort of meaningless figurehead president.

TED: (*with a British accent*): "I thought we were an autonomous collective!"

(*Beat.*)

MAZE: So you're just going to. Declare. Yourselves.

RAMZI (*simply*): What nation ever was begun in any other way?

MAZE: You're four people in a room!

TIMOTHY: We're five people. Can't you count? Five. Including you.

MAZE: In what conceivable way might this include me?

(LUIS *nods at* TIMOTHY, *who pulls out a key and uncuffs* MAZE. *During which* LUIS *produces several documents, and hands them over to* MAZE *one by one.* TIMOTHY *slips the key back into his pocket.*)

LUIS: We went ahead and prepared these documents. Here's mine that they didn't let you see before? And then here's something from Ramzi, and from Ted, and here's what Tim wrote. We built a fifty-year-long case. With all the evidence we personally witnessed. But this just the supporting materials. The official proposed resolution is here up top. All we need is representation. All we need? Is a lawyer.

(MAZE *looks at the papers. A silence. Then:*)

MAZE: You want to indict the United States federal government for racketeering?

RAMZI: Domestic as well as international.

MAZE: This is, uh, very thorough, you, wow, you cite statutes—

LUIS: Yeah, I guess that you could say I'm kinda familiar with the language of RICO prosecution.

TED: They must publish this in newspapers, read it aloud on television, post it on the Internet. And then we can discuss cessation of hostilities.

RAMZI: And so our courtroom will be everywhere. Our jury, everyone.

TIMOTHY: "There is no other case!" (*Beat.*) Paul Newman. *The Verdict.* Geez.

(*There is a pounding on the door. A moment.*)

LUIS (*to* RAMZI): See if he strapped. See if he wired. Stay behind
   him.

(RAMZI *nods and is gone amid a general flurry of activity as they
arrange themselves to prepare for the visitor.*)

TIMOTHY (*to* LUIS, *an earnest question.*): Who's running this? You?
LUIS: Yeah. You the muscle. Crazy. Could go off any second. (*To*
   TED.) And you the voice of reason. All like, "Oh, lemme
   explain."
TIMOTHY: The paranoid schizophrenic. Good choice.
TED: That label is part of a government plot to discredit me.
TIMOTHY: Oh, a secret government plot? Yeah, you don't *sound*
   schizophrenic.
TED: You know what, Tim—?
TIMOTHY (*high-pitched, girly*): "You know what, Tim—?"
TED: All right, that's it—
LUIS: Hey! Shut the fuck up! (*Pointing at each of them in turn:*)
   Muscle. Voice of reason. And I say almost nothing. Like I'm
   thinking really hard about everything? But he don't know what
   I'm thinking. (*To* MAZE.) And you? Represent.
MAZE: I—
TIMOTHY (*looking off*): Hey. Hey. Shh. Game face.

(*A moment.* NORMAN *enters.*)

NORMAN: Um. Hello there. Hello, Maze.
MAZE: Hey Mr. Norman.
NORMAN: I'm glad to see that you and Earl both are relatively
   unharmed.

TED: Well. Celebrity Row is of course bound by the Geneva
   Convention.

NORMAN: Um. Okay. You asked to speak to the person in charge
   of the prison? And I suppose technically that that's me. So I'm
   here to hear your terms for the release of—

TIMOTHY: Do you think we're fucking idiots?

NORMAN: No. No I certainly do not.

TIMOTHY: Then shut the fuck up!

TED: Tim? Please. (*To* NORMAN.) Our immediate need is for food
   and water. Which we will examine for hidden listening devices.

TIMOTHY: Yeah, we can skip the part where you bug the supplies,
   and the part where you ask us to release *just one* hostage as a
   gesture of goodwill, and the part where you try to drive a
   wedge between us by hinting at ways in which our interests
   may diverge.

NORMAN (*overlapping*): Yes. No. We, of course, we want simply
   to find some way to, uh, maybe by, say, improving your
   conditions, or by—

TIMOTHY: Oh, *now* he wants to talk about the conditions.

NORMAN: Some way to settle this. Peacefully.

LUIS: Oh well, you gonna have to direct further inquiries to our
   representation.

NORMAN: What?

(*Pause.*)

MAZE: They have a statement. And they, uh. They want it made
   public.

(MAZE *hands the documents to* NORMAN.)

NORMAN: Oh. Well, look, of course, prior to, we'd, uh, we'll have
to *review* the—
TIMOTHY: Shut your fucking mouth!
TED: Hey, hey, whoa.
LUIS: Maze?
MAZE: Uh. They will only accept unconditional capitulation to
their dem—

(LUIS *clears his throat noisily.*)

MAZE: Uh. Compliance. With the terms of the resolution.

(*Beat.*)

NORMAN: Um, okay, may I say something?
MAZE: Please.
NORMAN: Right now Timothy is the only person in this room with
a death sentence.
TIMOTHY: That is everybody's favorite topic for some reason.
NORMAN: But keep in mind that that kind of thing can always be
commuted with the right cooperation. Likewise, if this gets out
of hand, it can always be put back on the table for the rest of
you, so—
TIMOTHY: What did I *just say* about driving a wedge?
LUIS: Hey hey. Back up.

(NORMAN *takes a step back.*)

MAZE: I, uh. I think he meant figuratively.
LUIS: Yeah, first things first. Then we talk about what's next.
NORMAN: Well, but say we do this. (*Indicates the documents.*)

Then what? What are you promising in return? I just think
something, up front—

LUIS: Yeah, but unfortunately I got security considerations to
consider. What if I compromise and then you don't keep your
end? What I'm supposed to say to these guys? "What was I
supposed to do? Take precautions?"

(*Beat.*)

NORMAN: Okay, but, in the meantime, is there any way you could
release just *one*—

TIMOTHY: What did I just! Fucking! Say!

NORMAN (*turning away*): Okay, then.

LUIS: Hey. (*Pause.*) This is your prison?

NORMAN: This is a federal facility, Mr. Felipe. It belongs to
whoever pays for it. This is everybody's prison.

(NORMAN *goes. A moment.*)

LUIS: Okay. Let's get started.

MAZE: What? What's going on?

(TED *and* TIMOTHY *exit. A silence.*)

(TED *and* TIMOTHY *return, very carefully carrying a small wooden
box, with straps attached to it, and place it gingerly on the floor.
Meanwhile,* RAMZI *has returned.* TIMOTHY, RAMZI, *and* TED *gather
around the box and examine the contents.*)

MAZE: What are you doing? What is that? What's in that box?

RAMZI: When we fought the Soviets, they tried to turn the civilian population against us. The mujahedeen are not Afghani, they said. They hide amongst you so that our attacks kill your children, they said. But this tactic fails always. It binds instead together everyone against the aggressor out of shared hatred. Such that those who had not perhaps enough in common to begin with plot now as one. Always the aggressor forgets. Always he makes this mistake again. The fuse is ready. All that's needed is the flame.

(*Beat.*)

MAZE: You're going to blow up the prison.
RAMZI: I was speaking figuratively.
TED: But we are also literally going to blow up the prison, yes.
RAMZI: Yes, well that too.
MAZE: *Why?*
RAMZI: You yourself came here to destroy it.
MAZE: Not by blowing it up!
TIMOTHY: This way's faster.
MAZE: There are people inside of it!

(*They all look at her.*)

MAZE: You can't.
RAMZI: In fact we can.
MAZE: No, I mean you literally can't. Not with that. It's too small.
RAMZI: Have you noticed, Ms. Carroll, how temperate is the air here?
MAZE: What?
TIMOTHY: On its own, it's too small. But not when I attach it to the central environmental cooling system, which is full of nitroglycerine.

TED: "Opportunities tend to be those that the system provides." "Industrial Society and Its Future." Paragraph sixty-six.

(*The bomb is finished.* TIMOTHY *puts it on like a backpack.* LUIS *opens a panel in the floor.* TIMOTHY *cocks his gun.*)

TIMOTHY: There is one thing I'm gonna regret. What I was gonna do when they executed me? It was gonna be so . . . ! When they gave me a chance to say my last words? I was gonna just stare. Into the closed-circuit camera. Game face. And not say anything. Just look out at the witnesses, you know, the lawyers and the official and whoever, and the families of the victims, and my own family, Dad . . . Everybody that's out there. And just stare out. And not say anything.

(*A moment.* TIMOTHY *steps down into the open panel.*)

MAZE (*desperately*): Wait!
TIMOTHY (*peeking back out*): Yeah, we can also skip the part where you try to probe the roots of my pathology until I break down and change my mind—
MAZE: Okay, but, but, Tim, *think* about it. What does this gain you? What does this have to do with your cause?
TIMOTHY: Are you kidding? This is the most secure federal building in America.
MAZE: Well, okay, and maybe you'll take out some administrators or some guards, but mostly you'll kill federal prisoners. People just like you.
TIMOTHY: And Oklahoma City had a day care center. And if I'd have known that? I'd have picked a different building. Do you want to know why?

MAZE: Because you feel bad that you slaughtered dozens of children?

TIMOTHY: Because the label *child-murderer* kind of overshadows everything else, and when you're trying to send an important message—

MAZE: Well, that is an awfully cynical calculus, Tim.

TIMOTHY: When you're trying to send an important message—

MAZE: Oh yeah? What message? To who?

TIMOTHY: To *them*. That they routinely infringe on the rights of the very citizens—

MAZE: I'm sorry. Them? They?

LUIS: She's stalling, man. We don't have time.

TIMOTHY: Oh yeah? Then *you* go. (*A moment. Then, to* MAZE.) Don't play dumb. You know who.

MAZE: And "they" routinely infringe on who exactly?

TIMOTHY: Top of the list? Gun owner.

MAZE: Gun owners are at the top of the list.

TIMOTHY: Why are you doing that?

MAZE: What?

TIMOTHY: Repeating everything I say slightly slower than I'm saying it. Is that supposed to make it sound wrong, or something?

MAZE: I just want to make sure I've got it.

TIMOTHY: Yes. Gun owners.

MAZE: Why?

TIMOTHY: *Why?* Because *we're* the ones that can *protect* ourselves. They get rid of our guns? They have total power.

MAZE: Okay. So they get rid of the guns. They have total power. To do what?

TIMOTHY: What do you mean?

MAZE: Well, we have a saying where I come from, Timothy: There is no mountain so high that you can't take a nap next to it.

ITAMAR MOSES

(*Beat.*)

TIMOTHY: What?

MAZE: What do they do once all the gun owners lose their guns?

TIMOTHY (*overlapping*): Anything. That's the point. Then they could do anything. They could raise taxes as high as they want, they could start taking sixty, seventy, ninety percent of your income. What are you gonna do?

MAZE: Without all my guns? I guess not a damn thing.

TIMOTHY (*overlapping*): Okay, fine, this is not a joke—

MAZE: I know. Clearly. Okay? You made the point loud and clear that this is not a joke to you, I think. But—

TIMOTHY: They could throw you in jail. For no reason. Or any reason. Leave you there forever. They could do whatever they feel like.

MAZE: Why?

TIMOTHY: *Why what?*

MAZE: Why would they do that?

TIMOTHY: *What.*

MAZE: Why would they take ninety percent of my income and throw me in jail for no reason? To what end would the government do such a thing to me?

TIMOTHY: They probably wouldn't do it to you, Maze. You seem like a nice girl.

MAZE: Well, bless your heart, Tim, but—

TIMOTHY: Until you buy the wrong book, make the wrong phone call, end up on some list, show up for work one day, ATF tackles you, and you never see your family again.

TED: Now who sounds schizophrenic.

TIMOTHY: You shut the fuck up.

MAZE: A threat to what?

TIMOTHY: To their power.

MAZE: To their power to do what?

TIMOTHY: What is wrong with you? All the things I just explained. Is it me, or are we going over the same ground again and again?

MAZE: *Both*, Tim! We're going over the same ground again and again and it's *you*! 'Cause it's your contention, and please correct me, that they want the power to take absurd measures to keep the power to take absurd measures to hold on to their, I mean, *come on*! What have you got for me? What else have you friggin' got for me?

TIMOTHY: Do you really think that aggravating me is a good idea?

MAZE: Oh, what are you gonna do, *shoot* me?

TIMOTHY: They want the power. To *use* us. To make them rich.

MAZE: Okay. But. Do you honestly think that the President of the United States is worried about some guy in some barn with a rifle?

TIMOTHY: See, you're twisting it all around—

MAZE: No, Tim! The point is, the federal government can hold on to its power just fine *without* taking your guns away! In fact, if they can convince you to obsess over your guns instead of involving yourself in the political process, they can hold on to their power *better*!

TIMOTHY: Clearly they don't think so.

MAZE: What do you *mean*?

TIMOTHY: Because! They keep trying to pass all these laws! They keep hounding legitimate gun shows, and performing these raids. Why?

MAZE: To make it harder for criminals to get guns with which to perform robberies and murders?

TIMOTHY: Bullshit—

MAZE: To prevent accidents where children kill their parents or siblings?

TIMOTHY: Anyone trained properly—

MAZE: You don't think that *anybody* in the gun-control movement—?

TIMOTHY: Of course, of course, but they're just dupes, just bleeding-heart liberal dupes, like *you*, probably, putting a legitimized face on a really sinister agenda, on this new form of what's really domestic imperialism, like with the British and the colonies, and it calls for a second American Revolution, *calls* for, heck, it's already *started*, I can name you three battles: Ruby Ridge, Waco, Oklahoma City. So they're ahead two victories to one, but I think casualties are about even.

MAZE: And who's the government in here, Tim? Who has the power in the sovereign nation of Celebrity Row? And who's the dupe?

(*A long silence. Then* TIMOTHY *takes off the backpack and puts it on the ground. Then he flips the gun around and hands it to* LUIS. *Then he moves to a slight distance and sits on the floor.* LUIS *stares at* MAZE. MAZE *stares back.*)

(*A moment. Then* RAMZI *picks up the backpack.*)

RAMZI: "I will take the ring to Mordor. Though I do not know the way."

MAZE: Goddammit.

RAMZI: Yes, moving now to foreign policy—

MAZE: Oh my God, this is like the McLaughlin Group in hell.

RAMZI: ADX Florence must be destroyed because it is a mirror of how America sees its role in the world. The warden provides meals, shelter, protection, and in return we, the other nations, the lesser nations, may emerge from our cells, but only under strict supervision, to discuss movies and pop songs, but not our own ideas, not, God forbid, not *plans for escape!* Why would we want to? After all, from a distance, at least, the prison glitters in the sun.

(*During this* RAMZI *has strapped the bomb to his back. He now holds out his hand for the gun. A moment.* LUIS *hands it over.*)

MAZE: Okay, you're stretching this poor little metaphor awful far.
RAMZI: But! Though you wish for us to behave like prisoners *you are not willing to serve as a competent administrator!* Meals are missed! There is no prison library! Whole cellblocks go neglected for decades at a time! You are not a gentle beacon but a searchlight! Not Florence Nightingale but Nurse Ratched to our cuckoo's nest!
MAZE: You've read that book?

(*Beat.*)

RAMZI: Book?
MAZE: *One Flew over the Cuckoo's Nest.*
RAMZI: Oh. No. But I'll see anything with Jack Nicholson.
TED: Oh, me too. "You want answers?" "I want the truth!" "You can't handle the truth!"
MAZE (*bemused*): You hypocrite.
RAMZI (*not bemused*): What did you just call me?
LUIS: Ramzi—
MAZE: My understanding of Wahabbi Islam was, you don't believe in movies.
RAMZI: Whereas in America they're the only thing you do believe in, *imposing* these values economically, militarily—
MAZE: Um, try building an economy of your own! But no, you invest in terror networks instead of infrastructure, so—

RAMZI: Our network *provides* the infrastructure! We offer the services our leaders cannot! Hospitals, schools—!

MAZE: And militarily? That's awfully convenient now, Cold War's freakin' *over*, to pretend the Soviet Union was harmless or containment was really empire-building, or whatever, but I didn't hear *anybody* complaining when that wall came down.

RAMZI: Then perhaps you did not listen hard enough. To those you had *used* to achieve this great victory *for* you only to find that you want only to expand the territory in which to sell your cola. Whereas *we* are denied a home of *any* kind, we are *criminals*, any state that *harbors* us is *criminal*—

MAZE: You pursue your ends with violence.

RAMZI: So do you.

MAZE: Against civilians!

RAMZI: So do you!

MAZE: Without remorse!

RAMZI: All these things are true of you!

MAZE: It's not the same.

RAMZI: *Why not?*

MAZE: It's just *not!*

RAMZI: So the distinction in some way . . . defies articulation.

(*Beat.*)

MAZE: The distinction transcends simplistic moralizing.

RAMZI: Yes. Apparently all the way up to conveniently obfuscatory complexity.

MAZE: *We* have *rules*.

RAMZI: So do we. And ours are holy.

MAZE: Exactly! *We* have an apparatus in place to change and question—

RAMZI: Your Constitution.

MAZE: Yes.

RAMZI: Open to interpretation.

MAZE: Always.

RAMZI: So that it may mean whatever you wish for it to mean.

MAZE: Oh, you want to play *that* game? "He who slays anyone for any reason it shall be as though he slays all mankind." Surah five. Ayah thirty-two.

RAMZI: Impressive. You have memorized the Qu'ran?

MAZE: Honestly? Just that verse. In case I ever got to talk to someone like you.

RAMZI: Well, you are perhaps working from an incomplete translation. In fact, the Fifth Surah, it reads: "He who slays anyone for any reason *other than for murder or mischief in the land . . .*" Indeed, all of the Qu'ran's proscriptions against such acts make an exception for the execution of justice. You should understand perfectly. Having as you do a federal death penalty.

MAZE: I oppose the death penalty!

RAMZI: What's your point?

MAZE: That *I'm* allowed to *say* that.

RAMZI: Perhaps they allow you to say it to prevent you from acting. Perhaps you would be better off forbidden to say. And forced to act. Like a dog with its vocal cords removed.

MAZE: Like *you?* Like Tim?

RAMZI: Perhaps.

MAZE: You're *monsters!* *You* are a *fanatic!*

RAMZI: And what are you? A *nice* monster, yes?

MAZE: I don't know.

RAMZI: Who on occasion must be ugly to be secure.

MAZE: Maybe. Yeah.

RAMZI: Because let me tell you what *I* see. *I* see a frightened woman who knows the system must be shattered. She knows it. And she knows, furthermore, that change is not possible

ITAMAR MOSES

except through force, through explosive, violent force, but she *pretends* it is possible through talk, *endless* talks, like *this* one; for God's sake, my friend, at least *I* have *earned* their hatred through *behavior*! Your argument curves. It shifts its colors to frustrate perception. But I see you. *You* are the hypocrite. Your belief is idle. I act on mine.

MAZE: And then what? What then? I mean, yeah, we're ugly. We did some terrible things in the nineties and maybe some of them created Tim. And maybe we had to do them because of the terrible things we did in the eighties that maybe created you. Which maybe happened because of all the terrible things we maybe did since the Second World War that maybe created Ted. Only that is *nonsense*. Because analogous is not the same as equivalent. Cause and effect is not the size of nations. It is tiny, it is person-sized, it is some kid, some young kid, being told that he's not safe, not unless he joins, and don't you want to be a part of this, this thing, this perfect thing, that will make you safe, and now you've got him, now he's yours. And so then help me out, because then how can I compete if beating you will take becoming you? What am I supposed to do if trusting you's what makes me weak enough to lie to? How can I win? If the *only thing* that separates me from you is my willingness to lose? (*Pause.*) The world is not ADX Florence. Not yet. It's just the work camp, maybe the minimum, and you go right ahead and hate that prison, *hate* it. But if you *stab the guards* we will not let you *out*! We will just build a better one! So stop it!

RAMZI: I have stopped. They have stopped me. But it will happen.

MAZE: What?

RAMZI: It will. Happen. And you will not. Fucking. Believe it. You won't. You simply will not. (*Pause.*) Later that day it will happen again.

MAZE: What are you talking about?

RAMZI: No. Silence. (*He steps into the panel on the floor.*) Silence.

(*There is a pounding at the door. Everyone freezes. Everyone looks at one another. There is another pounding at the door.*)

MAZE: Is someone going to fucking *get* that?

(*A moment.* RAMZI *puts the bomb under the chair and moves toward the door.*)

TED: I'll go.

LUIS: Uhhh—

TED: See if he's strapped. See if he's wired. Stay behind him.

(*A moment.* LUIS *nods.* TED *moves towards the door. Then stops. Turns back.*)

TED (*to* MAZE): As a mathematician, I've never understood the phrase *cynical calculus*. Calculus is not cynical. Not at all. It's a labyrinth, yes, twisted, but not rigid, because mathematical systems can be both beautiful *and* secure. Rightness and wrongness are absolute and malleable. As with a continuous map of a boundary function in the complex plane. The unit disk can be stretched, smeared, folded, bent, but never shattered. Never broken and scattered. And where is the edge? The problem remains open. (*Beat.*) Did you know that my cabin in Montana was actually several square feet *smaller* than the cell in which I now reside?

(*There is one more pounding at the door.*)

TED: Close parenthesis. This is me.

(TED *goes.* LUIS *looks at* MAZE.)

LUIS: Silence.

(*There is a silence. Everyone waits. Then* EVAN *enters. He is holding a walkie-talkie.*)

EVAN: Hello. Luis. Timothy. (*A small smile.*) Ramzi.
RAMZI: Evan.
EVAN (*generally*): Hello. My name is—

(LUIS *points the gun at* EVAN.)

EVAN: Okay, so he's the muscle. Who's the voice of reason?
LUIS: Who are you? Where's Norman?
EVAN: Whoa, you can't be *both*, you have to—
LUIS: Where's our food? Our water?
EVAN: Okay—
LUIS: And you gonna print our statement? 'Cause if not—
EVAN (*overlapping*): Okay, hey, slow down there, *esse.*
LUIS: No, you slow down. We not doing anything or talking about
    anything or listening to anything till you do what you said you
    was gonna do. So back on out. Go get us food and water.
    Make our statement public. And *then* come back.
EVAN: So I'm gone long enough for you or Ramzi or Tim to get to
    the environmental cooling system? Yeah, we got guys there
    waiting. Or, um, "I'm afraid the deflector shield will be quite
    operational when your friends arrive." (*Beat.*) Yeah, you're
    very good at this, but let's not pretend, I mean, somebody
    holler at me when I get off track. You don't care if that stuff's

published. Heck! Kaczynski *got* his little treatise in the news, and all that happened was, his brother turned him in. There's an argument. *I* say we come in heavy right away. Dissenting opinion is, like, blah blah *hostages* blah blah *consensus* blah blah blah *exhaustion of remedies*, so I say, Fine, long as I get to decide what exactly *exhaustion of remedies* means. Guess what it means. (*Pause.*) Ted just surrendered at the door. And the rest of you will surrender now. Anybody?

(*A silence. Then* RAMZI *looks at* MAZE.)

RAMZI: Remember. You are in God's hands now. (*Beat. Then, generally*) This is, I think, a domestic problem.

(RAMZI *walks, hands raised, up to* EVAN. *A moment. Then, in an incredibly quick gesture, he snatches the sunglasses from* EVAN's *face. Puts them on. Then he turns back to look at* MAZE.)

RAMZI: "I'll be back."

(RAMZI *goes. A moment.*)

EVAN: Neat. Anybody else? Tim?

(TIMOTHY *stands, walks over to* LUIS, *takes the gun, and aims it at* EVAN.)

EVAN: Okay, so that's at best a strong maybe.
TIMOTHY: What are you? CIA?

(*Beat.*)

ITAMAR MOSES

EVAN: If my guys hear a shot? They will come in here and kill you all.

TIMOTHY: Is that right.

EVAN: Yeah. (*Holding up a walkie-talkie*) However? If they *don't* hear a shot? Then, in about ten seconds, I'm going to call for them, and they will come in here and kill you all.

TIMOTHY: That's okay. Because in ten seconds *I'm* going to shoot the bomb under that chair and kill everybody in the room.

(TIMOTHY *aims at the bomb.* EVAN *sees the bomb. A moment.*)

EVAN: Ten . . . nine . . . eight . . .

TIMOTHY (*overlapping, just behind*): Ten . . . nine . . . eight . . .

EVAN: Stop that.

TIMOTHY: You stop.

LUIS (*to* TIMOTHY): Tim, you don't have to do this.

TIMOTHY: Well. As my three options are now to die because of him, to die because of me, or to die because of a needle, I'm going to go with my gut, thank you.

EVAN: Seven . . . six . . .

TIMOTHY (*overlapping, just behind*): Seven . . . six . . .

EVAN: Stop!

TIMOTHY: You first!

MAZE (*to* EVAN): Evan, you don't have to do this!

EVAN: Yeah, you would say that.

MAZE: *What?*

EVAN: You think I don't *know* you, Ms. Carroll? You think I haven't seen your kind before? You waste our time up front talking to garbage like this. Then, once we're fucked, you want us to run away. You're not just a part of the problem. You're the worst part. The part that makes it *impossible* for the rest of us get it done. (*To* TIMOTHY.) You have five seconds.

TIMOTHY (*overlapping*): *You* have five seconds.

EVAN: Five . . . !

TIMOTHY (*overlapping, just behind*): Five . . . !

(*And suddenly, a searchlight hits* MAZE *and* LUIS, *who turn to face us.* EVAN *and* TIMOTHY *remain visible between them.*)

MAZE: In the name of God, the merciful, the compassionate.

EVAN: Fifth Surah.

TIMOTHY: *Al-Qaeda.* "The Cell."

LUIS: O believers! Remember!

EVAN: Four . . . !

MAZE: And he said:

LUIS: "This is a war."

TIMOTHY: Three . . . !

MAZE: And he went on, saying:

LUIS: "You don't get to pick one."

EVAN: Two . . . !

MAZE: And he said:

LUIS: "You have to pick both."

TIMOTHY: One . . . !

(MAZE *is now holding a knife.*)

(*Tableaux:* LUIS *staring at* MAZE, TIMOTHY *with a gun,* EVAN *with his walkie-talkie,* MAZE *between them with knife. A moment.*)

(*Darkness. Silence.*)

(*A phone rings. It rings again. It rings a third time.*)

(MAZE, *on the phone with* FENDELL.)

ITAMAR MOSES

MAZE: Hello?

FENDELL: Hey. How are you feeling?

MAZE: Better. Um. Physically better. A little better.

FENDELL: Good. That's good. (*Beat.*) So, I have good news. They're offering you immunity. And what I'd advise? Is that you take it. (*Beat.*) So long as you obey the gag order. And, I mean, never talk about this. Ever. (*Pause.*) Maze? (*Pause.*) Maze?

(*Pause.*)

MAZE: So they're all just exercising together again? Like nothing happened?

FENDELL: Yeah. Well, no. I mean, they pulled out Tim.

MAZE: Really? Why?

FENDELL: They're moving him to Indiana. The death house. They're going to kill him. August, I think.

MAZE: Oh. (*Pause.*) I mean: *Good.* You know? Good. He . . . deserves that. Probably. (*Pause.*) But it's also kind of sad.

FENDELL: Oh, I don't know. Apparently he's okay with it.

MAZE: Not sad for him. Sad for us.

(MAZE *remains, alone.* EARL *is at the door of a cell.*)

EARL: Hey, buddy, you ready? No rush, take your time, collect yourself, you just knock on the door when you're ready to come out. (*Pause.*) What's gonna happen is this: I'm gonna cuff you in the vestibule, take you out of the block. We'll be met there by four other guards, and the five of us'll escort you off the grounds, and then we'll turn you over to the federal marshals. So, you know: slap on the game face. They'll have a chopper on the helipad, and they'll fly you down to Indiana, and then . . . uh . . . (*Pause.*) Well: you know what then.

(*Pause.*) Okay? You ready? Tim? (*There is a knock from the other side of the door.*) Okay. Let's do it.

(TIMOTHY, RAMZI, *and* TED. *In separate spaces.*)

TED: " 'Industrial Society and Its Future.' Paragraph ninety-four: Freedom means being in control of the life-and-death issues of one's existence. Freedom means having power; not the power to control other people but the power to control the circumstances of one's own life. One does not have freedom if anyone else has power over one, no matter how benevolently, tolerantly and permissively that power may be exercised. It is important not to confuse freedom with permissiveness."

(TED *backs into darkness . . .*)

RAMZI: One-hundred-fourteenth Surah. *An-Nas.* "Mankind."

> *In the name of God, the merciful, the compassionate*
> *Say: I seek refuge in the lord of mankind*
> *The king of mankind*
> *The God of mankind*
> *From the evil of the sneaking whisperer*
> *Who whispers in the hearts of mankind*
> *Of the djinn and of mankind*

(RAMZI *backs into darkness . . .*)

(TIMOTHY *stares out . . . for a very long time . . . and says nothing . . .* MAZE *watches him . . . a long silence . . . then . . .*)

(*Blackout.*)

OUTRAGE

Outrage had its world premiere on February 18, 2003, at Portland Center Stage in Portland, Oregon (Chris Coleman, Artistic Director). Director: Chris Coleman. Set Designer: Klara Zieglerova. Lighting Designer: Daniel Ordower. Sound Designer: Jen Raynak. Costume Designer: Miranda Hoffman. Dramaturg: Mead Hunter. Stage Manager: Mark Tynan.

STEVEN/ARISTOTLE	Cody Nickell
BRECHT/GALILEO	Robert Dorfman
MENOCCHIO	Steve Wilkerson
KALE/ORACLE	Kate Levy
LOMAX/ARISTOPHANES	David Cromwell
LAURA	Kelly Tallent
BRETT/ALCIBIADES/VORAI	Jeffrey Jason Gilpin
RIVNINE/AGATHON	Christopher Burns
SOCRATES	Frank Lowe
POLITES/STEFANO/THE VOICE	Mark Schwahn
PLATO	Kevin Corstange

Outrage had its East Coast premiere on May 18, 2005, at the Wilma Theater in Philadelphia, Pennsylvania (Blanka Zizka and Jiri Zizka, Artistic Directors). Director: Jiri Zizka. Set Designer: Mimi Lien. Lighting Designer: Jerrold R. Forsyth. Composer: Adam Wernick. Sound and Music Designer: Bill Moriarty. Costume Designer: Janus Sefanowicz. Dramaturg: Walter Bilderback. Production Manager: Patrick Heydenburg. Stage Manager: Patreshettarlini Adams.

STEVEN/ARISTOTLE	Cody Nickell
BRECHT/GALILEO	Robert Dorfman
MENOCCHIO	William Zielinkski
KALE/ORACLE	Erika Rolfsrud
LOMAX/ARISTOPHANES	Joel Leffert
LAURA/PLATO	Caroline Tamas
BRETT/ALCIBIADES/VORAI	Matthew Humphreys
RIVNINE/AGATHON	Marc Wolf
SOCRATES	Gregg Almquist
POLITES/STEFANO/THE VOICE	Pete Pryor

CHARACTERS

STEVEN

A graduate student at a
New England University,
late twenties.

BERTOLT BRECHT

The German playwright
(1898–1956).

DOMENICO "MENOCCHIO" SCANDELLA

An Italian miller from the
village of Montereale
(1532–1599), forties–fifties.

ADRIANA KALE

The dean of the university,
forties.

EUGENE LOMAX

A classics professor, early
sixties.

LAURA

An undergraduate actress
at the same university,
twenties.

BRETT

A computer science
graduate student and
computing assistant,
twenties.

DANIEL RIVNINE

An English professor, late
thirties.

SOCRATES	The Athenian philosopher and social gadfly (468 BC–399 BC), age seventy.
POLITES INTERLOCUTOR AFFIRMAE	A devoted and agreeable disciple of Socrates.
PLATO	The young disciple of Socrates and a philosopher in his own right (427 BC–347 BC), twenties–thirties.
STEFANO DECANO	A young Italian priest.
AGATHON	Another Athenian playwright, younger than Aristophanes.
ARISTOPHANES	The Athenian playwright, older than Agathon.
ALCIBIADES	A stunningly handsome and charming young man, twenties.
ODORICO VORAI	Another stunningly handsome and charming young man, twenties.
THE ORACLE AT DELPHI	Ageless.
ARISTOTLE	The Athenian philosopher and student of Plato's Academy (384 BC–322 BC), in his precocious youth.

| GALILEO GALILEI | The Italian astronomer (1564–1642). |
| A VOICE | The conduit between Brecht and the world outside his door; THE VOICE is at times the critic Walter Benjamin and at other times the historian and critic Eric Bentley. |

Also: Various GRAD STUDENTS. Various CRITICS. CHORUS of judges.

A NOTE ON DOUBLING

Every single reading, workshop, and production to date has employed a slightly different system, due in part to circumstances specific to the ensemble in question. This is the arrangement preferred by the author, all things being equal:

1. SOCRATES
2. MENOCCHIO
3. BRECHT and GALILEO
4. STEVEN and ARISTOTLE
5. LOMAX and ARISTOPHANES
6. RIVNINE and AGATHON
7. BRETT and ALCIBIADES and VORAI
8. POLITES and DECANO and THE VOICE
9. KALE and THE ORACLE
10. LAURA and PLATO

The ensemble also shares, variously, the GRAD STUDENTS in Act 1, and the CRITICS in Act 2.

The CHORUS ought to be grandiose, thrilling, and somewhat scary. For whatever reason, this seems to be easiest to accomplish with live actors speaking in unison. Recorded sounds and fancy effects seem to diminish the impact and render it silly. Of course, the script undercuts the chorus with humor of its own, but we ought to have a real sense of danger from a powerful force sitting in judgment whenever the chorus is present.

THE VOICE, though "behind a door," ought to be visible onstage, perhaps in shadow or silhouette. The point is simply that, in Brecht's scenes, the characters speak "out" even when speaking "to" each other, as part of the conscious theatricality of that world in particular. (This also contributes to the impact of the moment when, at last THE VOICE "enters" and Brecht speaks directly to him.) Also, we can always tell whether THE VOICE is Benjamin or Bentley by his accent: Benjamin is German; Bentley, British.

A NOTE ON QUICK CHANGES

Almost all are covered by sufficient text. However, AGATHON and ARISTOPHANES must become RIVNINE and LOMAX almost instantaneously near the end of Act 1. Perhaps they wear their present-day costumes for this brief Greek interlude; in any case, treat this moment as a consequence of the ever-thinning membrane between these two eras in particular, just as when STEVEN stumbles repeatedly into Athens, then enters it more fully as ARIS-

TOTLE near the end, and just as LAURA eventually walks directly into Greece, becoming PLATO, and ALCIBIADES walks out of Greece, as BRETT.

A NOTE ON DESIGN

The set benefits from being variable and abstract, with many surfaces and playing spaces, and whatever "realistic" desks, chairs, and so on, are absolutely necessary to render the multiple settings. Klara Zieglerova's set at Portland Center Stage was symmetrical and ordered: three levels, joined by a single enormous circular staircase. Mimi Lien's set at the Wilma Theater was precisely the opposite, taking as a jumping-off point the line "It's like a bomb exploded in the center of history and we're stranded in the debris." Her set was asymmetrical and chaotic, dominated by a single ivory tower in the center. Either approach is effective; perhaps someday a production will use both, one for each act. One final thought about the set: Multiple levels are not, strictly speaking, a necessity, but it does help if it is possible for characters to "ascend" at times—say, to a precipice—so that Brecht and Rivnine can head for their respective windows, or so that there can be accessible vertical space through which to drop objects and so on. The play's final moments, especially, benefit from Rivnine's being able to ascend stairs during Lomax's and the Oracle's final speeches.

ACT 1

BRECHT'S PROLOGUE

An empty stage. A man enters, from behind the audience, dressed in the manner of a German intellectual from the 1930s. He carries a briefcase.

BRECHT: Hello. How is everybody tonight? Good? Aha.

(*Pause.*)

BRECHT: I see. Excuse me. I have something. Just a moment.

(BRECHT *puts the briefcase on the ground and opens it. He takes out a large placard with a length of twine running through it.*)

BRECHT: They assured me that you would know who I was. From the glasses, perhaps. Or the slight accent, which is supposed to indicate that I'm speaking German. But I wanted to be absolutely sure. Otherwise what's the point?

(BRECHT *puts the twine around his neck. The placard hangs at his stomach. It says, in large clear letters:* BERTOLT BRECHT.)

BRECHT: Is it clearer now? Good. Let's begin: Tonight there will be a play. I didn't write it, more's the pity. But I am *in* it. Which is very lucky, because there will be at least *one* person onstage who cares about making this a worthwhile experience for you, the audience. This play is a play about people who try to make the world a better place. As a result, rather a lot of those people are going to get killed. They die at every performance, and return, next time, to try again. And these deaths before your eyes, they will upset you. That's not prediction, it's an order. (*Shouted:*) They will! Upset! You! (*Mildly.*) Socrates is here. And he gets killed. The Italian miller Domenico Scandella, called Menocchio, is here, too. I know. I have never heard of him either. But he's here, and he dies. I am here. And I am forced, in fear of my life, to flee Nazi Germany. But I don't get killed. I have to survive until the end, you see, to deliver an epilogue. Also here is a young professor by the name of Daniel Rivnine. And although he is fictional, his death might upset you most of all. Which isn't to say that he dies. He may not. The element of surprise is, after all, important.

(*Throughout, as* BRECHT *has been talking, distantly, faintly, shadowy figures have been gathering in the background, a few at a time, until, by this point, ten indistinct figures are ranged around the stage, behind him. Their arrival has been accompanied by a slowly swelling, deep sound, a thrum or a rumble, which even now is quite subtle. At this point, he acknowledges their presence. Under what follows, the rumble swells.*)

BRECHT: Ah. You've noticed them. Yes. But don't worry. They're here, like you, as observers. To watch the performance. (*A beat, then:*) Enough from me. The play is about to begin.

(BRECHT *begins to back toward darkness. There is the distant sound, far away, of five hundred voices calling a name. The name is almost not possible to make out, but perhaps it is "Socrates!"*)

BRECHT: So don't close your eyes. Don't turn away.

(*The sound, likewise far away, of five hundred voices calling, "Domenico Scandella!"*)

BRECHT: For it will go on. Whether you're watching or not.

(*The sound, far away, of five hundred voices calling, "Bertolt Brecht!"* BRECHT *stands on the brink of darkness. Arms expansive, embracing the audience.*)

(*One of the figures steps forward, out of darkness. A young man,* STEVEN, *visible just long enough to be heard saying:*)

STEVEN: Outrage.
BRECHT *Act One!*

(*Blackout.*)

MENOCCHIO'S THEORY

A Renaissance Italian miller appears: DOMENICO "MENOCCHIO" SCANDELLA.

MENOCCHIO: In the beginning, the world was nothing. And then: the water of the sea whipped into a foam and coagulated. Like a cheese.

(*He produces a segment of cheese from inside his cloak.*)

MENOCCHIO: Inside the cheese were born a great number of worms, and these worms became angels, of which the most powerful and wise was God.

(*He throws his cheese into the darkness.*)

(*Blackout.*)

AN ATHENIAN FREEZE

Lights up on STEVEN. *He is gazing upward.*

Lights up on an Ancient Greek tableau: an old man reclines in an absurd pose of pontification, flanked by two young men, one writing on a scroll, the other playing a lyre. All three are in togas (technically, chitons, but let's call them togas), and surrounded by grapes, amphorae, wreaths, and so on.

Suddenly, MENOCCHIO's *cheese flies past.*

STEVEN *ducks and dodges, nearly stumbling, to avoid it. Regaining his equilibrium, he looks around wildly for the source. Seeing no one, he walks off.*

Blackout.

NEW ENGLAND, 1999

Lights up on Lomax's office. EUGENE LOMAX *is seated at his desk,*
paging through a thick document. Also here is ADRIANA KALE,
who stands, facing him.

KALE: Forty. Million. Dollars.

LOMAX: I'll be goddamned. (*He skims.*) New computers, new
software, new *buildings* . . . to put them in, I suppose . . . tech
support, Ethernet . . . (*He looks up.*) Ha. "Ethernet." As though
these people know what aether *is*. The Greeks, you know,
invented aether.

KALE: Yes, I know.

LOMAX: Well, *Dean* Kale. It's a lucky thing you're in charge now.

KALE: What do you mean?

LOMAX: It's funny, we always used to *say*, "When *we* run
things . . ." Years ago, you remember? How we'd *rescue* the
place. With a chuckle, yes, but part of me always *knew*—

KALE: What do you mean, "It's lucky—"

LOMAX: Because. It will be that much easier to do the right thing.

KALE: What's that?

LOMAX: My committee will vote to turn it down.

KALE: What?

LOMAX: So! How's the family? Your husband, your son?

KALE: They're both fine. Eugene—

LOMAX: Good. That's good.

KALE: I'm sorry: turn it down?

LOMAX: Yes.

KALE: You want us to turn down the Wallace grant?

ITAMAR MOSES

LOMAX: Yes.

KALE: You want us to turn down forty million dollars from Gabriel Wallace?

LOMAX: The *amount* is incidental, Adriana, the point—

KALE: I don't think it's incidental at all. It's enough money to change everything.

LOMAX: Exactly!

KALE: What?

LOMAX: I'm sorry: is it not clear to you what this is?

KALE: Yes. A powerful alumnus has made us a very, very generous offer.

LOMAX: Ah: "They weave its ribs with sawed-off beams of fir, pretending that it is an offering. Then, in the dark sides of the beast, they stuff their soldiers in its belly, deep." Virgil. The *Aeneid*.

KALE: Yes. Book two.

LOMAX: The Greeks, you know, invented the Trojan Horse.

KALE: Eugene, why must everything have some secret, sinister motivation?

LOMAX: I ask myself that question all the time.

KALE: Very funny.

LOMAX: It's not funny at all. This is the first step towards a hostile takeover.

KALE: It's an *opportunity*! We can attract top-notch faculty, we're projecting a jump in applications—

LOMAX: Of *course*. But in which *fields* are these wonderful things happening?

KALE: In computer science, in physics, at *first*, yes, but—

LOMAX: *So this will affect what we teach.* Until one day we're nothing but a factory, turning out employees for Gabriel Wallace's company.

KALE: *Or.* The stature this brings to a few departments spreads to others. Look, where do you think I learned about leadership?

LOMAX: Oh. Flattery.

KALE: Yes, in *your* seminars. Pericles! Alexander! Unite factions! Improve infrastructure, so the populace can thrive! Running the known world requires diplomacy.

LOMAX: But *first* you have to conquer it with an army.

KALE: Jesus. Why do you have to be such an absolutist?

LOMAX: When Alexander was faced with the impossible knot of Gordia, he cut it in half with his sword.

KALE: Yes, it's a hell of a story. Of course, the stories about Alexander being reasonable and flexible are less exciting, so nobody wrote them down.

LOMAX: He was flexible when it was the only way to win. Not when he was afraid of offending an acne-plagued multimillionaire. Alexander was a visionary.

KALE: Maybe so is Gabriel Wallace.

LOMAX: You think so? He's got awfully thick glasses for a visionary. (*Beat.*) And I am not an absolutist. I'm just deeply uncomfortable with relativism. And it looks to me like your model is not Pericles, but Alcibiades.

KALE: So now I'm a traitor? They're only *tools.* Tools are neutral. There's nothing to be afraid of.

LOMAX: Really? What about his proposal to turn us into a police state?

KALE (*wearily*): What?

LOMAX: This, this key-card system. Electronic doodads programmed to open all the doors on campus. But did you notice that they'll also allow the campus police to keep a record of who opens which doors at what times?

KALE: In case a card is stolen! I think it's very sensible to include in his gift some extra security.

ITAMAR MOSES

LOMAX: That's exactly what the Romans thought. "We need the
army to protect the Republic. Wait, is that Julius, wading
across the Rubicon?"

KALE: Electronic key cards don't have ambitions. Caesar did.

LOMAX: Maybe so does Gabriel Wallace. Adriana, this is invasive.
Things change. All right. But *we* decide *when* and *how*.

KALE: No, Eugene. *I* decide.

LOMAX: Yes. (*Pause.*) You know, I'd just barely gotten used to you
not being my student anymore. This might take longer.
(*Pause.*) Anyway, the Disbursement Committee still follows *my*
lead. And you won't be there tonight.

KALE: Yes, but I'll see the transcript.

LOMAX: Do you remember, what was it, six years ago, that old
woman gave us all that money to build a cathedral, and we
built a library that looked like a cathedral from the outside and
drove her past it in a car?

KALE: That was a unique situation. Don't abuse your authority to
advance your personal agenda.

LOMAX: Whose personal agenda should I abuse my authority to
advance?

KALE: You know what I mean. Don't go bullying your way into the
china shop. I need you on my team.

LOMAX: You're mixing metaphors.

KALE: What?

LOMAX: You don't want a bull on your team. Unless he's the
mascot.

KALE: I'll make a note. Are you finished?

LOMAX: No. But when I am, it seems *you*, of all people, may be
the cause. I always said you should have done your
dissertation with *me,* instead of skipping ahead to the
sixteenth century. It gave you strange, progressive ideas.

KALE: Eugene: "It is right that we seek out a foreign kingdom.

Stop your quarrel. It is not my own free will that leads to
Italy."

LOMAX: What?

KALE: Book four. After Aeneas *grows up* a little, he realizes that
the future is inevitable, and he'd better make his peace with it.

(*Beat.*)

LOMAX: That is *totally* out of context. Aeneas is *using* his trip to
Italy as an excuse to break up with his *girlfriend.* Did I not
teach you to employ textual sources *responsibly?* (*Pause.*)
Addy . . .

KALE: Don't call me that.

LOMAX: All right. The committee won't turn it down. I promise.

KALE: Thank you.

LOMAX: By the way, who's this new kid you just appointed?

KALE: Daniel Rivnine? Oh, you'll like him. You should meet him
first. Say hello.

LOMAX: I'll meet him this evening.

KALE: No, go make him feel welcome. Play nice.

LOMAX: He's junior faculty, yes? Fifth-floor office? No elevator? I
don't think so.

KALE (*turning to go*): I will pick my battles.

(BRECHT *appears, unseen. He is holding a dismantled telescope.*
During the following, he begins to assemble it.)

LOMAX: Tools are *not* neutral, Adriana. They have *purpose.* I have
never used a gun to clean my ear. Though I am now
considering it. And they make us *lazy.* "Spell-checking" has
not eliminated the inability to spell. So forgive me for
wondering how we might more egregiously coddle these

ITAMAR MOSES

young minds. Honestly, why don't we just reclassify stupidity as a learning disability, and wave them all through! So when a Ph.D. candidate stands before me, babbling incomprehensibly, not qualified to *spell literature*, let alone be dubbed a doctor of it, I think of primitive man, a sharpened rock his only tool, slaughtering a ravenous tiger. And then I imagine the tiger devouring this idiotic student. Who is, of course, defenseless. Having had all of his sharpened rocks stripped away, by years and years of *progress*. *That's* a metaphor. You seem to need reminding.

KALE: Eugene—

LOMAX: What?

KALE: That's an allegory.

(KALE *goes. Blackout on* LOMAX's *office.*)

(*Lights up on a table in a café.* STEVEN *is seated here.* LAURA *sits opposite, finishing up a small meal.*)

STEVEN: You have to do it.

LAURA: I don't want to.

STEVEN: I get that. But you have to.

LAURA: That's fascist. And it sucks.

STEVEN: It's *not* fascist. It's an intractable rule that must be obeyed. (*Beat.*) Everybody has to do a final essay for the course.

LAURA: Not me.

STEVEN: Well. Then. (*Gravely.*) I may have to fail you.

LAURA (*casually*): Go ahead.

STEVEN: Wow, that . . . That threat's really supposed to carry a lot more weight.

LAURA: You think I give a shit about grades? I have *passions*. The

only reason *anybody* takes this stupid Western Civ survey
course is because it's required. This is not my major.

STEVEN: Wait, I thought this *was* your major.

LAURA: Sure, back at the *beginning* of the *semester*, 'cause I
heard this professor was the greatest thing in the whole entire
history of, well, of history. But it wasn't *me*. And I have to be
true to myself.

STEVEN: What's your major now?

LAURA: Acting.

STEVEN: Ah.

LAURA: Yeah. It rocks. The chair? Professor Marcus? Is the *best*.
We are so on the same wavelength that he's always finishing
my sentences. With ideas I haven't even *thought* of. With *him* I
feel like I have a chance to create something very unique.

STEVEN: That's impossible, actually.

LAURA: See, that's exactly the galling attitude I'm talking about.

STEVEN: No: a thing can't be "very" unique, it's either—

LAURA: I want to do work that is *extremely* unique. *You* want me
to write an *essay*.

STEVEN: I wish I could help you. Obviously, I . . . (*Pause. Then,
carefully:*) I can't allow our personal relationship to—

LAURA: That's a convenient excuse. The *real* issue is, you're so
beholden to the system that any kind of subversive behavior
makes you uncomfortable.

STEVEN: I am not . . . beholden—

LAURA: Oh, you so are. So I'll go over your head. I'll go to the
professor.

STEVEN: All right. *Go* to the professor. But don't waste time
complaining about having to write an essay. Tell him you have
the perfect topic *already*.

LAURA: But I—

ITAMAR MOSES

STEVEN: *And*, while you're talking, take a look around his office at his *bookshelves*. Because what's on his bookshelves?

LAURA: Books?

STEVEN: *His* books. Books he *owns*. Books he *likes*. Write down a few titles, and tell him *that's* your bibliography. Be sure to select totally at random, so that the list of books makes no obvious sense. *That* means you're performing *highly* original scholarship. And then, as you get him talking about them, he will unwittingly reveal to you how the books connect. Just fellow his lead, and voilà! Essay topic!

(*Beat.*)

LAURA: What the hell is wrong with you?

STEVEN: What.

LAURA: If I wanted just *any* topic, I'd make one up myself.

STEVEN: No, no, no, this works *much* better than making one up yourself. Preparation is a trap. A hundred pages in, the professor has a fight with his wife or something, decides he hates your essay, and you're screwed. Who wins? The slacker. "Thank God," he says, "that I was *lying* about having a hundred pages." (*Beat.*) Oh, it *might* help to prepare, like, a dossier on the professor? Find out everything you can about him before the meeting? You can probably get somebody from UCA to do the research *for* you, those computer guys'll do anything—

LAURA: *Why?*

STEVEN: I guess they just like the challenge?

LAURA: No: what kind of a person would *do* something like that?

STEVEN: Well, yeah, no, I mean, I guess it is kind of . . . extreme.

(*Beat.*)

LAURA: You know what? I think I've got my topic!

STEVEN: Oh!

LAURA: Well, more of a . . . project, actually.

STEVEN: Good. What is it?

LAURA: I'll surprise you. But thanks, this was very helpful.

STEVEN: I'm . . . glad.

LAURA (*standing*): Want to go to a party this weekend? You need a costume.

STEVEN: Why?

LAURA: Because it's a costume party. (*Handing it over:*) Here. I have a flyer.

STEVEN: No, I mean . . . We've *talked* about this: as long as we keep it . . . But: a *public* party, I . . . I think it would appear grossly inappropriate.

LAURA: So the fact that your behavior already *is* grossly inappropriate is fine so long as it doesn't appear that way.

STEVEN: Yes.

LAURA: Steven, people could care less about TAs . . . *fraternizing*, or whatever.

STEVEN: You mean they could *not* care less. And they *could.* I'd lose my job.

LAURA: The semester's practically *over*, so for all intensive purposes—

STEVEN: Oh my God. You're doing it on *purpose.* (*Beat.*) I don't have a costume.

LAURA: Fine. What are you doing right now?

STEVEN: Oh, uh: actually I, uh . . . I have a meeting with a potential thesis adviser.

LAURA: Do you have a pen?

STEVEN: What? Of course I have a *pen.*

LAURA: Why? "Preparation is a trap." "Just follow his lead."

STEVEN: Laura—

LAURA: Professor Marcus says that being a yes-man is the worst
   of all crimes. And pretty much all the drama majors agree
   with him.

(LAURA *goes, leaving behind an apple.* BRETT, *twenties,*
approaches the table.)

BRETT: Hey.
STEVEN: Oh. Hey, Brett.
BRETT: Who was that?
STEVEN: Oh, that's my protégée. (*Beat.*) Do you have it?

(BRETT *produces a folder overflowing with documents and drops*
it on the table.)

BRETT: One dossier. As requested.
STEVEN: Looks . . . thorough.
BRETT: Oh, yeah, what do you take me for? E-mail archive,
   collected publications, every mention in the campus paper—
STEVEN: You're probably wondering why I need all this.
BRETT: Uh: not really.
STEVEN: Okay. So: what are the highlights?

(BRETT *opens the folder. Lights up on* RIVNINE'*s office. Bookcases,*
a desk with a computer. RIVNINE *is here, gazing out his window.*
He goes to his desk, and sits.)

BRETT: His name is Daniel Rivnine.
STEVEN: Uh: yeah.
BRETT: He's a Milton scholar.
STEVEN: Doesn't he teach a course entirely on Milton? Called
   "Milton"?

BRETT: He likes having a good view.

STEVEN: What?

BRETT: His office is on the fifth floor of Horton Parker Hall. There's no elevators in that building.

STEVEN: Maybe he likes exercise.

BRETT: He's married for reasons that are unclear.

STEVEN: Not because he loves his wife?

BRETT: Rumor has it, it's to help him get tenure. To make him seem more . . . settled? I mean: they don't have any kids. Also—

STEVEN: Uh, you know what? Thanks, I'll . . . peruse it on my own.

BRETT: Okay. (*He turns to go.*)

STEVEN: Oh, hey, anything in here about what his favorite *books* are?

BRETT: I don't . . . I mean: not specifically, no. But I can—

STEVEN: Doesn't matter. I'll be fine.

(BRETT *goes.* RIVNINE *pulls a cardboard box from beneath his desk, goes to his bookshelves, and begins tossing his books into the box. By the end of the scene,* RIVNINE *has packed all but three of his books.* STEVEN *remains, studying the folder.* KALE *enters Rivnine's office.*)

KALE: Professor Rivnine.

RIVNINE: Dean Kale! To what do I owe the honor?

KALE: To the stairs.

RIVNINE: What?

KALE: I wanted to see if you had any *questions*: about the committee, about . . . Sometimes new members are made to feel—

(LOMAX *enters, behind* KALE.)

LOMAX: Daniel Rivnine, is it?

RIVNINE: Oh! Hello. Yes.

KALE: And *other* times—

LOMAX: I'm Eugene Lomax.

RIVNINE: I know who you are, Professor Lomax. It's nice to . . . In
fact, I didn't expect to meet you until this evening.

LOMAX: Well I like to make people feel welcome.

KALE: Yes. So. I'll leave you boys to talk. (*To* RIVNINE.) If he gives
you a hard time, you come to me.

LOMAX: I certainly will.

KALE: Very funny.

(KALE *goes.*)

LOMAX: Going somewhere?

RIVNINE: What? Oh, just: new office.

LOMAX: Ah yes: those are the perks.

RIVNINE: What?

LOMAX: You're on my committee now. Excited?

RIVNINE: I don't know. I mean, I just look at this as sort of a, you
know, a—

LOMAX: No. I don't know.

RIVNINE: A formality. We're all required to do *some*
administrative . . . I figured I'd just get it out of . . . so I can
concentrate on . . .

LOMAX: On what?

RIVNINE: On my students.

LOMAX: Ah. Them.

RIVNINE: I'm sorry to disappoint you. That I'm not exactly *zealous.*

LOMAX: No, no, no, I was just wondering . . . I mean, there's
plenty of committees, Daniel. Endless. Why funding
disbursement?

RIVNINE: I just asked Dean Kale to put me wherever there was a spot available.

LOMAX: And until now, you've avoided administrative work altogether?

RIVNINE: Well, I've only been here two, two and a half years, so—

LOMAX: At rise: the woods! Enter: babe!

RIVNINE: Pardon?

LOMAX: Complete. *Anyway*: before tonight's vote, you should have a look at this.

(LOMAX *drops the Wallace proposal on* RIVNINE's *desk with a thump.*)

RIVNINE: I have appointments this afternoon.

LOMAX: It's ten o'clock in the morning.

RIVNINE: And I'm lecturing tomorrow. *Paradise Lost.*

LOMAX: We're meeting *today*.

RIVNINE: I like to *rehearse*, onstage, in advance. To get at the purity of the ideas before they're warped by the fact that, you know: people are listening.

LOMAX: All right, but surely, before this evening—

RIVNINE: And there's this thing with my wife—

LOMAX: But in case you *do* find the time—

RIVNINE: I'd rather not abscond with your copy.

LOMAX: This is *your* copy. Look, my intent is not to unduly influence—

RIVNINE: I'm sure it's not. Look: you've been chairing this committee how long?

LOMAX: I prefer not to think about it.

RIVNINE: Exactly. So I'm just planning to . . . follow your lead.

LOMAX: I see. (*Pause.*) Well. It's a unique situation, actually. Unique.

RIVNINE: How so?

LOMAX: This donor wants us to spend the money on very particular things. But what he's suggesting is . . . unacceptable. So we have to find a way to use it instead on something more *appropriate* for this university's mission.

RIVNINE: Sounds very reasonable. Look, like I said, I just want to teach. And dispense with this chore as painlessly as I can.

LOMAX: All right. (*He turns to go, then hesitates.*) Rehearsing your lectures, I admire that, I remember when *I* . . . But recently, increasingly, I find that I am faced with a kind of . . . laziness, an almost *aggressive* apathy among the students. And that my energies are more effectively directed here. And that, finally, what seems a chore, these days, is not dealing with *this*, but rather . . . dealing with *them.*

RIVNINE: Many of them are brilliant.

LOMAX: That doesn't mean they're not idiots.

RIVNINE: They're wonderful students.

LOMAX: They're charming young people. Which is not the same thing. It's an easy mistake to make. In the beginning.

RIVNINE: Well. That is, of course, where I am.

LOMAX: Delicately put. I appreciate that. And look: need we always agree?

RIVNINE: Oh, the best way to destroy another professor is to agree with him. It diminishes the importance of everything he has to say.

LOMAX: Then let us always disagree. So long as we always vote the same way.

RIVNINE: The very heart of democracy.

(*They shake hands.*)

LOMAX: Yes! The Greeks, you know, invented democracy.

(STEVEN *stands. He picks up the apple.*)

(*Blackout.*)

(BRECHT *comes forward, gazing through the telescope out at the audience.*)

BRECHT: It's research. For my new play. Hot-worked metal. Glass
curved like shells from the shore. An electrical pulse: mind,
eye, machine. And my eyes . . . I see . . . the end of Earth . . .
and the beginning . . . and . . .

(BRECHT *turns his gaze toward the Greek frieze, and vanishes.*)

ATHENS, BC

Lights up on the Athenian frieze. The men come to life, as though animated by BRECHT's *telescopic gaze. The young man with the lyre,* POLITES INTERLOCUTOR AFFIRMAE, *begins to strum. The young man with the scroll,* PLATO, *wets his writing implement against his tongue. The old man,* SOCRATES, *leans back into a more comfortable position on the couch.* PLATO *writes frantically whenever anyone speaks.*

SOCRATES: Polites! You visited the marketplace today, did you not?

POLITES: Yes, Socrates!

SOCRATES: And there was talk of me among the citizens, is that not so?

POLITES: Indeed there was, Socrates, yes!

SOCRATES: And they discussed, did they not, the most recent and momentous news?

POLITES: I do not see how things could be otherwise, Socrates. And so it must be as you say.

SOCRATES: And what did you hear?

(Beat.)

POLITES: By Zeus's thunderbolt, Socrates, I do not know!

SOCRATES: Is it true that there has been a call for my arrest and imprisonment?

POLITES: By Hera's wrath, so there has!

SOCRATES: And what is the charge against me?

OUTRAGE

POLITES: By Poseidon's kelp-laden trident, Socrates, I do not know!

SOCRATES: Do they contend that I have corrupted the young, by encouraging them to question commonly held beliefs?

POLITES: Yes, Socrates!

SOCRATES: But the necessity of my inquiries only grows in the face of this resistance, and I have vowed to speak out, thus inspiring others to *think* for themselves! (*Beat.*) Right?

POLITES: To dispute you on this point, as on any other, would be to place myself very deeply into the nebulous folds of error, Socrates.

SOCRATES: I'm so glad that you agree, Polites Interlocutor Affirmae. (*Pause.*) But . . . tell me . . . Did you happen to learn at what time, or on what day, the arrest is to take place?

POLITES: By the vicelike twin threats of Scylla and Charybdis, I do not know!

SOCRATES: What time is it now, Polites?

POLITES: By Chronos, I do not know.

SOCRATES: There is a *window*, if you recall, not far from where you are standing, is there not?

POLITES (*amazed*): By the glittering breastplate of brow-borne Athena, so there is!

SOCRATES: Can you look through it?

POLITES: So I can!

SOCRATES: And where is the sun?

POLITES: It is near setting, Socrates. By the red-flaming chariot of Apollo.

SOCRATES (*quietly*): Safe, then. For another day. Unless they come by night.

POLITES: To say that you are correct is to raise the standard for rectitude, Socrates.

SOCRATES: That wasn't a question, Polites.

POLITES: How very true.

SOCRATES: Are you still staring at the sun?

POLITES: Yes.

SOCRATES: And are you blind, Polites?

POLITES: Oh yes.

SOCRATES: And so you have learned several things, have you not?

POLITES: By the ruined clops-eye of Polyphemus, so I have.

SOCRATES: My aim is not to teach you, but to teach you how little
you know.

POLITES: Yes, Socrates! Each day under your tutelage, I know less
and less!

SOCRATES: Then you are approaching wisdom. (*To* PLATO.) Did
you get all that?

(PLATO *nods, massaging his hands.*)

(STEVEN *enters from below, tired from climbing several flights of
stairs, surveys the room: togas, amphorae, ancient garb. The
others look at him.*)

SOCRATES: A messenger!

POLITES: By the feathered ankles of Hermes, so it is!

SOCRATES: See what he has brought us!

(PLATO *approaches* STEVEN.)

STEVEN: Hello. (*Pause.*) Is this . . . (*He leans back to check the
door.*) I'm sorry, I must be on the wrong floor. (*Pause.*) Is this
the classics department? (*Pause.*) Listen, I need a pen, could I
borrow . . . that?

(PLATO *nods, and hands over his stylus.* STEVEN *holds out the party flyer.*)

STEVEN: Thanks, um . . . Here. It's a . . . costume party. Costumes.
   (*Pause.*) Uh . . . Thanks.

(STEVEN *leaves.* PLATO *hands the flyer to* SOCRATES.)

SOCRATES: An invitation! Agathon, the playwright, is hosting a
   symposium tonight. "Wine. No women. And song." Tempting.
   But . . . I suppose that I should not brave the streets tonight,
   what with so many seeking me out, enraged.
POLITES: I concur wholeheartedly, Socrates!
SOCRATES: On the other hand . . . Alcibiades is a close friend of
   Agathon's, is he not?
POLITES: He is, Socrates, yes.
SOCRATES: Then perhaps I ought to go after all.
POLITES: I see no course of action save the one you describe.
SOCRATES: Very well. Plato! My wreath and my good toga! We are
   going to a party! And, Plato? Bring something to write with!

(SOCRATES *strolls out, followed by* POLITES. PLATO *searches.*)

(*Blackout.*)

NEW ENGLAND, 1999

Lights up on GRAD STUDENT #1, *who stands ready to address the audience.*

GS1: Hi. My name is Simon Peck. I'm a Ph.D. candidate in art history. My thesis is an analysis of crayon drawings from a colony of autistic children in Tangier in the late 1920s. And the myriad things these drawings can teach us. It's called *Little Rain Men*. The subtitle is: "The Crayon Art of the Tangier Colony and the Myriad Things These Drawings Can Teach Us." Because I wanted my goals to be clear. To you guys. Okay: Here goes:

(*Blackout.*)

(*Lights up on* RIVNINE*'s office. Several sealed boxes are on the floor by the desk. The bookshelves are empty, with the exception of three books lying on their sides at the edge of one shelf.* STEVEN *stands looking at this, in disbelief. Sitting at his desk, looking at his computer, is* RIVNINE. *Hovering over his shoulder is* BRETT.)

BRETT: So when you click—
RIVNINE: On . . . on the . . . I have to click—
BRETT: Twice, remember, you have to double-click.
RIVNINE (*trying*): Right. (*Pause.*) Why isn't it—
BRETT: Faster, you . . . You're not just clicking twice, you're *double*-clicking.
RIVNINE: I'm familiar with the semantic distinction, I just—

BRETT: *There* you go.

RIVNINE: Oh my. There I go. (*To* STEVEN.) I'm so sorry about this. I'm having a bit of computer trouble. I should have been ready for you.

STEVEN (*looking at the shelves*): It's fine. I'm not quite . . . ready for you.

RIVNINE: Steven, is it?

STEVEN: Yes. Right. Yes.

RIVNINE: Professor Rivnine.

STEVEN: I know.

RIVNINE: Oh, and this is—

BRETT: Brett. Hi.

STEVEN: Hi.

BRETT: This won't take long. (*To* RIVNINE.) Careful!

RIVNINE: What, why, what, what?

BRETT: We're in a sensitive area. You don't want to erase your entire memory.

RIVNINE: You'd be surprised.

(*Meanwhile,* STEVEN *has gone to the shelves. He writes down the titles of the three remaining books, and then sits, just in time for* RIVNINE *to turn back to him with:*)

RIVNINE: There's these departmental Web pages, for reading lists, discussion threads, little biographies for each professor, and they're supposed to make everything work faster, but they keep crashing my computer.

BRETT: Hey, the *reason* they crash is not design flaws, okay? You think I *want* the sites to look like ass, and freeze all the time? Maybe you ought to think about this frustrating experience when you're voting on that big donation.

RIVNINE: What?

BRETT: Never mind. (*The computer:*) Hey! You're all set. You may now partake of the sweet milk of the motherboard.

RIVNINE: Thank you. For your help.

BRETT: My pleasure. Remember: double-click. Different than just clicking twice.

(BRETT *exits. Pause.* STEVEN *fidgets uncomfortably.*)

RIVNINE: Steven. Alone at last. So: what have you brought me?

(*Blackout.*)

MONTEREALE, SIXTEENTH CENTURY

Lights up on a young Italian Renaissance priest. This is STEFANO
DECANO. *He addresses the audience.*

STEFANO: My sermon is nearly at an end. And thus, as always . . .
Time for a joke! Once, a man came to Rome, and approached
four citizens on the street. One was a merchant, one a pirate,
one a scientist, and one a priest. The man said to them,
"Pardon me, but can I ask you a question? What is the reason
for the high price of Bibles?" All four of the men looked
confused. The merchant said, "What do you mean, 'high
price'?" The scientist said, "What are 'Bibles'?" The pirate
said, "What does this mean, 'Pardon me'?" And the priest, he
said, "What is a question?"

(*Lights up on* MENOCCHIO, *at a simple wooden table, building a
model: pulleys, levers, wheels, weights, gears, playing cards, etc.
Several books are stacked nearby.* STEFANO *turns into the scene.*)

STEFANO: Menocchio.
MENOCCHIO: Hello, Stefano!
STEFANO: You were not at my sermon today.
MENOCCHIO: Yes, I apologize. But I was, as you can see, otherwise
engaged.
STEFANO: A new model. What is it?
MENOCCHIO: It's not finished. Give me time. (*Pause.*) I am glad
you are here, Stefano, for I have been meaning to ask you:
who do you suppose *wrote* the Bible? Most people now

contend, do they not, that it was God, but I have been reading it, and I wonder—

STEFANO: Sadly, I am not at liberty to engage in our customary spirited debate.

MENOCCHIO: How unusual. You are ordinarily a generous listener, for a priest.

STEFANO: I was disappointed by your absence this morning.

MENOCCHIO: Yes, I do regret missing this week's joke. After all, one can only hear a competent delivery from *you*, as the joke is invariably *bastardized* and *ruined* by everyone who attempts to interpret it secondhand. But there will be a new joke next week, I trust? I hope so. The Bible, you see, contains only very old ones.

STEFANO: Yes, I . . . My friend, I have an important matter to discuss with you.

MENOCCHIO: And *I* have an important matter to discuss with *you*—

STEFANO: Menocchio—

MENOCCHIO: Most people contend, do they not, that God is all-powerful, and all-knowing, and has been so *always*, but—

STEFANO: But you wonder, yes, Menocchio, you have told me before—

MENOCCHIO: And I have had, just today, a new thought, Stefano. What if God was at first as an infant in the womb: without understanding or even life. And he, like us, over time, began to live, and grow, and understand?

STEFANO (*intrigued*): Well, I . . . (*Beat.*) No, Menocchio, you must calm yourself, I—

MENOCCHIO: Yes! God, the sightless worm, wriggling out of the cheese!

STEFANO: I am leaving Montereale.

(*Pause.*)

MENOCCHIO: What? Leaving?

STEFANO: It is . . . not of my own accord. (*Pause.*) You know, of course, that this is not a village of the devout. My superiors have determined that this place requires the guidance of a firm hand, a vigilant eye. A priest less progressive than myself.

MENOCCHIO: Stefano, no one could accuse you of being progressive. In six years I have observed no progress in your opinions whatsoever. I will vouch for that, on your behalf, if you like. I've long dreamed of addressing the Holy Office, discussing my theories directly with them—

STEFANO: In this matter you are not, I'm afraid, the ideal character witness.

(*Beat.*)

MENOCCHIO: Is this *my* fault?

STEFANO: It's mine. You are not the only resident of this village who remains unmoved by my work here. You are only my most spectacular failure.

MENOCCHIO: And the Holy Office is angry.

STEFANO: The cure, they tell me, will be direct and swift.

MENOCCHIO: How do they propose to cure us?

STEFANO: His name is Odorico Vorai. He arrives from Rome in two days. And he is . . . unlike me. When faced with . . . blasphemy . . . Vorai will not hesitate to turn the matter over to the Inquisition.

MENOCCHIO: But, Stefano, as you say, we are a *village* of failures. They cannot take us all away.

STEFANO: They will take only you. The others are blessed with a profound lack of imagination, and can muster only inattentiveness, not heresy. This will keep them safe, for *apathy*, you see, is not a crime. But you . . . Your wish to stand before the Holy Office could very well come true. Think of your wife, your daughter . . .

MENOCCHIO: What must I do?

STEFANO: You must not speak about your ideas. You must stop building models. You must attend his sermons.

MENOCCHIO: Well, of *course* I will attend the sermons, I—

STEFANO: Vorai does not tell jokes.

MENOCCHIO: None? Really. (*Pause.*) I cannot discuss *any* of my ideas?

STEFANO: Is there anything on which you and the church agree?

MENOCCHIO: I don't know. I suppose . . . Our worlds spring from the same premise. That, in the beginning, there was nothing.

STEFANO: Excellent.

MENOCCHIO: Although frankly, Stefano, I fail to see how even God could create where there is nothing to begin with. Perhaps it is more accurate to say that in the beginning there was a kind of *chaos*, an unformed milky substance, like cheese prior to coagulation!

STEFANO: You *must* not phrase it in such colorful—

MENOCCHIO: On the other hand! Far to the east, I'm told, they have an entirely different philosophy which, at the risk of redundancy, I will call "Eastern." *There*, it seems, beginnings and endings merge into a kind of eternal continuum, rendering history both cyclical *and* linear.

STEFANO: Enough! Menocchio, I cannot protect you anymore! Promise me you'll *try*, if not for your sake, then for mine. So that I might sleep more soundly.

(*Pause.*)

MENOCCHIO: I'll try, Stefano.

STEFANO: Thank you. (*Pause.*) You missed an excellent joke today. One I'd never told before in my sermon, for fear of repercussions.

MENOCCHIO: My interest is piqued.

STEFANO: I have a theory, in fact, that the only worthwhile jokes aren't jokes at all. (*Beat.*) I am beginning to sound like you, Menocchio. I think it is time for me to go.

MENOCCHIO: No, stay awhile. Tell me your joke, while I complete my model.

STEFANO: I cannot. (*Pause.*) What will it be, when it is finished?

MENOCCHIO: Beautiful, Signore Decano. It will be beautiful. It will have wheels in motion. The rise and fall of organic matter, in the form of sweet fruit and sharp cheese. Paper aflame, star-bright. A dozen mice in the agony of birth. It will sway with the wind, and the soil underneath will boil with worms, and its perpetual motion will rock all of Italy. But most of all: it will be beautiful. For this is a model of our universe, Stefano. For this is the universe.

(*Blackout.*)

NEW ENGLAND, 1999

Lights up on GRAD STUDENT #2, *who addresses the audience.*

GS2: My name is Lars Ericksen. I'm a Ph.D. candidate in African-American studies. My thesis asserts that jazz has its roots in the traveling musicians of medieval Europe. It's tentatively entitled *Minstrel Show.* (*Amending.*) That's not supposed to be offensive or anything. It's tentative, like I said. I'm not married to it. I mean, it's not etched in stone. Obviously. Oh God, can I start over?

(*Blackout.*)

(*Lights up on* RIVNINE*'s office, where* STEVEN *sits across from* RIVNINE.)

STEVEN: So . . . ah. Yeah. So. Um. (*Rescued!*) Hey, what "donation"?

RIVNINE: Excuse me?

STEVEN: That guy, um, Brett. He said something about a big donation?

RIVNINE: He's referring to an anonymous gift.

STEVEN: Ah. From whom?

RIVNINE: What?

STEVEN: No, I know, *anonymous*, but aren't you on the committee, that, um—

RIVNINE: How did you know that?

STEVEN: Know what?

RIVNINE: That I'm on the Disbursement Committee. I haven't even been to my first meeting. Nobody really knows yet that I'm even involved.

STEVEN: Then why are you telling me?

RIVNINE: I'm obviously very confused. Let's move on.

STEVEN: Of course. So: this committee. What's it like?

RIVNINE: I meant, let's move on to you.

STEVEN: *I* don't know what it's like. You're the one on the committee.

RIVNINE: Well, Steven, I *imagine* that like any entity that's supposed to transcend politics, it's highly political. Everyone voting party line, as it were. (*Beat.*) But this is *your* time. Wow me.

STEVEN: "Wow" you?

RIVNINE: I'm very busy. If you want to convince me to take you on, I'm going to need to hear something very unusual.

STEVEN: You just might.

RIVNINE: Well then.

STEVEN: I couldn't help noticing that your bookshelves are pretty much empty.

RIVNINE: Yes.

STEVEN: It's just that everything's in boxes.

RIVNINE: That's because I'm changing offices. I mean, fifth floor? No elevator? Who'd want this?

STEVEN: Well there's the, uh . . . exercise.

RIVNINE: What?

STEVEN: You're leaving a few books behind.

RIVNINE: Yes. Don't want them anymore.

STEVEN: I see.

(STEVEN *crumples up his "bibliography" and stuffs it into his bag.*)

RIVNINE: Listen, I'm lecturing, and I also have an appointment at
the hospital, so if we could—

STEVEN: The hospital? Is everything all right?

RIVNINE: It's my wife.

STEVEN: Oh no.

RIVNINE: She's not ill, she's pregnant.

STEVEN: Your wife is pregnant.

RIVNINE: Yes.

STEVEN: Congratulations. Is it a boy or a girl?

RIVNINE: A girl.

STEVEN: Do you have a name?

RIVNINE: We haven't . . . What the hell is going on here?

STEVEN: What do you mean?

RIVNINE: You're very good at this, Steven.

STEVEN: What, good? Good at what? (*As though he has
misheard:*) What?

RIVNINE: Usually, it's clumsier. What are you doing, exactly?
Working out final thoughts in your head while asking inane
questions to keep me occupied?

STEVEN: Not exactly.

RIVNINE: What, then? You forgot to bring a pen?

STEVEN: Of course not.

RIVNINE: So what is it? Do you just have *nothing*? You simply
decided to come to the meeting with nothing at all prepared,
is that it? (*Pause.*) Is that *it*? You actually have nothing? (*Long
pause. Then, evenly:*) You're fucking kidding me.

STEVEN: Yeah, well.

RIVNINE (*lighting up*): Nothing? Really nothing?

STEVEN: Yes.

RIVNINE: Wow.

STEVEN (*standing*): So maybe I should just—

RIVNINE: No, stay, stay. (*Pause.*) You have no idea what to write about.

STEVEN: That's correct.

RIVNINE: And you came here anyway.

STEVEN: Yes.

RIVNINE: All right, then. Now we're getting somewhere.

STEVEN: What?

RIVNINE: Well, did you hear it? I actually said "wow." So I guess you're over the first hurdle. Let's move on.

STEVEN: Oh. (*Pause. He sits.*) Uh . . . to where?

RIVNINE: Yes. Right. What happens now?

(*Blackout. There is the sound of frantic typing.*)

GERMANY, 1933

Lights up on BRECHT, *seated at a plain wooden desk, working on a black typewriter. Books and papers are piled around him.*

BRECHT (*to the audience*): Now: a scene for me.

(BRECHT *resumes typing. There is a violent pounding on a nearby door.*)

BRECHT: Hello?

(*The pounding stops.* THE VOICE *speaks from behind the door. The actor is perhaps visible in silhouette, or dim light, and has a German accent.*)

VOICE: Herr Brecht?
BRECHT: Yes?
VOICE: I've just come from the premiere of your new play, Herr Brecht.
BRECHT: Really? It seems implausible that I'd have been here writing while that was going on.

(*Pause.*)

VOICE: What?
BRECHT: Never mind. How was it received?
VOICE: It wasn't. The play was interrupted.
BRECHT: By whom?
VOICE: By the Nazis, Herr Brecht.

BRECHT: Why are you calling me Herr Brecht?

VOICE: What? That's . . . it's . . . isn't that your name?

BRECHT: Brecht is my name, yes. But we're having a conversation in English.

VOICE: I don't—

BRECHT: *Herr* is the only German word you're using! Is this supposed to make the people think that we're speaking German? You're not fooling anyone. And don't say it was the *premiere* of my new play, I'd have *been* there. You are shattering the reality of the scene!

VOICE: No, *you* are shattering the reality of the scene, by calling attention to these insignificant errors!

BRECHT: No, you are!

VOICE: No, you! (*Beat.*) Wait, *I* see what you're trying to do.

BRECHT: What's that?

VOICE: You are transforming the apparatus of bourgeois culture! After all, revolutionary content requires revolutionary forms.

BRECHT (*to the audience*): This is my friend Walter Benjamin, with whom I haunt the cafés of Berlin.

VOICE: Hello.

BRECHT: We're in Germany. It's 1933. Which means that we *are* speaking German, and also that if the Nazis want to disrupt my plays, they have the right. (*To* THE VOICE.) What gives the Nazis the right to disrupt my plays?

VOICE: Bertolt, they are thinly veiled allegories condemning the government. Your stated goal is to destroy the German people.

BRECHT: When did I state such a goal?

VOICE: No, *they* have stated that it is your goal.

BRECHT: But it is not true! I am a devout Communist! It is the people I protect!

VOICE: Nevertheless, there is talk of placing a price on your head.

BRECHT: Where?

VOICE: Among the policemen waiting downstairs.

BRECHT: Excuse me?

VOICE: I don't think that excusing you is what they have in mind, Herr Brecht. Indeed: the only reason I dared interrupt your writing was to suggest that you leave for your evening walk through the window tonight. And perhaps also that you walk all the way to Prague, or to Zurich, and not come back. They have the power to alter history, Bertolt. I think that not even the dead will be safe from this enemy if he wins.

(BRECHT *loads his belongings into his briefcase, and heads for the window.*)

BRECHT: Will you follow me, Walter?

VOICE: As soon as I can.

BRECHT: Then I'll see you on the other side of the border, my friend.

VOICE: What shall I tell them?

BRECHT (*opening the window*): Tell them I am at work on a simple historical character study.

VOICE: Is that so?

BRECHT (*with one leg out the window*): Yes. And that hopefully they will not interpret it as a thinly veiled allegory.

VOICE: We can only count on their indulgence. What, pray tell, is it called?

BRECHT (*with the other leg out the window*): It's called: *The Life of Galileo.*

(BRECHT *disappears out the window.*)

(*Blackout.*)

NEW ENGLAND, 1999

Lights up on GRAD STUDENT #3.

GS3: Hi, my name is Paula Gretchen Sanders, and I'm a graduate
   student in economics. My dissertation is a predictive study of
   the likely effects of the legalization of prostitution on the
   American economy. My goal is to determine whether or not
   prostitution's regulation by the federal government can
   provide useful revenue for social programs. My dissertation is
   entitled: *Bitch, That's My Corner.*

(*Lights up on* RIVNINE's *office.* RIVNINE *and* STEVEN *are both
laughing hysterically. The laughter dies down. A beat.*)

RIVNINE: Nothing!

(*They both burst into renewed hysterics, which gradually die
down to amused sighs.*)

STEVEN: You know, actually, I expected you to be . . . angrier . . .
   about this.
RIVNINE: I'm not a judge, Steven, I'm a scholar. Like you.

(*A beat. More laughter.* RIVNINE *clears his throat and takes
control.*)

RIVNINE: No, this is great. You could write about *anything*. What
   would you like to write about?

STEVEN: Um. Milton?

RIVNINE: Oh dear God, no.

STEVEN: I . . . I mean—

RIVNINE: If I have to advise one more thesis on Milton—

STEVEN: No, I . . . Not Milton.

RIVNINE: You're coming very close to wrecking this. Listen: what do *you* want to write about?

STEVEN: I don't know.

RIVNINE: How about this: what do you want your thesis to *do*?

STEVEN: I don't know. "Change the world"?

RIVNINE: All right. How does one do that?

STEVEN: I don't know. But rarely, I think, by writing an essay.

RIVNINE: Then by doing what?

STEVEN: I don't know.

RIVNINE: Could writing an essay help you find out?

STEVEN: Why are you helping me so much?

RIVNINE: I like you. I like that you came here totally unprepared.

STEVEN: Um. Why?

RIVNINE: It's not often that a student surprises me. That's very important.

STEVEN: I assumed you'd think I was wasting your time.

RIVNINE: Steven, scholarship has *always* been about reverse reasoning. Students writing essays, if they're smart, learn to write the introduction *last*. You've taken it to a . . . refreshing extreme, but the principle is the same. I think you came here like this because you're not willing to commit yourself to anything that doesn't interest you.

STEVEN: No no. *Nothing* interests me.

RIVNINE: Even better! Tell me about that.

STEVEN: I chose humanities because it sounded awfully broad. But it turns out to be less all-inclusive than the name suggests.

RIVNINE: Oh, but you can do whatever you want! Ideally, the
humanities isn't so much a discipline as it is a lack thereof.

STEVEN: Then perhaps it does not exist here in its ideal form.

RIVNINE: What does that mean?

STEVEN: Well, there's an authority on every subject, and straying
too far outside of what they already have to say is sort of . . .
forbidden. It's . . . There's pressure to vote the party line. As it
were.

RIVNINE: Huh. (*Pause.*) It's a shame if that's what we're teaching
you. New ideas come *from* the students. When they come
at all.

STEVEN: Well, then why—

RIVNINE: "Why then was this forbid?"

STEVEN: Yes. What?

RIVNINE: "Why but to awe, / Why but to keep ye low and
ignorant, / His worshippers."

STEVEN: Excuse me?

RIVNINE: So, of *course* you become apathetic, of *course* you feel
your only recourse is just to sail through, trying to fulfill your
requirements as painlessly as . . .

STEVEN: Professor Rivnine?

(RIVNINE *has taken his copy of the Wallace proposal out of his
desk, and tucked it under his arm, as he stands and prepares
to go.*)

RIVNINE: Call me Daniel.

STEVEN: Daniel?

RIVNINE: I've had a thought.

STEVEN: What is it?

RIVNINE: I'll be your adviser.

STEVEN: It's brilliant.

ITAMAR MOSES

RIVNINE: That wasn't the thought.

STEVEN: Ah.

RIVNINE: I think this might work best if the advising duties
were . . . shared. Do you know anything about Professor
Eugene Lomax?

STEVEN: Yes. That's why I'm meeting with *you.*

RIVNINE: When you have a topic, talk to him. Ask him to co-
advise your essay. Tell him I sent you. Now, unfortunately, I
have another appointment.

STEVEN: Right. Which comes first? The committee or your wife?

RIVNINE: Actually, I'm hoping I won't have to choose.

STEVEN: No, I—

RIVNINE: That was a joke.

STEVEN (*awkwardly*): A-ha-ha . . . ha.

RIVNINE (*heading for the door*): You can have those leftover
books, by the way.

STEVEN: Oh yes. The ones you don't like.

RIVNINE: I don't think I said that. Which ones are they?

STEVEN: *The Apology of Socrates* by Plato . . . *The Cheese and
the Worms* by Carlo Ginzburg . . . and *The Life of Galileo* by
Bertolt Brecht.

RIVNINE: No, they're some of my favorites. I bought brand-new
editions. Take them.

(*On his way out,* RIVNINE *stops by his window.*)

RIVNINE: There is one thing I'll miss about this office. The view.
It's not described this way in Milton, but I've seen drawings,
from the Renaissance, of the Garden perched on top of a rocky
summit. And I like that. The idea that Eden, you know, was a
mountain.

(RIVNINE *exits.*)

(STEVEN *puts the three books into his bag. He feels something
beneath them. He pulls* LAURA*'s apple out of the bag, and puts it
into a drawer in* RIVNINE*'s desk.)*

ITAMAR MOSES

RIVNINE'S LECTURE

RIVNINE *appears at a podium. Lights fade on* STEVEN *as the lecture begins.*

RIVNINE: Why does Eve eat the apple? It's a good question. Her whole world is God, who has told her to obey Adam, and Adam, who has told her to obey God. And yet Satan, in the guise of a talking snake, changes her mind. He says:

Why then was this forbid? Why but to awe,
Why but to keep ye low and ignorant,
His worshippers; he knows that in the day
Ye Eate thereof, your Eyes that seem so cleere
Yet are but dim, shall perfetly be then
Op'nd and cleerd, and ye shall be as Gods . . .

Satan is a little biased, of course. Here is a former angel, indeed God's most trusted adviser, cast down for the unforgivable crime of . . . revolutionary activity. He'd grown tired of God's arbitrary rules: All praise Me; Everyone play golden harps and sing major thirds; and, the last straw, Everyone worship My Son. And when Satan lost the war in heaven, he looked out over the abyss, God's ferocious forces at his heels, and *chose* to fling himself over the edge. Who is the hero of Milton's rendition of Western civilization's first story? The distant, impulsive, and arrogant God? Dim-witted Adam? Manipulative Eve? God's obedient Son? Every creature here is intellectually blind. Except for one. And he wins. Simply by persuading Adam and Eve to disobey God's edicts *at all*, for spurring them to *act*. And so: Adam and Eve are cast out. But I say to hell with it: we're better off. The first moment in this story when anyone does anything remotely human is when Milton tells us: "Reaching to the Fruit, she pluck'd, she eat." So why does Eve eat the apple? Because the hero teaches her she can. Because he makes her human.

(*Beat. A single person applauds.* RIVNINE *is startled.* LOMAX *approaches.*)

LOMAX: Brilliant.
RIVNINE: Oh! Hello. Thank you.
LOMAX: Well done. The students will love it.
RIVNINE: I didn't, uh, realize anyone was—
LOMAX: Yes, sorry, I just thought I'd walk you over to the meeting.
    Make sure you find it. It *is* your first one.
RIVNINE: You're very kind.
LOMAX: Are you ready?
RIVNINE: Yes. Oh yes.

(*Blackout.*)

(BRECHT *enters, dressed for travel, carrying his briefcase.*)

BRECHT: I'm on the move. The Nazis control the government, the newspapers. Their stories are the only stories, and what can I say in response? Only: "That is not true." And what good is that? So I flee. First: Prague! Have you ever been to Prague? Such luxurious beer. Bittersweet. Such beautiful women. High elfin cheekbones. Such ugly, ugly men. But it was not my scene. Then: Zurich! Here, the prevailing attitude is that it's good to remain neutral. And I tell them only: "That is not true." I must leave Europe altogether, because it's not my scene. And I reach the shore.

(BRECHT *is at an edge of the stage. He produces an apple and a large, round cheese from his briefcase.*)

BRECHT: The research continues. Two objects, unalike in size, weight, and density. A pulse: mind, hand, sphere . . .

(BRECHT *drops the two objects off the stage.*)

BRECHT: And my ears . . . I hear . . . the roar . . . and the whistle . . . and . . .

(BRECHT *vanishes.*)

ATHENS, BC

Sounds of revelry. Lights up on another comically exaggerated Ancient Greek scene. Reclining on couches, eating grapes, are several men in togas. SOCRATES *is in the center. Standing in the background are* PLATO *and* POLITES. *Two other men are here as well:* AGATHON *and* ARISTOPHANES. *Everyone is drunk.* PLATO *transcribes.*

AGATHON: Brilliant, Socrates! Well done!

SOCRATES: You are a kind host, Agathon. But has my contribution at least been satisfactory?

POLITES: By the youthful but corpulent midriff of Eros, the challenge was no match for your genius.

SOCRATES: I leave the genius to Agathon, and his award-winning plays.

ARISTOPHANES: Ha.

AGATHON: Oh, be gracious in defeat, Aristophanes. My satire won the prize fairly. Furthermore, the Oracle predicted this outcome.

ARISTOPHANES: She most certainly did not. She said, "Submit a play, and the most deserving dramatist will be victorious." And yet the opposite seems to have come about.

SOCRATES: My friend, you are a man of lofty concerns. Surely insulting young playwrights cannot be one of them?

ARISTOPHANES: On the contrary. *This* insulting young playwright is one of my primary concerns.

SOCRATES: But have you learned nothing from the playwrights who precede you? Sophocles revealed that the Oracle at Delphi gives us rope only so that we might hang ourselves.

ARISTOPHANES: Perhaps, to secure victory next year, I ought to write a satire about *you.*

SOCRATES: I would be an enormously unpopular subject.

ARISTOPHANES: You think so as well? Excellent. I shall begin at once.

(ALCIBIADES, *young, handsome, drunk, appears in the doorway, wearing a wreath.*)

ALCIBIADES: Gentlemen!

AGATHON: Alcibiades! Where have you been? You said you'd be here on time.

ALCIBIADES: I say many things, Agathon. Then I seem to do others. Tonight, for example, I have been trying to find some decent guests for your party. I approached only the most respectable citizens, and they ran from me! Although I am the most beautiful man in Athens!

ARISTOPHANES: That is no doubt why they ran.

ALCIBIADES: It is intimidating, isn't it. (*Beat.*) Oh. Socrates. Hello.

SOCRATES: Alcibiades. You look well.

ALCIBIADES: So. (*Pause.*) So! Gentlemen! What have we accomplished this evening?

ARISTOPHANES: Agathon has challenged each of us to give a speech in praise of love. Thus far, Socrates has delivered the best.

ALCIBIADES: Love, you say? How serendipitous. For I have a story concerning the highest form of love, and Socrates himself is at its heart.

ARISTOPHANES: What story?

ALCIBIADES: You've never told them the story, Socrates?

SOCRATES: A story *about* me is more effectively told by someone else, is it not?

POLITES: By Hephaestus and the self-evident heat of his volcanic forge—

SOCRATES: Not now.

ALCIBIADES: You must know, all of you, that for a long time I have been deeply and passionately in love . . . with Socrates. He was distant. Aloof. A challenge. But how could he resist *me*? The most desired man in all Athens? (*Beat.*) They hang on my every word, Socrates. You know why? It's the *drama*. Teach that to your scribe, and you'll be immortal.

ARISTOPHANES: If you have something to tell, boy: tell it!

ALCIBIADES: You see? (*Pause.*) Now: where to begin?

SOCRATES: Don't ask the playwrights. They'll tell you to start in the middle.

ALCIBIADES: Then I shall begin, like a philosopher, at the beginning.

(*The lights shift, and we are in* ALCIBIADES' *bedroom. The other guests fade into the background, to listen.*)

ALCIBIADES (*to the listeners*): After a party much like this one, we returned late to my room. And . . . (*To* SOCRATES.) More wine?

SOCRATES: The hour is late, Alcibiades. I should go.

(ALCIBIADES *pours him more wine.*)

ALCIBIADES: It's too late for even that. You should stay. There is plenty of room.

SOCRATES: I may sleep here on your couches?

ALCIBIADES: Some host I would be then! Exiling my guest alone to the couches! No, you may sleep in my room. With me.

(*Pause.*)

SOCRATES: I have a long day of questioning people tomorrow—

ALCIBIADES: All the more reason you should be well rested.

SOCRATES: Do you hope that we'll be lovers, Alcibiades?

ALCIBIADES: Yes. No. (*Beat.*) I did not intend to reveal so much so quickly. Premature extrapolation.

SOCRATES: Be thankful you're so young, and can extrapolate at all.

ALCIBIADES: Socrates, I only want . . . to spend the night with you. Whatever else happens . . . happens.

SOCRATES: That, my friend, is a tautology.

ALCIBIADES: I have seen you watching me. Why not? I am beautiful. Can you deny it?

SOCRATES: I cannot.

ALCIBIADES: And you are so wise. I listen intently when you speak. Have you noticed?

SOCRATES: I have.

ALCIBIADES: Well then. Think of it as . . . an exchange.

SOCRATES: But, Alcibiades: the mind's eye can remain razor-sharp long after the body's eyes are blurred and useless. My wisdom in *exchange* for your physical form? You offer me bronze in exchange for gold.

ALCIBIADES: Other men would not agree.

SOCRATES: But that is an appeal to false authority: what if the other men are wrong?

ALCIBIADES: Socrates. Please.

SOCRATES: Pleading, Alcibiades, is a sign of argumentative desperation. Have you run out of strategies already? (*Pause.*) Are you *crying*?

ALCIBIADES: *No.*

SOCRATES: An appeal to pity is a *truly* feeble tactic.

ALCIBIADES: I should throw you out of my house for this.

SOCRATES: Ah yes. The last refuge of the defeated: force.

ALCIBIADES: Get out! (*But when* SOCRATES *has nearly reached the door.*) *Wait!* (*Pause.*) Yes. Oh, yes, I see.

SOCRATES: What do you see?

ALCIBIADES: The Oracle at Delphi told me: "Socrates will give himself to you." Now, as you were leaving, I resolved to return to her and cut that liar's throat, but then . . . I saw . . . She was right. You *have* given me your gold. Already. In exchange, not for bronze, but for *nothing*. By your *example*. Is that it? (*Pause.*) Have I rendered the great Socrates speechless? Can you only ask questions and not answer them?

SOCRATES: I am . . . impressed. (*He turns to go.*) And now—

ALCIBIADES: No. I think you *will* spend the night with me. After all.

SOCRATES: Some use my example would be *then*—

ALCIBIADES: Only to talk. I have earned that much. We will huddle together. Under my blankets. And you will whisper your golden wisdom in my ears.

SOCRATES: And whatever else happens . . . happens? (*Pause. His resolve is weakening.*) Alcibiades, you are already wiser than you are beautiful. The combination terrifies me. Promise me that you'll use both well.

ALCIBIADES: I promise.

(*Blackout.*)

NEW ENGLAND, 1999

Lights up on GRAD STUDENT #4.

GS4: My name is Timothy Lauterman, and I'm a Ph.D. candidate in
medieval literature. My thesis is an examination of the practice
of dueling during the Arthurian period. My focus is the
throwing down of the gauntlet as both a literal and figurative
gesture. My thesis is called: *What's Glove Got to Do With
It?* I will now present it as a story-song, in the style of the
itinerant bard-troubadours of the day. Ahem. (*He sings:*)
"Tra-la-a-a-a—"

(*Blackout.*)

(*Lights up on* KALE*'s office.* KALE *is here, behind her desk, holding
a bound document.* LOMAX *and* RIVNINE *are facing her.*)

LOMAX: Humiliating, Adriana! And deviously done!
RIVNINE: You know: be *gracious.* The vote was *fair.* And
furthermore—
KALE: Oh God, I knew this would happen.
LOMAX (*overlapping*): I am not talking to *you.* The dean has—
RIVNINE (*overlapping*): Because, I think, your *real* concern ought
to—
KALE: I need you *and* you to *stop* this! I did not *bring* you here to
make a *scene! I'm* just wondering why this is not *over* yet!
LOMAX: Do you *know* what he *said* to me?
KALE: Well, what with the shouting match in front of me, I haven't
had time to read the transcript yet, no, but—

LOMAX (*taking it*): Give me that.

RIVNINE: If I may—

LOMAX: Quiet, young man. Here it is. You *said*: "To call our field, Dr. Lomax, the study of 'humanities' is to greatly underestimate what it means, in this day and age, to be human." You challenged me on what it *means to be human!* And *then* you *threw* a glass of water!

RIVNINE: I spilled it by *accident.*

LOMAX: *Years* I've been running this committee. And with a well-chosen phrase *you* trigger a revolt.

RIVNINE: I didn't *make* anyone vote my way. They *chose. And* you're quoting me out of context. (*Taking it.*) Give me that.

KALE: If only I'd made copies for everybody.

RIVNINE: I was responding to *you*: "We ought to accept young Mr. Wallace's gift only on condition that we be allowed to spend it on the humanities. These funds are, after all, only a tool. The Greeks, you know, invented money."

LOMAX: They *did.*

RIVNINE: He would have rescinded his offer! Are we better off empty-handed?

LOMAX: Yes!

KALE: Oh dear. I see. Daniel? May I speak to Professor Lomax alone?

RIVNINE: Oh. Of course, I'm . . . Of course.

(RIVNINE *goes.*)

LOMAX: So now it's "Daniel," is it?

KALE (*rounding on him*): You *promised—*

LOMAX: I *promised* we wouldn't turn it *down.*

KALE: This is crazy, what you tried to do.

LOMAX: Oh? What if *another* donor did the same thing? But for the humanities?

KALE: What kind of a question is that? We'd *accept* it.

LOMAX: You don't get my meaning. What if another donor did the *same thing?* Endowed a new program, *specifically* for the humanities, with a specific *reading* list, named specific *faculty* to run it—

KALE: Oh. *Then* we'd have to turn it down.

LOMAX: Why?

KALE: Because it would completely undermine our intellectual integrity to allow a *donor* to dictate *content*.

LOMAX: Wallace's money came with conditions.

KALE: It's not the same thing, actually.

LOMAX: What's the difference?

KALE: What's the difference between giving me a specific kind of computer and forcing me to read Thucydides?

LOMAX: Yes.

KALE: A computer is a piece of equipment.

LOMAX: So is having read Thucydides! Not a wildly popular one. But knowledge *is* a tool.

KALE: This is very insidious, what you're suggesting.

LOMAX: Why?

KALE: Because it's a completely specious argument, Eugene! Knowledge is a tool, sure, but it's not *only* a tool.

LOMAX: What does that mean?

KALE: It *means*: we use tools on *purpose*. But knowledge affects our *decisions*, every day, without our even being aware of it! We *make* tools. Knowledge makes *us*. And we have to be *very careful* what we teach these kids, because there's no off switch for things you've *learned*.

LOMAX: Of course there is! Free will!

KALE: Yes. But. *We also have to teach them that.*

LOMAX: Well said! I agree! But *my* question is: *What's the difference?* In both cases an outside entity is teaching our students to take important things for granted! You want them to question whether the Great Books are great books, but you *don't* want them to question whether books ought to be replaced altogether. That's nonsense! Either *both* scenarios are acceptable or *neither* one is!

KALE: No. *Yours* isn't.

LOMAX: Why? Because you *say* so? I don't think you've made your case, Adriana. I'm asking: fundamentally, philosophically—

KALE: *Oh my dear God!* This is not about *philosophy,* Eugene, this is for *real!*

(*Beat.*)

LOMAX: Well, it's true, these big donations can be few and far between, but, years from now, we may have to have *this* fight for real.

KALE: Eugene, I think we *are* having this fight for real. And I think . . . (*Pause.*) You may not be here. Years from now.

LOMAX: What? What are you saying?

KALE: This could have been a very public disaster. And at that point, we're talking about *my* job. There are consequences for me. And for you.

LOMAX: Hold on. Addy, this is what we do for *fun,* we—

KALE: I'm not in your goddamn seminar! We're not in *your* office, we're in *mine!* We're in the *present,* and I am your dean, and you fucked up. *Very* badly. (*Pause.*) Now. Obviously, you can finish out this academic year. But after that—

LOMAX: After *what.* I have tenure. You can't force me to leave.

KALE: But I can eliminate your reasons to stay. I can hire younger scholars in your discipline. I can assign you to teach introductory language sections. I can take away your committee.

LOMAX: All right, all right, I . . . I knew that it would make you angry. But I never imagined that it would make you . . . *angry,* I . . . Don't do this because you're angry.

KALE: I'm *doing* it because it's *right.* I'm *capable* of doing it because I'm angry. (*Pause.*) You have no *idea* . . . My first big coup as dean. I came straight to you. I thought you'd be . . . proud.

LOMAX: I *am,* I . . . I was. But given my *principles*—

KALE: It's not principles. It's fear. In Aristotle's universe, the Earth stands comfortingly still. But read ahead sometime. In the sixteenth century, we discover that the Earth *moves.* And *that's* what scares you. But you know what Benjamin used to say about new beginnings?

LOMAX: Walter Benjamin? Are you *serious?* Don't quote that trendy, existentialist, nihilistic, suicidal fuck at me! I don't have to *sit* here and—

KALE: Eugene—

LOMAX (*heading for the door*): You know, Horton Parker is on campus next week. It breaks my heart that he'll have to see what's become of this place. The beautiful thing he built is dying.

KALE: *Horton Parker* is dying. He's a very sick man. And his time is past.

LOMAX: I'm going to fight this.

KALE: Don't. If you go to war, a great career will be destroyed.

LOMAX: That's what I'm counting on.

(*Blackout.*)

MONTEREALE, SIXTEENTH CENTURY

Lights up on another young Italian priest. This is ODORICO VORAI.

VORAI: Some empty seats. (*Pause.*) Not good. Not good at *all*.
   (*Pause.*) Let us pray. *Especially* for those who are not here.
   Those who stayed at home.

(*Lights up on* MENOCCHIO, *at his simple wooden table.* VORAI
turns into the scene.)

VORAI: Scandella.
MENOCCHIO: Hello, Signor Vorai. Call me Menocchio.
VORAI: Scandella, you did not come to confession today.
MENOCCHIO: Yes, that's right.
VORAI: You also did not come to confession last week. Or the
   week before.
MENOCCHIO: It's true. I did not.
VORAI: Signor Scandella. Have you stopped coming to
   confession?
MENOCCHIO: I suppose, my friend, that I have.
VORAI: I am not your friend.
MENOCCHIO: Ah. Perhaps that is why I have stopped coming.
VORAI: You have also stopped attending my sermons.
MENOCCHIO: They are useless to me.
VORAI: They are *what?*
MENOCCHIO: I only mean that I am happy with my own reading of
   the Bible.
VORAI: You do not need your own reading! You already have
   mine!

MENOCCHIO: Yes, but does not it seem inadvisable to obey a
mandate from a book one knows only secondhand, while
deferring for its explication to the very person whose second
hands those are?

(*Beat.*)

VORAI: What?
MENOCCHIO: I find it hard to believe what you tell me.
VORAI: So you prefer to believe instead that God was at first
unaware?
MENOCCHIO: Is it not possible?
VORAI: No, it is not possible.
MENOCCHIO: Why?
VORAI: Because it is blasphemous!
MENOCCHIO: Your logic is somewhat Eastern, Vorai. Cyclical, if not
linear.
VORAI: Silence! Know your place! God is perfect and eternal!
MENOCCHIO: But if drawn from the same *source*, cannot our two
interpretations coexist? As two worms that burrow happily
through the same cheese?
VORAI: The true intent of Holy Writ is laid down by the Church!
You cannot simply *alter* the meaning with interpretation!
MENOCCHIO: On the contrary, Signore, I cannot seem to avoid
altering the meaning.
VORAI: Then I will have you taken. And it will go badly for you,
Scandella. The Inquisition has . . . instruments. Imagine: the
gears and pulleys of your flimsy models on a grand scale. Put
to excruciating use.

(VORAI *turns to go.*)

MENOCCHIO: Wait! Please—

VORAI: I have no choice. (*Pause.*) Unless . . . (*Pause.*) Your . . .
daughter, Scandella. (*Pause.*) She is very . . . pretty.

MENOCCHIO: Why, thank you! Though I find your sudden switch
to flattery perplexing.

VORAI: I think you grasp my meaning.

MENOCCHIO: Well, Vorai, I would not want to *impose* an
interpretation of my own. Perhaps it is best if you explicate the
meaning *for* me.

VORAI: If we cannot come to an agreement, your soul is out of my
hands.

MENOCCHIO: Well then. We agree on one thing at least.

(*Blackout.*)

NEW ENGLAND, 1999

Lights up on GRAD STUDENT #5.

GS5: Hello. My name is Derrick Lombard, and I'm a graduate
   student in religious studies. My dissertation is on the methods
   of torture used on victims of religious persecution throughout
   history. I explore how these methods can be updated for use
   in today's society, where, frankly, they are more sorely needed
   than ever before. I even have some prototypes here with me,
   and later on I will be asking for volunteers. My paper is called:
   The Hand of God.

(*Blackout.*)

(*Lights up on* LOMAX*'s office.* STEVEN *is here, sitting and waiting,
while* LOMAX *is helped by* BRETT, *who is leaning over his
shoulder.*)

BRETT: No, you have to drag it.
LOMAX: Yes, but *how* . . . you see I—
BRETT: Click and . . . you have to click and then—
LOMAX: I'm clicking. Are you watching me click?
BRETT: Yes, but you have to click and then *hold.*
LOMAX: Oh, yes yes yes. (*Pause.*) Nothing's happening.
BRETT: Well, then you drag it.
LOMAX: Ah. See? What.
BRETT: You let go, man.
LOMAX: Fuck it. Go away. This student is waiting, and that's at
   least technically what my office hours are for, so—

BRETT: All right. (*He begins to pack his things. To* STEVEN.) Hi,
Steven. Busy week for the both of us, eh? How's Rivnine
working out?

STEVEN: Um . . . fine.

BRETT (*to* LOMAX): Don't forget, I still need your bio for the Web
page. "Eugene Lomax, Professor of . . . Whatever." You fill in
the blank.

LOMAX: How about Professor of Pre-Virtual Textuality. (*Pause.*)
Books.

BRETT: Let me know when you have something real you want me
to use.

LOMAX: Something "real." Are you aware of how staggeringly
ironic that is?

BRETT: No. But that's probably what makes it ironic.

LOMAX: Don't be clever with me. The Greeks, you know, invented
irony.

BRETT: Yeah, well, I invented a new online interface. Remember:
click and hold.

(BRETT *exits.*)

LOMAX: So. Steven, is it?

STEVEN: Yes.

LOMAX: What's this about Rivnine?

STEVEN: He's my adviser. For my dissertation.

LOMAX: We all have our misfortunes, Steven. What does that
have to do with me?

STEVEN: He sent me here. He thought you'd be a good co-adviser.

LOMAX: He did *what*?

STEVEN: He—

LOMAX: He sent me a *student*?

STEVEN: Well, I met with him yesterday, and—

LOMAX: And he sent you to me.

STEVEN: Yes.

LOMAX: I see. (*Pause.*) Why?

STEVEN: I . . . he . . . I guess because he thought my topic would
be of interest to you.

LOMAX: I see. And what is it?

STEVEN: Excuse me?

LOMAX: What is it?

STEVEN: What is what?

LOMAX: What?

STEVEN: I'm sorry, what?

LOMAX: *What is your topic?*

(*Pause.* STEVEN *reaches into his bag, takes out his slightly
crumpled "bibliography." He holds it out.* LOMAX *takes it.*)

STEVEN: Let me answer your question with a question, Professor
Lomax. Three different men. Three different periods of history.
What's the link?

(*Pause.*)

LOMAX: Okay. I'll bite. Where does this lead?

STEVEN: Let's see if you can guess. I'll tell you if you get it right.

LOMAX: Intriguing. The Greeks, you know, invented the mystery.

(*Blackout.*)

ACT 1 FINALE

BRECHT *appears, carrying his briefcase in one hand and his typewriter in the other.*

BRECHT: Fresh off the boat. I am a tired, poor, and huddled mass. Yearning. And here, at long last, I may breathe free. Hawaii! I arrive by boat, and we come to rest inside a beautiful harbor that glitters in the sun . . . much like the pearl, from which the inlet takes its name! And I know that I am safe, at last. (*He looks up.*) Only to find that here, it begins again. Only to confirm the fatal knowledge we endeavor to keep secret from ourselves: that it *always*. Begins. Again.

(STEVEN *and* LAURA *enter* STEVEN*'s bedroom, wearing nothing but fig leaves, and looking for all the world like Adam and Eve.*)

BRECHT: Don't worry. We haven't gone back quite as far as you think.
LAURA: So did you have a good time?
STEVEN: You told me we were going to a costume party. That was a *rally* to protest funding cuts for the theater department.
LAURA: With *costumes.*
STEVEN: But didn't the school just get some huge donation—
LAURA: Not for us! Not for theater! Didn't you look at the flyer?
STEVEN: No. And why was everybody throwing *cheese*?
LAURA: It's a *symbol.*
STEVEN: Of *what*?
LAURA: There was a whole article in the paper!
STEVEN: I don't read the paper.

ITAMAR MOSES

LAURA: See? This is the *whole point* of my project.

STEVEN: Your—?

LAURA: For your class.

STEVEN: You never told me what that was.

LAURA: Oh! It's you.

STEVEN: Excuse me?

LAURA: It's you.

STEVEN: Okay. Um. I'm not sure I can give you credit for that.

LAURA: I already did the paperwork.

STEVEN: What? But . . . How is it even relevant to the course?

LAURA: My proposal delineates how the history of Western civilization is essentially a string of master-disciple relationships in which the line between intellectual and emotional passion is constantly blurred and wherein, as often as not, it is the student who inspires the teacher.

STEVEN: Wow.

LAURA: Okay! Let's make out.

STEVEN: The Greeks, you know, invented nudity.

LAURA: Nah: it's much older.

STEVEN: Yeah?

LAURA: Oh yeah. Original sin.

(LAURA *leans in to kiss* STEVEN *on the mouth, but he turns his head slightly, and her lips meet his cheek instead. During the following,* LAURA *leaves* STEVEN *alone.*)

(SOCRATES *and* ALCIBIADES *appear, surrounded by* AGATHON, ARISTOPHANES, *and* POLITES.)

ALCIBIADES: And that is my story of the night Socrates spent at my home. And it is also my speech, in praise of the highest form of love.

ARISTOPHANES (*moved, but trying to hide it*): Beginner's luck.

AGATHON: (*simply moved*): Yes. How lucky. To be at the
   beginning.

ALCIBIAD: Socrates, I am so . . . I am sorry.

SOCRATES: What is it, my friend? What's wrong?

ALCIBIADES: I tried to stop them, but I could not, they . . . they
   threatened me, Socrates. They are coming for you. They are
   already here.

(ALCIBIADES *puts a hand to* SOCRATES' *face, and kisses him gently
on the cheek. The symposium guests all back away into the
darkness, leaving* SOCRATES *alone.*)

BRECHT: I cross the water to the mainland, hoping to continue to
   the East. New York! But here too, now, the war is under way.
   And I am German. They will not let me cross the border.

(*Lights up on* LOMAX's *office.* AGATHON *and* ARISTOPHANES *enter
the office, becoming* RIVNINE *and* LOMAX *as they do so.*)

LOMAX: Look. I'm sorry that we didn't see eye-to-eye at the
   meeting—

RIVNINE: We didn't, did we. And the dean seemed pretty upset. I
   hope you—

LOMAX: Oh, we're old friends. (*Beat.*) Anyway: that's not what I
   wanted to talk to you about. I have some good news.

(LOMAX *pulls out a sheaf of papers, and drops it onto his
desk.*)

RIVNINE: What is that?

LOMAX: It's the last will and testament of one of our trustees. He wants to endow a new program. A new center for the humanities. Isn't that marvelous?

RIVNINE: It sounds . . . Yes! May I see it?

LOMAX: By all means. (*He hands it over.*) Now, the man is still *alive*. So no one else has *seen* this yet. So, Daniel, listen: I'm showing this to you because I . . . I'm prepared to look at our little disagreement as . . . a *lapse*. You understand? I was hoping we could have: a new beginning.

RIVNINE (*looking up from the pages*): He names you.

LOMAX: What was that?

RIVNINE: He names you specifically. As director of this center. An endowed chair.

LOMAX: Yes, that's right. I'm extremely flattered.

RIVNINE: Well, is he allowed to *do* that?

LOMAX: Oh, that's not for me to say. I'm just a soldier. In the belly of the beast.

RIVNINE: What?

LOMAX: Can I count on your support?

RIVNINE: I don't know.

LOMAX: I can promise to look with kindness on your little practical joke.

RIVNINE: What are you talking about?

LOMAX: That student you sent me? That boy?

RIVNINE (*he remembers*): Oh yes. Steven. What about him?

LOMAX: Yes, him. "Steven." My new pal. Thank you.

RIVNINE: He came to see you *already*?

LOMAX: What are you talking about? You *sent* him.

RIVNINE: Yes, I'm just surprised that he felt . . . *ready* to—

LOMAX: You sent that boy to me on *purpose*.

RIVNINE: I . . . Pardon?

LOMAX: It was a *symbol*. You're trying to make some kind of a clever *point*.

RIVNINE: And what's that?

LOMAX: *I am a university professor!* And yet you *insist* on *wasting my time* with *students!*

RIVNINE: Well, it's hardly a waste of your time if you say no to every—

LOMAX: I said yes.

RIVNINE: I'm sorry, you did what?

LOMAX: His topic interested me.

RIVNINE: His "topic" interested you.

LOMAX: Is that so unthinkable?

RIVNINE: No, I'm just . . . curious how he went about . . . presenting this "topic."

LOMAX: Oh, it was a bit of a guessing game, actually. He gave me his bibliography, and challenged me to connect the dots. Most inventive pitch I've ever had.

RIVNINE: And, presumably, you were able to do so.

LOMAX: For Christ's sake, Daniel, don't start a pissing contest. But yes, I was. And, if you must know, he said I was much better at it than you were.

RIVNINE: And, so, ultimately, when you'd put it all together, you liked what . . . Steven had come up with?

LOMAX: Socrates! Menocchio! Brecht! The link between them jumps right out.

RIVNINE: Their books all have recent new editions?

(MENOCCHIO *appears, building his model, joining* SOCRATES *and* BRECHT *on stage.* STEVEN *also remains, and a loose tableau now seems to be forming. And, once again, shadowy figures begin to gather, ranged in the misty background, watching, accompanied by a subtle, growing thrum.*)

LOMAX: I'll grant you this: it's apropos. The Greeks, you know,
    invented the trial. And the trial invented the martyr. Figures
    who weren't afraid to stand up, nobly, in the face of a stifling
    regime!

RIVNINE: Oh, *I* see. You imagine that *you* fall into this category.

LOMAX: Yes! Good lord, you've all become so "open-minded"
    that your brains have fallen out! Who's on trial now? It's us,
    Daniel. It's *us!*

RIVNINE: I'm sorry: "us"?

LOMAX: Yes! If you stand in the way of this, you'll be harming
    your own *field*. Your *career*. You cannot possibly consider
    turning this down.

(*Beat.*)

RIVNINE: I'll advise Steven alone. He shouldn't be in the middle of
    this.

LOMAX: Then *you* shouldn't have put him there! And, given your
    teaching, perhaps he'd be better off with me.

RIVNINE: You don't know the first thing about my teaching.

LOMAX: I saw your lecture. Misguided from start to finish. Milton
    was a deeply religious man. He would never have made Satan
    the hero of his story.

RIVNINE: Maybe the story didn't give him a choice.

LOMAX: Well: *I* am giving one to *you*.

(*A booming* CHORUS *of five hundred voices calls out, now very
near:*)

CHORUS: Socrates. You are under arrest by the authority of the
    Archon.

LOMAX: I have the support of powerful faculty.

CHORUS: Domenico Scandella. You are under arrest by order of the Grand Inquisitor.

LOMAX: I have wealthy alumni. The board of trustees.

CHORUS: Bertolt Brecht. Welcome to Hollywood.

LOMAX: I have two thousand years of Judeo-Christian tradition. What do you have?

RIVNINE (*turning back*): Outrage.

(RIVNINE *and* LOMAX *stare at each other across the office.* STEVEN *stands to gaze out his bedroom window.* SOCRATES, MENOCCHIO, *and* BRECHT *are each alone.*)

BRECHT: *Intermission!*

(*Blackout.*)

ACT 2

BRECHT'S INTERLOGUE

The sound of typing.

Lights up on SOCRATES, *in a prison cell: a bare room, stone walls. The wall is partially covered with white chalk diagrams. Prominently in the center of the wall is a drawing of the sun. A stick-figure man stands underneath the sun, arms raised. Elsewhere on the wall is a drawing of other stick figures bound together inside a cave.*

Lights up on MENOCCHIO, *in a prison cell of his own.*

Lights up on BRECHT, *sitting at a desk, typing. He is wearing a Hawaiian shirt and sunglasses. Palm trees are visible in the background. A beach ball bounces slowly past.*

BRECHT: And so I ask: which of us has it the worst? Welcome back. Those of you who returned. History, as you may have noticed, is invariably written by the winners. And because winners so often rely on lying and cheating, they are untrustworthy as a group. Their lies become the facts, or, at any rate, the record of the facts. Records *exist*, you see, whereas facts may not. Stories, on the other hand. Stories are the *opposite* of history. They are filled with invention to begin with, and then misinterpreted, and then rewritten, and nevertheless can contain throughout a kind of truth. As you might imagine, this presents a problem for *stories about* history. Which comes first? The *story* or the *facts*? This play cannot seem to decide, and thus is neither factual nor true. I expected you to rise to your feet during the first act and decry it, but you've proven to be a fairly apathetic group so far. It is very lucky for history's inevitable children, that sometimes a visionary observer can stand above all of this. Naturally, by *children* I refer to all of you, and by *visionary* I refer to myself. I am in Los Angeles. It is wartime. And I am hard at work on *The Life of Galileo*.

(*There is a sudden loud banging at the door.*)

VOICE: Herr Brecht!
BRECHT: *What?* I am hard at work on *The Life of Galileo*!
VOICE: Oh, yes. God help any rebellion that depends heavily on its artists.

(*It is clear from his accent that this* VOICE *is a different person: British, not German.*)

BRECHT (*to the audience*): This is not Walter. Walter was not able . . . (*Pause.*) In the mountains between France and Spain, Walter Benjamin, my friend, found the border closed. The Gestapo were at his heels. And he chose . . . he chose to . . . I wrote these lines for him:

In the end, driven to an impassable frontier,
you, we hear, passed over a passable one.

He had a briefcase in his hand when they found him. And even in death, he would not let it go. None of us ever learned what was inside.

VOICE: Finish quickly, Bertolt. That way, if the Nazis arrive, we can deploy your play, and distract them for a few hours.

BRECHT: This is my new friend, Eric Bentley. With whom I haunt the poolsides of Santa Monica. And even in English, I am:

VOICE: Herr Brecht! Like most artists, you greatly overestimate the impact of art on society.

BRECHT: And like all critics, *you* greatly overestimate the value of your own opinion.

VOICE: If you wish to effect science, or politics, then you ought to become a scientist, or a politician!

BRECHT: Unfortunately, I am a playwright. (*Beat.*) And my play is finished!

(BRECHT *pulls pages out of his typewriter.*)

VOICE: We must find a director! Someone who not only has the wisdom to fathom your work, but who also lives in Los Angeles.

(*Beat.*)

BRECHT: I will direct the play myself. Scene thirteen! Galileo, as an old man, receives a visit from his former pupil, Andrea, who is angry that the Inquisition was able to force his old teacher to recant. I need an Andrea and a Galileo!

(*The actors playing* LOMAX *and* RIVNINE *appear, as we last saw them.*)

BRECHT (*handing over the pages*): Now! This is the final scene. It must therefore be extremely powerful, or the audience will wonder why the play is not yet over. Go!

LOMAX (*reading, awkwardly*): "Andrea, my former pupil. How strange to see you after these many years, though I do not see so well as I once did."

RIVNINE (*likewise*): "Silence, old man! You should have died for the truth, and instead you live here, inside this house. This house . . . of lies!"

LOMAX: "But look, Andrea!"

BRECHT: Galileo holds out a dusty bound volume.

RIVNINE: "Silence, old man! I'll not look at your dusty bound volume . . . of lies!"

LOMAX: "Silence, young man! These are the *Discorsi*, a work very useful to mankind, created in secret, secretly, at great personal risk!"

RIVNINE: "Praise be! Your hands are better off stained than empty! Your work will lead to miracles of science that will one day save mankind!"

BRECHT: Brilliant!

LOMAX: Thank you.

BRECHT: Not you. It's lucky I'm so *brilliant*. (*Beat.*) And now: cells locked!

LOMAX: I have the support of powerful faculty.

BRECHT: Fates sealed!

LOMAX: Wealthy alumni. I have the board of trustees.

BRECHT: Travels ended!

LOMAX: I have two thousand years of Judeo-Christian tradition. What do you have?

BRECHT: Next semester!

RIVNINE: Outrage.

BRECHT (*shouting*): Act two!

LOMAX: Outrage? What is that supposed to mean? You have . . . your own outrage?

RIVNINE: Not *mine*.

LOMAX: Oh. Whose, then?

RIVNINE: I . . . Never mind. You totally . . . deflated the moment.

(RIVNINE *leaves.*)

LOMAX: Outrage? What the hell does that mean?

(*Blackout.*)

NEW ENGLAND, 2000

Lights up on BRETT, *facing the audience.*

BRETT: Hi, I'm Brett, I'm a double major, in computer science and, uh, fantastical Norse mythology. My thesis combines these variegated areas of expertise into a single project, wherein I have created a pantheon, as it were, of autonomous computer programs, each endowed with the powers and temperament of a particular Norse god. Tonight, I shall set them loose on the Internet, whereupon I will track their bitter struggle for supremacy, from which only one can emerge unscathed, and lord eternally over *Virtual Valhalla*. Which is the project's title.

(*Lights up on* RIVNINE*'s new first-floor office.* RIVNINE *is sitting at his desk, checking e-mail.* BRETT *is hovering over his shoulder.* STEVEN *is across from them.*)

RIVNINE: Sorry about this. I'm swamped. Suddenly, I'm getting hundreds of e-mails every day.

BRETT: The new software can handle the higher volume. It'll revolutionize the way the university is administered.

RIVNINE: You mean modernize. Hell unleashed couldn't revolutionize it.

BRETT: Look at the animation on that icon. I did that one myself.

RIVNINE: It's . . . very festive.

BRETT: Well, it's all thanks to you: new computers, new software, Ethernet. Word is, you stood up for us.

RIVNINE: You shouldn't believe everything you read.

BRETT: I know, but I kinda do.

ITAMAR MOSES

STEVEN: Everything you read where?

BRETT: In the paper. You didn't see it?

STEVEN: No.

RIVNINE: The campus paper made a budget meeting sound a lot more dramatic than it actually was. And now my in-box reaches capacity every six hours.

BRETT: Say what you want, man. I saw the transcript. (*Reverently*:) "To call our field, Dr. Lomax, the study of humanities is to greatly underestimate what it means, in this day and age, to be human." We're putting that on a banner. We're gonna hang it on the wall at UCA.

RIVNINE: That's, um . . . terrifying.

BRETT (*to* STEVEN): At one point in the meeting? He got up and threw a glass of water in the other guy's face. Brutal.

RIVNINE: That's not in the transcript.

BRETT: Well, apparently that's because it went down while you were, you know, off the record.

RIVNINE: It's not in the transcript because it didn't happen.

BRETT: Whatever. Doesn't matter.

RIVNINE: What happened doesn't matter?

BRETT: We've been drooling for this money for a long time. As long as we get new toys to play with, I could care less how it "really happened."

RIVNINE: I think you mean, you could *not* care less.

BRETT: Irregardless. (*The computer.*) There. All fixed.

RIVNINE: Thank you. Sorry to be so incompetent. I'd just mastered the old one, and now my skills are obsolete.

BRETT: Hey, it's nothing to be ashamed of. There's a reason it's called the cutting edge. Try to hold it back and it'll slice your hands.

RIVNINE: Did you make that up?

BRETT: Yeah. Uh . . . no. This friend of mine has it on a T-shirt.

(BRETT *exits.*)

STEVEN: What the hell is he talking about?

RIVNINE: Nothing. It's only politics. It has nothing to do with you.

STEVEN: That's what I like to hear.

RIVNINE: Yeah. (*Pause.*) I read the pages you gave me.

STEVEN: Something wrong?

RIVNINE: It's mainly that the people you're writing about in your martyrdom study aren't actually martyrs.

STEVEN: What?

(*Beep. Another e-mail has arrived.*)

RIVNINE: Oh, you have to hear some of these: "Professor Rivnine, you are a role model for all those who—"

STEVEN: What do you mean they're not actually martyrs?

RIVNINE: I meant that they're not. Which isn't surprising, given how you arrived at your choices.

STEVEN: I . . . uh . . . Well, shit. I mean . . . shit.

RIVNINE: Oh, it's not a big problem.

STEVEN: It's not a big problem? The title of the paper is *Three Martyrs!*

RIVNINE: So change the title of the paper! What did I teach you about scholarship?

(*Beep.*)

RIVNINE: Ooh. "You are responsible for the intellectual decay of a great institution."

STEVEN (*of his paper*): I don't understand.

RIVNINE: Martyrs die for their beliefs. Brecht died of natural causes.

ITAMAR MOSES

STEVEN: But he wrote *The Life of Galileo*! He identified with it!

RIVNINE: Galileo *recanted* his beliefs, and *then* died of natural causes. And you know what Brecht thought of that? This is a quote: "The recantation was a crime against humanity on the order of original sin."

STEVEN: I . . . He said that, really—?

RIVNINE: I mean, did you *read* the *play*?

STEVEN: *Yeah.*

RIVNINE: In scene thirteen, Galileo *condemns* himself: "Any man who does what I have done must not be tolerated in the ranks of Science."

STEVEN: When he started writing the play, he was running from the Nazis, it was his metaphor, or allegory, or—

RIVNINE: Yeah, well, something changed his mind before he finished it. What?

STEVEN: I don't know.

RIVNINE: Exactly. You don't.

(*Beep.*)

RIVNINE: Oh dear: "I am the Hand of God. And you strike me as an ideal subject for the newly updated methods of torture I have—"

STEVEN (*agitated*): Please stop reading me your e-mail.

RIVNINE: Okay: Menocchio.

STEVEN: He stood up to the Inquisition! At his trial he criticized the Church!

RIVNINE: But after they found him *guilty*, he said: again, this is a quote:—

STEVEN: I think you mean "quotation." (*Beat.*) You know what? Go ahead.

RIVNINE *Quote*: "I am deeply repentant that I have offended my

Lord God, and I wish now that I had not said the follies that I said, into which I fell, blinded by the Devil." So they let him *go*.

STEVEN: They killed him . . . eventually.

RIVNINE: After a *second* trial. *Fifteen years* later.

STEVEN: So what?

RIVNINE: So doesn't it compromise your status as a martyr if you take time out from standing up for your ideas to *live* a while longer? And incidentally, your death is supposed to galvanize ·followers. Menocchio didn't *have* any.

STEVEN: Well . . . (*Beat.*) What about Socrates? He could have defended himself, or backed down, but he didn't. He *provoked* the jury. So clearly, he—

RIVNINE: Yes. Socrates was a martyr. Clearly. *Too* clearly, if you see what I mean.

STEVEN: Right. (*Beat.*) What do you mean?

RIVNINE: On the page, everything is two-dimensional. Plato wrote just about everything we have, and his Socrates is fearless, *perfect* . . . But real life has *three* dimensions. *Real* people have fears, weaknesses, and you cannot fathom the *real* reasons a person might . . . why someone might . . . *risk* . . .

(*Pause.* RIVNINE *is staring at* STEVEN.)

STEVEN: Professor Rivnine?

RIVNINE: Sorry, I just . . . It's Daniel. Please.

STEVEN: So . . . You're saying these people aren't martyrs.

RIVNINE: I'm *saying* it's the wrong question. Look: when Socrates drank the hemlock, what happened next?

STEVEN: He, uh, died.

RIVNINE: No. What did *Plato* do *next*?

STEVEN: I don't know.

RIVNINE: Exactly. You don't.

STEVEN: I've got a *hundred pages* already. What are you asking me to do?

RIVNINE: *Christ! I'm* not asking *you* to do anything! That's the *whole point*! Look: what are you doing here?

STEVEN: What do you mean?

RIVNINE: What is it, you just want to get this done, just do what I say so you can get this done, get your degree, and get out of here, is that it? Because I thought . . . I thought you came to me with something unique.

STEVEN: I came to you with *nothing*. I told you: nothing interests me. It's not my fault if you chose to *interpret* that as—

RIVNINE: No, no, you're right, it's not. I thought the apathy was a pose. I thought you were brave. Silly me, the apathy is real. You're not brave. You're just lazy. I mean, why *me*? Really. Why did you *pick* me?

STEVEN: Because. I heard you had a spot available. (*Pause.*) I'm going to be late.

RIVNINE: What for?

STEVEN: A party.

RIVNINE: Ah. That's important. You ought to get going, then.

STEVEN (*heading for the door*): Yeah.

RIVNINE: Aren't you even going to argue with me? About how brave you are?

(*Pause.*)

STEVEN: Would you . . .

RIVNINE: Would I what?

STEVEN: Would you like to come with me?

RIVNINE: What?

(*Beep.*)

STEVEN: Hey, another one. Nothing threatening, I hope.

RIVNINE: You want me to go with you to a party?

STEVEN: With my . . . friend Laura and me. It's a costume party. (*Pause.*) Costumes.

RIVNINE: Well. I don't have a costume. (*Pause.*) Anyway, I shouldn't. My *wife*, she's . . . she's close.

STEVEN: To what?

RIVNINE: The delivery.

STEVEN: Oh. Do you know what you're going to name her?

RIVNINE: Oh, we haven't . . . I think . . . (*Pause.*) Eve. We're going to name her Eve.

(*Blackout.*)

ATHENS, BC

Lights up on SOCRATES, *in his cell.* ALCIBIADES *enters, followed by* PLATO *and* POLITES. *Their entrance brings with it a shaft of bright light from outside, against which the old man shields his eyes.* PLATO *transcribes all that occurs.*

SOCRATES: Who's there?

ALCIBIADES: Socrates? Your friends are here.

SOCRATES: Shut the door. My eyes are not accustomed to the light.

POLITES: Yes, Socrates.

(POLITES *shuts the door.*)

SOCRATES: What time is it? In here . . . I no longer . . .

ALCIBIADES: It's early, Socrates. Early dawn.

SOCRATES: I'm surprised that the warden was willing to admit you.

ALCIBIADES: He . . . ah . . . (*Pause.*) He was willing, Socrates. (*Pause.*) How are you?

SOCRATES: Are you here to help me escape?

ALCIBIADES: Yes. No. (*Beat.*) You're good at that.

SOCRATES: I cannot go, my friend, until the laws have set me free. Is that not so?

POLITES: By the circling carrion birds of Ares, your logic is as airtight as this cell.

ALCIBIADES: The *law* bends to the convenience of those in power! Like twine, it can tie your hands, or be lowered as a rope to rescue those in need!

SOCRATES (*loftily*): No! I must remain here, nobly imprisoned, no matter how they might impinge upon the freedom of the outspoken individual. (*Beat. Then, to* PLATO:) Stop writing.

(*Stunned,* PLATO *does so.*)

SOCRATES: All right. How are you getting me out of here?

ALCIBIADES: What? Oh! I . . . Well! We've bribed the appropriate parties, and arranged safe passage for you on a ship to Thessaly.

SOCRATES: Excellent.

ALCIBIADES (*ushering him to the door*): There we can live in bliss, and forget Athens!

SOCRATES (*hesitating*): Forget Athens?

ALCIBIADES: Yes! And forget all else, too! As I've always said: The examined life is not worth living.

SOCRATES: But . . . Alcibiades, surely, you believe that you ought to *act* according to the ideals I am imprisoned for *espousing*? That you ought to *do* as I *say*?

POLITES: *I* will do as you say, Socrates.

SOCRATES (*realizing*): No. No, that . . . *I* . . . must do as I say.

ALCIBIADES: Oh, of course, of course. But let us discuss this further on the boat, as we are *most* unwelcome here. Aristophanes, no less, has written a new satirical play! Portraying you as a madman, with your head in *The Clouds*. It seems that no one here was ever truly able to learn from you.

(*Pause.*)

SOCRATES: So it seems.

PLATO: What is this drawing?

(*Stunned, they all turn to* PLATO, *who, no longer occupied with his writing, has wandered away from the door.*)

SOCRATES: This? Ah. Men. Bound in a cave. Their only light is a
  great fire that lies behind and above them. And so they see
  only shadows, not what casts them, and they think those
  shadows are all there are to the world. Then: one man breaks
  free. He claws his way up into the light. Past the fire. To the
  outside. At first he is blinded by the sun, but gradually his
  eyes adjust and he is able, for the first time, to see. He plunges
  back into the cave to share his great discovery, but when the
  return to darkness blinds him once again, the others don't
  believe him. His journey upward, they tell him, has ruined his
  sight. And so: wouldn't they ridicule him? If he tried to drag
  them upward, wouldn't they fight him off? And, if he began to
  succeed, wouldn't they kill him?
POLITES: Yes. As surely as if Clotho, Lachesis, and Atropos had
  spun, measured, and snipped his fate themselves.
ALCIBIADES: Interesting. But this is no time for philosophy. *This is
  important!*
SOCRATES: I have reconsidered. Perhaps I'll stay after all.
ALCIBIADES: What? (*Pause.*) Your sudden vacillations feel like a
  cruelty aimed at me.
SOCRATES: That's not my fault, Alcibiades. That's narcissism.
  Plato. You may resume.

(PLATO *does.*)

ALCIBIADES: You cannot stay and die! You alone can lead us!
SOCRATES: And that is why I must.
ALCIBIADES: If you have a better plan, then tell me what it is!
SOCRATES: And sacrifice the element of surprise?

ALCIBIADES: Surely *I* needn't be surprised.

SOCRATES: Success may depend on it. Watch the trial, Alcibiades. Promise me.

(*Pause.*)

ALCIBIADES: I promise.

(BRECHT *appears.*)

BRECHT: This is not true! Socrates received a visit in prison, yes. But not from Alcibiades. Do you want to know why? It will break your heart. No, really, it will. Armed with the teachings of Socrates, he became a beloved general. But when the wars began between Athens and Sparta, he switched sides. Twice. Then he fled to the coast, where he was slaughtered by assassins. When Athens arrested Socrates, Alcibiades had been dead for five years. But his actions were used as proof that Socrates had corrupted the young. I thought you ought to know the facts as well as the story. I thought you'd like to know both.

(*Blackout.*)

NEW ENGLAND, 2000

Lights up LOMAX's *office.* LOMAX *is here.* KALE *enters, slamming papers on his desk.*

KALE: I am shocked.

LOMAX (*looking at the pages*): Ah. Not too shocked, I hope. He was very sick.

KALE: Stop it. (*She reads.*) "Forty-one million dollars, which money is to be devoted to the refurbishment of the humanities program, securing a place at my alma mater for the study of dead white men such as myself."

LOMAX: That *is* shocking. Takes quite a man to have a sense of humor in his will.

KALE: What have you done?

LOMAX: What are you talking about?

KALE: What did you *do*? Kneel by his deathbed and *dictate* this to him?

LOMAX: *What?*

KALE: It includes *all* of the things you mentioned: the humanities, the reading lists, and, oh yes, an ongoing position for *you*.

LOMAX: I'm pleased by his generosity, but Horton Parker's motives, like those of so many great men, are forever lost to history.

KALE: Do I strike you as an idiot? Your hand in this is clear, in the terms, the *amount* even, the forty-one million as opposed to forty—

LOMAX: Saddened by the man's *death* as I am, I haven't yet given it much thought, but it seems Parker was as put out by

Wallace's gift as I was. All right? Why don't we just treat this as an *opportunity*?

KALE: Keeping you here, as you know, would undermine my authority.

LOMAX: Not if no one else finds out you wanted me to leave.

KALE: And you know how I feel about these kinds of restrictions.

LOMAX: Do I?

KALE: *Yes.* We *talked* about it.

LOMAX: That was hypothetical. Those were virtual dollars. The fact that they're now very real doesn't affect your stance at all?

KALE: *No.* And I think some members of your committee might agree with me.

LOMAX: That's my concern.

KALE: Well, the *trustees* are *mine.*

LOMAX: Then you'll be pleased to hear that they're very much in support of this.

KALE: They . . . (*Beat.*) I'm sorry: You've spoken to them?

LOMAX: Well, yes, several of them telephoned me personally to give me the news of Horton's passing. He was . . . one of their own.

KALE: You discussed this with the trustees before speaking to me?

LOMAX: Very . . . informally. I just thought my . . . relationship with them might allow me to slice through some of the knotty bureaucracy.

KALE: Then I'll speak to them myself, about the likelihood of impropriety in—

LOMAX: If you feel you must.

KALE: Oh. I see. You *want* me to. You think they'll side with *you.* But they chose *me* to be their dean. Not you.

LOMAX: But don't you see? They *chose* you because they couldn't get *away* with choosing me. They *thought* they were getting the next best thing: me in acceptable disguise. Everyone *knows* you were my—

KALE: What. Your what.

LOMAX: My protégée.

KALE: No. You've crossed a line. I'll make them see that. *Alea iacta est.*

LOMAX: What?

KALE: Julius Caesar.

LOMAX: I know who *said* it.

KALE: And I thought you'd *hear* me if I quoted one of *yours*. He rolled the dice. And wound up vomiting blood on the steps of the Senate.

LOMAX: But, Addy: Caesar died when the powerful men who'd supported him decided they wanted their Republic back. Which of us does *that* sound like? You should know better. After all, Shakespeare's one of *yours*: "Stoop, Romans, stoop, and let us bathe our hands in Caesar's blood. How many ages hence shall this, our lofty scene, be acted over in states unborn and accents yet unknown." *Julius Caesar.*

KALE: Act three, scene one: "If I could pray to move, prayers would move me. But I am constant as the northern star."

(*Blackout.*)

ROME, SIXTEENTH CENTURY

Lights up on MENOCCHIO, *in his cell. His wrists are shackled.*
STEFANO *enters.*

STEFANO: Menocchio.
MENOCCHIO: Stefano? (*Pause.*) Stefano, my friend. Hello. (*Pause.*)
Stefano, why are you still in Rome? I thought, surely, by now
you'd be far off, in some Italian village, with a new flock to
tend.

(STEFANO *lifts his hands from beneath his cloak. His wrists are
also shackled.*)

STEFANO: When I heard that you had come, I, I knew I had to find
you. They will come soon, to take me back, but I must . . .
I, I must ask you—
MENOCCHIO: You are . . . a prisoner? (*Pause.*) What have they
done to you?
STEFANO: They? They have done nothing. But they are not, ha-ha,
not yet convinced that I am fit to be a shepherd again. No
sheep for Stefano. (*Sheep noise:*) No-o-o-o-o-o!
MENOCCHIO: What has . . . happened to you?
STEFANO: I don't know, I . . . Ever since I left Montereale, I have
had dreams . . . nightmares, I have been plagued, I . . . In these
dreams, I stare into the mirror, and my limbs fall from their
sockets, one by one. I tear myself apart with my own gaze.
I . . . (*Beat.*) Would you like to hear a joke?
MENOCCHIO: No.

STEFANO: Once, a man went to the doctor of small village. He was
a stranger there, but the doctor nevertheless saw that the man
was deeply troubled.

MENOCCHIO: Stefano, please—

STEFANO: He asked: "What is the matter?" And the stranger
replied, "Doctor, I am sad and frightened. Can you help me?"
And the doctor said: "Every year, a traveling circus, from the
east, passes through, moving west. By chance, they are in
town tonight, and this year the festival includes the world's
most famous clown. Yes! An evening with the great Pagliacci
is precisely what you need."

MENOCCHIO: *Enough!* (*Pause.*) Stefano, what can I do to . . . to
help you . . . to . . . ?

STEFANO: You *can* help me!

MENOCCHIO: How?

STEFANO: I must ask: you have said that God and his angels, at
first unknowing, gradually grew in wisdom.

MENOCCHIO: I . . . I don't—

STEFANO: *That is what you have said, is it not?*

MENOCCHIO: I . . . have said that, yes. But—

STEFANO: Well, my friend: I have my *own* interpretation, and you
must, you *must* tell me if I am correct, or, or else—

MENOCCHIO: I don't understand.

STEFANO: Most contend, do they not, that you mean to suggest,
blasphemously, that God is imperfect, as we are. But is it not
possible, just possible, that you mean precisely the opposite?
That we, like God, are capable of growing in understanding, of
striving gradually towards perfection, of creating, out of chaos,
something entirely new! That your God is a metaphor for
man!

MENOCCHIO (*intrigued*): Well, I . . . (*Beat.*) No, you must calm
yourself—

STEFANO: Tell me if I am correct!

MENOCCHIO: *Why?*

STEFANO: Because then I would know that *I* . . . can . . . heal myself.

MENOCCHIO: Stefano, heal yourself, and *then* you will know you can.

STEFANO: But it is *your* theory! *Why will you not reveal the true meaning?*

MENOCCHIO: *Why must there be only one?*

(*Pause.*)

STEFANO: Perhaps I lack your capacity for doubt. Priests must have answers. I have only questions. If I cannot . . . They may never let me leave Rome.

MENOCCHIO: It's a beautiful city. The Greeks, you know, invented Rome. (*Pause.*) What is the ending of your joke, Stefano? After the doctor has told the stranger that the great Pagliacci can cure his sadness?

STEFANO: Oh! Oh yes, it is so funny! The stranger, he burst into tears. The doctor said, "What's wrong, my friend? What have I said?" And the man replied, "You don't understand. You don't understand at all. Doctor. I *am* Pagliacci."

(BRECHT *appears.*)

BRECHT: This is not true! Oh yes, poor Menocchio! Imprisoned in Rome, and visited only by the priest he once befriended, now an insane prisoner himself. Except, of course, it never happened! I learned a number of things about him, you see, doing research for my own play. He and Galileo were contemporaries. Though thankfully, they never met. Sparing us, I hope, the obligatory scene in which they encounter one another, and influence each other's lives in some all-too-convenient manner. No doubt one on his way in to see the Inquisitors and one on his way out, though in fact their trials were separated by decades! I would object strenuously to that kind of cheap effect!

(*Lights out on* MENOCCHIO *and* STEFANO. *Smoke, lasers, music . . .*)

NEW ENGLAND, 2000

Lights up on Steven's bedroom. STEVEN *is here, dressed as Obi-Wan Kenobi from Star Wars. Also here is someone dressed as Darth Vader.*

BRECHT (*leaving*): Don't worry. We haven't gone as far . . . far away as you think.
STEVEN: I hope you had a good time.

(*"Darth Vader" removes his mask, revealing* RIVNINE.)

RIVNINE: I did. I'm glad, though, that I could make an appearance incognito.
STEVEN: I, uh . . . I figured. You want a drink?
RIVNINE: No, thanks, I had plenty already.

(STEVEN *gets two beers, and hands one to* RIVNINE. BRECHT *storms back in.*)

BRECHT: And don't think I'm not perfectly aware how much more quickly you recognized them than you recognized me!

(BRECHT *vanishes.*)

RIVNINE: I can't stay long. I'm lecturing in the morning. *Paradise Lost.*
STEVEN: I like that one.
RIVNINE: When did you see it?
STEVEN: No, yeah, I . . . guess I didn't.

RIVNINE: Thanks for the costume.

STEVEN: Thank Laura. She got them.

RIVNINE: Ah. Pity she couldn't make it.

STEVEN: Yeah, she had something to do, some . . . thing.

RIVNINE: Listen, I'm sorry. I was a little harsh with you this morning.

STEVEN: Oh. So . . . My paper's really fine?

RIVNINE: No, it sucks. I just wish I'd been nicer about it.

STEVEN: It *sucks*?

RIVNINE: Come on. You put these three texts side by side, like you expect parallels to just . . . emerge! What's *your* contribution? Where are *you* in there?

STEVEN: Actually, my strategy is to kind of just stay out of the way. You know, let the great minds do their own talking.

RIVNINE: So why should anyone read you instead of just reading them?

STEVEN: No one *should* read me. My ideas are *ridiculous*.

RIVNINE: That's a marvelous attitude, Steven.

STEVEN: It's not an attitude, "Daniel." It's a fact.

RIVNINE: People thought Galileo's ideas were ridiculous.

STEVEN: Yes, but his only *seemed* ridiculous, whereas mine, in fact, *are*.

RIVNINE: Who can tell, at the time? New ideas *always* look ridiculous next to older ones. When Galileo revised the universe, he was revising Aristotle, right?

STEVEN: Right.

RIVNINE: But who was Aristotle's teacher?

STEVEN: Plato.

RIVNINE: And Plato's?

STEVEN: Socrates.

RIVNINE: Sounds like you're saying the outcasts of one era become the authorities of the next. Am I right?

STEVEN: Yes, I guess that is what I'm saying, Daniel.

RIVNINE: And how does an individual *do* that, do you think? Go from exile to icon? It's because people like *you* have learned the wrong lesson. You *should* say: "From Aristotle, I learned about the *spirit of inquiry* that allows for something as *marvelous* as a new model for the heavens!" But instead you spend your life parroting: "From Aristotle, I learned about the crystal spheres!" And then you set fire to anyone who disagrees. It's much more comforting to be *sheep*, so when you reject the tyrant and adopt the maverick, all you've done is *swap shepherds*. Because: "My ideas are ridiculous." But when Aristotle appeared, he didn't say, "My name is Aristotle. I'm the greatest philosopher of all time, and I'm going to change the world." He didn't see *himself* as an unquestionable authority, he didn't see *anyone* that way! Have you ever read his commentary on Plato? It's *brutal*! Which must have made Plato very proud, because the fondest wish of anyone like that is for someone to come along and render him obsolete! When they were *made*, Greek sculptures were whole, and brightly colored. We recreate them in plain white marble, with missing arms. We think that's how they're supposed to look because, over time, paint fades and limbs fall off. Reverence is *wasted* on the past! Write your fucking essay!

STEVEN: It's not even a real topic! It's nonsense! I picked the books at random!

RIVNINE: Look at our *campus*! Modernist towers, medieval arches, Athenian tableaux: it's like a *bomb* exploded in the center of history and we're stranded in the *debris*. You read works of genius, and your own work is so *messy*. But *life* is *messy*. So, all due respect to *them, we're* the ones who have to go out and *live* in this mess every day. And that makes us . . . geniuses. That makes *you*. A genius.

(*Pause.*)

STEVEN: You don't have the faintest idea how to fix my essay.
RIVNINE: Yes I do.
STEVEN: No you don't.

(*During the following,* STEVEN *surreptitiously begins to take notes.*)

RIVNINE: All right, smart-ass. Let's say *you've* got a vision. And that vision earns you a following. And there's *nothing* more powerful than that collective group mind. Disciples. A congregation. An audience. A classroom! And then: somebody *kills* you. How do your followers feel now?
STEVEN: Well, they're . . . sad. Um. Angry. Thirsty.
RIVNINE: Let's go with angry. Which isn't strong enough. But: Let's say they're angry enough to rise up, and take over. Now they're in charge. But you're dead. You're not around anymore to think for them. You *taught* them, but you also *used* them, so they only learned to be tools. You raised them to question everything, but the one thing they *won't* question is the memory of you. Anger makes them strong, but it doesn't make them smart. *Now* the group mind is judge. And jury. And . . . when the next visionary comes along, your mob burns him alive. In your name. And once it starts, it never stops. We take for granted that every Plato needs a Socrates, but which one has more control over what happens a hundred years later? A thousand? Your own group of followers is *tiny* compared to the largest audience there is: all the generations to come. And they only know what your Plato wrote down. If he got it right, and if they read it right, and if nobody comes along later and *changes* it. So how do you avoid that cycle, and make them,

not a mob, but: an ocean of Aristotles? *How do you make them furious, and wise, at the same time?*

(*Pause.*)

STEVEN: You can't.

RIVNINE: What?

STEVEN: You can't. They have to choose.

RIVNINE: Between the two.

STEVEN: No. They have to choose to be both. They have to decide.

(*A moment. Then:*)

RIVNINE: Wait, are you taking notes?

STEVEN (*starting to laugh*): Um. No?

RIVNINE: Great, nicely done. I'm giving all of my wisdom away, for free. And you're laughing at me.

STEVEN: I'm laughing because it's kinda hard to take you seriously in that costume.

RIVNINE: Right. Anakin Skywalker, noble Jedi knight, turned to the Dark Side.

STEVEN: Don't blame me. I, Obi-Wan, taught you what to use your power *for*, but you became obsessed with it, for its own sake. And then you killed me.

RIVNINE: But then *I* die. Saving my son. Who catches me when I fall. (*Pause.*) It's a hell of a story.

STEVEN: Maybe we should switch costumes.

RIVNINE: I can play either part.

(RIVNINE *wields an imaginary lightsaber, with sound effects.* STEVEN *does likewise.*)

RIVNINE (*in Darth Vader voice*): "I've been waiting for you, Obi-Wan. We meet again, at last. The circle is now complete. When I left you, I was but the learner; now I am the master."
STEVEN (*in Obi-Wan voice*): "Only a master of evil, Darth."

(*Imaginary sabers clash three times.*)

RIVNINE: "Your powers are weak, old man."
STEVEN: "You can't win, Darth. If you strike me down, I shall become more powerful than you can possibly imagine."
RIVNINE: Yes. (*Pause.*) That's the whole idea, isn't it? Yes.

(*Pause.*)

STEVEN (*turning away*): Do you want another, uh—

(RIVNINE *reaches for* STEVEN, *turning him back.*)

(*Blackout. Lights up on* LAURA.)

LAURA: Hi, I'm Laura! Thanks everybody for coming to my play! It's really great to see all of you here. A few warnings before we get started. There will be smoke and flame onstage, and also strobe lighting, so if you have a respiratory condition, or epilepsy, or if you don't like rapidly projected subliminal images of horrific atrocities, um, just keep that in mind. There will also be nudity, so any, like, puritanical hypocrites out there should just be warned. And the first eight rows will be getting wet, and, no, it's not water. Also, the exits are now locked. Please enjoy the show.

(*Blackout.*)

LOS ANGELES, WARTIME

Lights up on Brecht's office. BRECHT *is here, working with a small model.*

BRECHT: This is a set design. Onstage, it will appear much larger. (*Generally*) I need Andrea and Galileo! Dress rehearsal! Scene thirteen!

(*The actors appear, but this time they are* RIVNINE *and* STEVEN. *They have a simple set now.* STEVEN *sits at a simple wooden table, with a telescope, some papers, etc.* RIVNINE *stands beside him. They begin the scene.*)

RIVNINE: "Silence, old man! I'll not look at your dusty bound volume of lies!"
STEVEN: "Silence, young man!—"
BRECHT: Wait, wait, wait! (*Pause.*) Who are you? What happened to my Galileo?
STEVEN: He had some problem with the union. So.
BRECHT: The "union"? The one legitimate attempt at communism in this country, and it ruins my play.
STEVEN: I guess the casting doesn't make much sense.
BRECHT: You have created a chronological paradox which threatens to tear apart the fabric of space-time.
RIVNINE: Look, I can do either.
BRECHT: Also! Notes from last time! (*To* RIVNINE.) You! In scene one. Your line: "The millennium of faith is ended. This is the millennium of doubt."
RIVNINE: Actually that wasn't *my* line—

BRECHT: Well, you've been saying it all wrong. Emphasize! "The
   millennium of *faith* is ended! This is the millennium of *doubt!*"
RIVNINE: If I overplay it like that, it'll be obvious that I'm . . .
BRECHT: What?
RIVNINE: Acting.
BRECHT: I'm glad we understand each other. Now: final scene!
   Go!

(*The acting is no longer awkward. It's polished, heartfelt. During
the scene, however, the sound of a plane's engine gradually
becomes audible, joined shortly by the whistle of an object
plummeting from a great height.*)

RIVNINE: "Silence, young man! These are the *Discorsi,* a work
   very useful to mankind, created in secret, at great personal
   risk!"

(RIVNINE *holds out an actual prop: the dusty bound volume.*
STEVEN *takes it reverently, and tucks it safely away inside a
briefcase.*)

STEVEN: "Praise be! Your work will lead to miracles of science
   that will one day save mankind!"

(*The massive roar of an explosion. A sudden, blinding light. A
fading rumble. Darkness. Silence. Then, in faintly returning light:*)

VOICE: Herr Brecht! The war is over! We have triumphed!
BRECHT: But how? What was that blinding light? That terrible
   noise?
VOICE: It was a weapon. A miracle of science has saved mankind!
BRECHT: How many people were killed?

VOICE: None, Herr Brecht. Only the enemy.

BRECHT: Dear God.

VOICE: No. It was a man of German blood. Just like you. Only: he is a scientist. In the employ of politicians.

BRECHT: My script . . . my hand . . . the pen . . . the page . . . and . . .

(*The lights suddenly swell as . . .*)

TRIAL

A banging, very loud, now more like a judge's gavel than like a knock at the door. The shadowy gathered CHORUS *is suddenly here, with its attendant rumble.*

SOCRATES *appears.*

CHORUS: Socrates! You are here to stand trial!

(*The banging, again.*)

(MENOCCHIO *appears.*)

CHORUS: Domenico Scandella! You are here to stand trial!

(*The banging, once more.*)

(BRECHT *looks up from his work.*)

CHORUS: Bertolt Brecht! You're in previews!
BRECHT: I have rewritten scene thirteen! Actors!

(STEVEN *and* RIVNINE *enter the Galileo set.* RIVNINE *takes a seat at the table and* STEVEN *stands facing him, holding the briefcase.* BRECHT *gives them new pages.*)

RIVNINE: Isn't it kind of late for a rewrite?
BRECHT: I changed my mind. Go!

(RIVNINE *hands over the* Discorsi. STEVEN *tucks it into his briefcase.*)

STEVEN: "Your hands are better off stained than empty. Had you
  burned at the stake, they would have won."

RIVNINE: "No, Andrea. They *have* won."

STEVEN: "But science has only one commandment: contribution.
  You have contributed more than any man for a hundred
  years!"

RIVNINE: "Have I? I surrendered my knowledge to the powers that
  be, to use it, abuse it, as it suits their ends."

STEVEN: "Then why did you recant?"

RIVNINE: "They showed me their . . . instruments. They simply
  showed them to me. And I was afraid."

STEVEN: "It was not a plan?"

RIVNINE: "No, Andrea. And any man who does what I have done
  must not be tolerated in the ranks of science."

SOCRATES: I'm not sure how to defend myself against these
  charges. But perhaps I can tell you a story: in Delphi, as you
  know, lives our prophet, the Oracle, to whom suppliants
  come daily.

(*A woman appears. This is* THE ORACLE AT DELPHI.)

ORACLE: *Ask your question. And I shall answer.*

SOCRATES: Should we go to war?

ORACLE: *If you go to war, a great nation will be destroyed.*

MENOCCHIO: When did the universe come to be?

ORACLE: *The universe came to be at the beginning.*

BRECHT: Can I show them what I see?

ORACLE: *If they're willing to purchase tickets.*

SOCRATES: The Oracle, you see, cannot be relied upon for a
  simple yes or no.

BRECHT: By the way, the Oracle was nothing like this. In fact, she was a teenage girl, kept delirious on hallucinogenic drugs.

SOCRATES: But one day, a man came to her and asked, "Is there any man wiser than Socrates?" And she said:

ORACLE: *No. There isn't. (Pause. For a moment, she is* KALE.) It goes without saying that blindly accepting this kind of gift would completely undermine our intellectual integrity. But what troubles me more is the question of motive. As I'm sure every member of this board understands.

SOCRATES: I assumed she was mistaken. And so: I set out to test her.

BRECHT: We open in Los Angeles!

VOICE: Herr Brecht! I've just come from the premiere of your new play.

BRECHT: An English translation of a German play set in Italy. The characters don't know *what* to call each other. (*To* THE VOICE.) How was it received?

VOICE: Very well. The audience was greatly moved by the sacrifice of Herr Signore Mr. Galilei.

BRECHT: What?

VOICE: They think he's an inspiring hero.

BRECHT: They are mistaken!

VOICE: I don't know what you mean. They're responding to *your* work.

BRECHT: I'll have to try again. New York!

CRITIC 1: Galileo is a brave man, suffering in silence for decades to share his knowledge with the world!

BRECHT: Sometimes I hate this country. Where writing is a tool, and not an art.

STEVEN: Actually? I think it's a problem with your play.

BRECHT: It *is* a problem that you're thinking about my play.

STEVEN (*retreating*): He doesn't want to hear my idea.

RIVNINE: I do.

STEVEN (*turning back*): With all due respect? We're the ones who actually have to go out there, and perform it every day, and, in that sense: it's our play.

BRECHT: What did you just say?

STEVEN: Listen: you can't change the world's opinion of Galileo by adding a speech to the end of your script where he *tells* us not to like him. The audience only gets what you *show* them.

BRECHT: Where did you learn that? Graduate school?

RIVNINE: He's right, you're contradicting Aristotle. To the audience, Galileo still looks the same.

BRECHT: I don't care what he *looks like*! This is what he *is*! A coward, who allowed science to become a tool, and not an art! He committed a crime against humanity, on the order of original sin!

STEVEN: Maybe from some distant perspective? But we're seeing him in, you know, in a frail human moment. People don't do things based on principle, they do things because they're afraid, or because they want to have sex, or whatever. So, I mean, *realistically*, what else could Galileo have done?

MENOCCHIO: I will discuss my theories, as you ask. But first, let me say that recently, increasingly, I have observed that the Church does not act properly. It is not governed lovingly, as it was when it was founded. There are pompous masses. And I do not think that God wants this. My mind is lofty. I wish for a new world, and a new way of life.

BRECHT: He could have told the truth.

VOICE: Herr Brecht! A phone call. From a man called Joseph.

BRECHT: Joseph who?

VOICE: Joseph McCarthy.

BRECHT: What does he want?

ITAMAR MOSES

VOICE: Have you ever made application to join the Communist Party?

BRECHT (*long pause*): No. Never.

MENOCCHIO: And now: I will tell you about the cheese.

BRECHT: I . . . I must cross an ocean, again. I will take my play to Europe. Where perhaps they will understand it. We open in Marseilles!

CRITIC 2: I cannot help but empathize with the plight of the brilliant physicist.

SOCRATES: Each day, I approach men who think themselves wise, and question them. And each day, to my surprise, these men prove to know nothing. Thus far: the Oracle is right. I am the wisest. And as a result, I have become somewhat unpopular.

BRECHT: I must hand down edicts! I will *tell* the audience how they are permitted to feel! It's my goddamn play! Paris!

CRITIC 3: The press is incensed at your arrogance, Monsieur Brecht. They demand to determine how they feel about your play only after having seen it.

BRECHT: Dammit!

STEVEN: Maybe it would help if we filled in the blanks about these characters.

BRECHT: It is not complicated. He was your teacher. And why did you select him as your teacher?

STEVEN: I liked you.

RIVNINE: You'd never even met me.

BRECHT: No: you recognized that he was a great scientist.

STEVEN: Yes, but . . . I didn't tell you this . . . then I saw you lecture. That afternoon, after we met. I went to the auditorium.

BRECHT: What play are you talking about?

STEVEN: You were onstage. Lecturing to no one. I mean, *I* was listening, but you didn't know that. I watched you lecture to an empty room.

SOCRATES: No doubt you think that, by silencing me, you are
    rescued from giving an account of yourselves. But others will
    stand up in my place. In fact, perhaps one is here today.

BRECHT: Berlin! At last, my play is performed for German people,
    who felt the tremors of those bombs falling on their allies in
    Japan. That beast of science tearing at the earth. And what did
    they see?

CRITIC 4: I see a man who has weakened his eyes at the telescope
    and who is now almost blind.

SOCRATES: Alcibiades? Stand up!

CRITIC 4: A man who has nevertheless worked, illegally,
    dangerously, by moonlight, in order to make a copy of a work
    extremely useful to mankind.

SOCRATES: Alcibiades? My friend? Where are you?

CRITIC 4: And I am supposed to hate this man? To condemn him?
    I don't care how many directives are issued demanding that I
    do so, I simply cannot!

SOCRATES: You promised! You promised you would stay!

VOICE: Herr Brecht!

BRECHT: *What is it?*

VOICE: You have been awarded a prize! The prize is named for
    Joseph.

BRECHT: Joseph who?

VOICE: Joseph Stalin.

BRECHT: What is it for?

VOICE: For your achievements, as an artist and a Communist. As a
    result, of course, your theater company has been banned from
    the United States.

CHORUS: The jury has reached a verdict!

(*The critics, and all other onlookers who remain, exit.* BRECHT
sinks into a chair at the simple wooden table from the GALILEO

set, with the notes, the telescope. PLATO *enters, and approaches*
SOCRATES.)

PLATO: Socrates.
SOCRATES: Alcibiades? Is that you? My eyes, they . . .
PLATO: Yes. Here I am.
SOCRATES: Oh! My friend! Thank you. I thought you had left me.
PLATO: Yes. Yes, I know.

(PLATO *gives* SOCRATES *a bowl of hemlock.* SOCRATES *drinks. They
wait, together,* PLATO *stroking* SOCRATES' *brow. There is a gentle
knock.*)

VOICE: Herr Brecht?
BRECHT: Who's there?

(THE VOICE *"enters." He approaches* BRECHT, *at the table, and
faces him for the first time. And when he speaks, it is once again
with a German accent.*)

VOICE: Bertolt?
BRECHT: Eric? Is that you? My eyes, they . . . Andrea? (*Pause.*)
   Walter?
VOICE: Yes. Here I am.
BRECHT: Walter. (*Pause.*) Why can't they see? He should have let
   them kill him.
VOICE: Then we would have lost a great man.
BRECHT: But we *did*, Walter. He became a coward, who allowed . . .
   his craft . . . to become a tool, instead of an art.
VOICE: No, Bertolt. No. When the fascist enemy, with rallies, book
   burnings, executions, has made an artistic spectacle of politics,
   there is no choice but to retaliate by politicizing your art.

Remember what you always used to say to me about new
beginnings?

BRECHT: I don't know. I . . . suddenly I feel quite . . .

(SOCRATES *swoons.* PLATO *cradles him in his arms.*)

BRECHT (*holding out script pages*): Here. Take these.

VOICE: What's this?

BRECHT: The *Life of Galileo* has a fourteenth scene. In scene
fourteen, Andrea arrives at the border, bearing Galileo's
precious final work. Meanwhile, in a nearby tent, a girl is
cooking over a fire, and her shadow appears monstrous
against the cloth. A mob of young boys gathers, taunts the
girl, insisting that she is a witch! But: Andrea lifts one boy to a
rip in the fabric, and he sees the girl for what she truly is. But
the moment Andrea lets him go, the boy runs off with his
friends, insisting the girl is a witch after all. And Andrea
crosses the border.

MENOCCHIO: I am deeply repentant that I have offended my Lord
God. And I wish now that I had not said the follies that I said.
Into which I fell. Blinded by the Devil.

(BRECHT *gives the new pages to* THE VOICE, *who tucks them into
his briefcase.*)

BRECHT: Make sure this new final scene is added to the play. (*To
the audience.*) And my throat . . . and my lungs . . . and my
heart . . . I'll try again. Next time.

(BRECHT *slumps,* THE VOICE*'s hand on his head.* MENOCCHIO *walks
slowly out.* PLATO *lowers* SOCRATES *gently onto his back.*)

FINALE

Lights up on Lomax's office. STEVEN *is here.* LOMAX *is looking at his essay.*

STEVEN: I, uh . . . Is this a bad time? Maybe I should come back later.

LOMAX: Later than you already are, you mean?

STEVEN: I, uh . . . I forgot to set my alarm. (*Pause.*) I know that needs a lot of work.

LOMAX: On the contrary. I think it's wonderful.

STEVEN: What?

LOMAX: It's very insightful. Full of . . . argumentative panache!

STEVEN: Oh. I mean, I thought it was kind of . . . I mean, I had this whole plan to, uh, to kind of insert *myself* into the, uh—

LOMAX: No, no. I love the way the parallels emerge when you simply place these texts side by side. So far, so good!

STEVEN: Oh. Okay.

LOMAX: I'm starting to think you'll even make a splendid professor someday. (*Beat.*) Though hopefully, I'll be able to help you by redressing certain curricular shortcomings at this university. Which I am in the process of trying to do, as I imagine you are aware.

STEVEN: What are you talking about?

LOMAX: The Parker estate. I assumed Rivnine had told you.

STEVEN: No.

LOMAX: Oh, it's a crucial matter that my committee is voting on in a few weeks. Actually, now that you bring it up—

STEVEN: You brought it up.

LOMAX: In any case, Steven, I suspect that you and I don't really
disagree.

STEVEN: About what?

LOMAX: You're a scholar in the humanist tradition! And I think
you'll be surprised to hear that Rivnine is planning to vote
against this wonderful gift.

STEVEN (*rising*): I don't really think I should be having this
discussion with you.

LOMAX: Why? I'm giving you a chance. To be on the right side.

STEVEN: And how do you propose I decide which one that is?

LOMAX: The same way history will, Steven. Pick the one that's
going to win.

(*Pause.*)

STEVEN: What makes you think I can even help you?

LOMAX: I . . . nothing. (*Beat.*) Did I ask you to help me?

STEVEN: I . . . No, I guess you didn't. (*Pause.*) Look, why don't I
just—

LOMAX: Wait. (*Pause.*) *Can* you help me? To persuade him to see
things our way?

STEVEN: No . . . I mean . . . how could I possibly—

LOMAX: Do you want this degree?

STEVEN (*hesitating*): What?

(RIVNINE *appears, at his podium.*)

RIVNINE: So why does Eve eat the apple?

LOMAX: I only mean: I'd be very grateful. If you could. (*Pause.*) No
one is neutral at wartime, Steven. Not even those who stand
aside. (*Pause.*) If you have something to tell me: tell it.

ITAMAR MOSES

(*During the following,* STEVEN *goes, and* LOMAX *remains.*)

RIVNINE: Because the hero . . . because he teaches her . . . (*He
looks at his notes.*) You know, I've been giving this lecture the
same way for years, but this semester I've . . . *revised* it, so
bear with me . . . I used to say he makes her human. But she's
human already. The apple does exactly what he says it will. It
makes her eyes open, and clear, and he cannot control what
she'll do next, no one can. She has to decide. And from that
moment forward Eve, beautiful Eve, is as a God. Just as the
serpent promised.

LOMAX: I know that you're a good teacher. Students compete to
get into your courses, your evaluations are always favorable. I
can appreciate that ability, to have a real *connection* with one's
pupils. That's not just teaching, that's *mentorship*. And it's
something that becomes increasingly difficult for me as I get
older.

(RIVNINE *has turned into the scene.*)

RIVNINE: I *am* a good teacher.

LOMAX: Yes. The Greeks, you know, invented mentorship. But
they had some odd ideas about what exactly it entailed. And,
apparently, so do you.

RIVNINE: What? (*Pause.*) I assumed . . . Is this about next week's
vote?

LOMAX: No. Well, in a manner of speaking.

(*Pause.* LOMAX *reaches into his desk and pulls out a thick
computer printout.*)

RIVNINE: What is that?

LOMAX: Did you know that the new electronic key-card system is connected to the computer at the campus police department? It keeps a record of which cards open what doors at which time. Say, which floor of the graduate student dormitory you go to at night, and when you leave the next morning. As in this highlighted portion. Of course, what happens between arrival and departure is, as it were, "off the record," so maybe there's a better explanation than what this looks like.

RIVNINE: I'm sure there is. I'm sure that you're misreading it.

LOMAX: It's possible. I don't really understand these things. I might have to pass it along to more experienced people. To confirm what I think it says. (*Pause.*) But I don't *have* to do that. You understand? It can be enough that I simply showed it to you. (*Pause.*) After all, it's the kind of thing over which someone might be terminated. And I don't want that, Daniel.

RIVNINE: You don't.

LOMAX: Well, I have different concerns now. (*Beat.*) Oh! I suppose you haven't heard! The trustees have selected me to replace Adriana Kale as dean. And, as dean, it will be in my best interest to keep *this* sort of thing quiet. *After*, of course, one last meeting with my old committee.

RIVNINE: You want me to support you.

LOMAX: I said nothing of the kind. But if you've had a change of heart, by all means: vote your conscience, Daniel.

RIVNINE: And then you want me off the committee.

LOMAX: You're quite wrong. My step up leaves a vacancy. I want you to chair it.

RIVNINE: What? (*Pause.*) Oh. I see. So long as we always vote the same way.

LOMAX: I could help you get tenure. And perhaps, when I've taken the big step up, you could have my job.

RIVNINE: I don't want your job. I want to teach.

LOMAX: And you can. For the rest of your life. (*Pause.*) You don't have to decide anything immediately. You have until the meeting.

RIVNINE (*leaving*): Excuse me.

LOMAX: I saw your *revised* lecture, by the way. And I had a thought. The way you interpret Eve's eyes: it's wrong.

RIVNINE: It's *what*?

LOMAX: Well, as you *must* know, by the time he finished writing *Paradise Lost*, Milton himself had gone completely blind. All our visionaries seem to do that, don't they? Heh. But the point is, he's not expressing some grand statement about human agency. He's just wishing something. For himself. It's an easy mistake to make, in the beginning.

RIVNINE: The Greeks, you know, stole almost everything you say they invented.

LOMAX: That's true. Nevertheless, they excelled at everything they stole.

(RIVNINE *leaves.* LOMAX *remains visible.*)

(*Lights up on* STEVEN *and* LAURA, *at the café.* LAURA *is wearing a* toga.)

STEVEN: So . . . um . . . I'm sorry I missed your play. I've been—

LAURA: You didn't miss anything.

STEVEN: No, I'm sure you—

LAURA: No, you really didn't miss *anything*. The administration shut us down. Too controversial. I mean, you know, they said something about the set blocking the fire exits, and toxic smoke, or some bullshit, but that was just an excuse to send in their storm troopers and pull the plug:

STEVEN: You're mixing . . . uh . . . (*Beat.*) What are you wearing?

LAURA: What do you mean? For the protest!

STEVEN: The, uh—?

LAURA: Our program might get cut. Like: entirely. Funding.

STEVEN: But wait, isn't there another huge gift—

LAURA: Not for theater! Never for theater! Alan says it's a liberal arts education that's not liberal and involves no arts.

STEVEN: What are you gonna do?

LAURA: Well, the committee's approving this whole travesty of justice tonight, so, you know, basically all the different little groups that feel screwed are gonna stand outside and yell. But: long-term? Steven, there's only one thing I *can* do.

STEVEN: Of course.

LAURA: Change majors *again*.

STEVEN: Yes. What?

LAURA: Well there's this new professor who's taking over the journalism program? And studying with him is an experience you can only understand once you've done it. I'm told. (*Beat.*) And so I asked myself: Why do I do theater? To reveal truth. So why, like, *cloak* it in drama, when I can just do journalism and get the facts out? So I started writing for the campus paper! (*She holds up a copy.*) Look, my first story!

STEVEN: Wow.

LAURA: Yeah. Actually, it's about your adviser and, you know, how he's leaving.

(*Lights up on* RIVNINE, *at the desk in his old fifth-floor office, which is now totally empty. He's attached a laptop computer to the phone line, and is e-mailing.*)

STEVEN (*taking the newspaper*): Daniel's leaving?

LAURA: Oh, it's "Daniel" now?

STEVEN: Is this for real?

LAURA: It's in the paper, isn't it? Anyway, so I'm disputing the
C-minus you gave me last semester. I mean, I still don't care
about grades, but all the good journalism schools do, so—

STEVEN: I'm sorry, Laura, I have to go.

(STEVEN *goes*. POLITES *and* ALCIBIADES *enter, joining* LAURA, *now*
PLATO.)

ALCIBIADES: Where shall we go?

PLATO: Go? There is work to be done! We must remain.

POLITES: Plato, your accuracy recalls the silver arrows of Artemis.

ALCIBIADES: To stay is *madness*! They will turn on *us* next!
Polites, tell him.

POLITES: Um. By the as yet unconfirmed mountains and craters
on Diana's face—

PLATO: You're wrong. Isn't he, Polites?

POLITES: By the, uh . . . earthly summers and Hades-bound
winters of Persephone, devourer of pomegranates, I, uh . . .
(*He points.*) Look! The Hydra!

(*They look.* POLITES *runs from the room.*)

ALCIBIADES: Plato—

(STEVEN *enters.*)

STEVEN: You're leaving?

ALCIBIADES: Yes.

PLATO: No. (*Beat.*) Who are you?

STEVEN: I . . . uh. Sorry, I . . . must be on the wrong floor . . .

(STEVEN *leaves, perplexed.*)

PLATO: I'm staying.

ALCIBIADES (*turning away*): If you change your mind. I know a
place, on the coast. It's safe, and you're welcome to . . .
(*Pause.*) Good luck, Plato.

(ALCIBIADES *leaves, and walks into* LOMAX*'s office, as* BRETT.)

LOMAX: So you're leaving us. (*Beat.*) What on earth are you
wearing?

BRETT: Oh, it's for this, uh, protest.

(*Beat.*)

LOMAX: Are there *any* events at this school that don't involve
costumes?

BRETT: Not really.

LOMAX: What are you protesting?

BRETT: Oh, nothing. I mean: I'm not. It's just a . . . good way to
meet girls. (*Beat.*) *Anyway:* I just wanted to thank you in
person. For getting me the job.

LOMAX: You *earned* it. I just put you in contact with the right
people.

BRETT: Even *that*. Not everybody can make a phone call and get
some grad student an interview with Gabriel Wallace.

LOMAX: Oh, I've reopened our dialogue with his company. If I'm
going to make any changes around here, I'm going to need,
what is it? "Tech support."

BRETT: Hey! Nice!

LOMAX: Well, it's all still not-Greek to me. But I'm not too old to
learn.

BRETT: That's right. There's nothing to be afraid of. We just provide the tools. (*Beat.*) Hey, you find what you needed in those key-card records?

LOMAX: Yes. Thank you, Brett. You go have fun.

(*Fade out on* LOMAX*'s office.* STEVEN *enters* RIVNINE*'s office.*)

STEVEN: You're leaving? (*Pause.*) What are you doing up *here?*

RIVNINE: Incognito. Nobody ever moved in. I guess no one wanted the stairs.

STEVEN: Where are you going?

RIVNINE: I'm taking another job. A college on the Coast. So. You know. I guess I can't finish advising you on your *essay.*

STEVEN: Is this my fault? (*Pause.*) At your new job, they don't know—

RIVNINE: No. There are laws, since I'm leaving voluntarily. Nondisclosure. (*Pause.*) What do you want?

STEVEN: I don't know. I wanted to talk to you. To convince you to stay.

RIVNINE: What did you *think* would happen? If this isn't what you wanted, then why did you *do* this?

STEVEN: Do what?

RIVNINE: If you hadn't gone around *telling* people—

STEVEN: I didn't tell anyone. (*Pause.*) Wait, so you're *angry* at me?

RIVNINE: I don't know, Steven. You know what Aristotle said about anger, right?

STEVEN: No.

RIVNINE: Look it up.

(*Pause.*)

STEVENS: Don't go. Stay.

RIVNINE: I'm sorry. (*He reaches for* STEVEN's *face.*) Steven—

STEVEN (*slapping the hand away*): Don't walk away! *Argue*
with me!

RIVNINE: *What am I supposed to do?* I have a wife and child,
Steven. The Earth does not orbit *you.* I mean, maybe, when
you're *older,* you'll understand the, the *principles* . . . When
you ask: Which comes first—

STEVEN: You're not *principled,* you're *afraid!* God, you people are
unbelievable! "Humanities." "*Univer*sity." Terms so huge for
such a tiny little world. You have your *ideas,* sure, but God
forbid you base any *choices* on them in your actual *life!*

RIVNINE: Is *that* what you think? Steven: I could care less what
people—

STEVEN: *So why are you doing this?*

RIVNINE (*simply*): You're my student. I'd lose my job.

STEVEN: You're losing it anyway!

RIVNINE: No. I'd *lose* my *job.* I won't be allowed to teach.
Anywhere. Do you have the *slightest* idea what that would be
like for me?

STEVEN: So go. Go to your safe new job. Because, you know, I
don't *need* your help. It's done. My essay is done.

(*Beat.*)

RIVNINE: You revised a hundred pages already?

STEVEN: I, uh . . . I was lying about having a hundred pages. And
actually, it's not finished, I just have a new outline. Based on
helpful, uh, notes. (*Beat.*) I have it with me. Do you want to
see it?

(STEVEN *takes a copy of the outline out of his bag.*)

RIVNINE: Yes. I'd like that. (*He takes it.*) Thank you. (*Reading.*)
I like the new title. I'll try to read it before I go. (*Pause.*) Oh,
Steven. If only I were a professor of Eastern Civ. I could
promise to get it right *next* time. (*Pause.*) You really didn't tell
anyone.

STEVEN: No.

RIVNINE: Well then, Steven, um. Would you . . . (*He breathes.*)
Would you . . .

STEVEN: Would I what?

(*Beep.* RIVNINE *looks at his e-mail. He reads.*)

RIVNINE: Oh my God.

STEVEN: What is it?

RIVNINE: It's from my new school, they, uh . . . Some reporter
from our campus paper called them, she, uh, had some
questions about, um, "the circumstances under which . . ."
She's working on the story. They're rescinding the offer. Oh
God. (*Pause.*) Oh my God. Eve.

STEVEN (*approaching the desk*): Hey. Hey, can I . . . what can I . . .

RIVNINE: Could you go now? Please? Just go.

STEVEN: But . . . I . . . (*Pause.*) Sure.

(STEVEN *turns to go.*)

RIVNINE: Steven. (*He holds out the new outline.*) Promise me
you'll finish this.

STEVEN (*taking it*): I promise.

(STEVEN *exits.* RIVNINE *finds the apple* STEVEN *left behind earlier
and picks it up.*)

(*The* ORACLE *appears, off to the side, and oversees these last few scenes.*)

(*Fade up on* PLATO's *office at the Athenian University.* PLATO *is seated behind a desk;* POLITES *faces him.*)

PLATO: Do we have sufficient resources, Polites?

POLITES: Yes, Plato! (*With difficulty.*) In fact: no. We do not. We're short of ink, and also papyrus. And we require five more philosophers for the faculty.

PLATO: Send a runner to Sparta.

POLITES: I'll try. The last one collapsed and died the moment he arrived.

PLATO: Do your best, my friend.

POLITES: By all nine muses who dwell on Parnassus, by astronomical Urania and dancing Terpsichore, by the tragicomic embrace of Thalia and Melpomene, by the varied verse of Euterpe, Calliope, and Erato, by Polyhymnia's song, and most of all, by Clio, who governs history: I will.

PLATO: As we discussed, let's keep the divine invocations to a minimum while we're inside the school, all right?

POLITES: Yes, Plato.

(POLITES *leaves, passing a young man on his way in. This is* ARISTOTLE.)

PLATO: Can I help you?

ARISTOTLE: Am I in the right place? Is this the Academy for Philosophers?

PLATO: It is. Though I'm thinking of changing that. "Academy" isn't quite—

ARISTOTLE: Are you Plato?

ITAMAR MOSES

PLATO: Yes.

ARISTOTLE: I read your *Republic*. The allegory of the men in the
cave is truly brilliant.

PLATO: Yes, I'm . . . proud of that.

ARISTOTLE: The rest I hated. It made me quite angry. Though,
as I always say, anybody can be angry. But to be angry at the
right person, at the right time, the right amount, for the right
reason . . . That is much more difficult.

PLATO: Who are you?

ARISTOTLE: My name is Aristotle. I'm the greatest philosopher of
all time and I'm going to change the world.

ORACLE: From *The Apology of Socrates:* "There will be more
people to test you. And they will be more difficult, as they will
be younger."

(*Fade out on* PLATO's *office.*)

(MENOCCHIO *enters, on his way out of his trial. He collides with*
GALILEO, *and causes him to drop the charts and telescope he*
carries.)

MENOCCHIO: Oh no! I'm sorry! Let me help you.

GALILEO: No, please. It's delicate equipment.

MENOCCHIO: What is it?

GALILEO: It's a miraculous metal tube, which allows those who
look through it to see far-off objects in great detail.

MENOCCHIO: My God!

GALILEO: No sign of him yet. But! I have discovered miraculous
new stars, and moons around Jupiter. Would you like to look?

MENOCCHIO: I . . . No. I cannot.

GALILEO: Are you sure? Above us there are wonders. Mars, Venus,
Saturn: each circles the sun! And spins! As does our own dear

Earth! Indeed: the path of all celestial bodies seems to be both cyclical and linear!

MENOCCHIO: Is that so?

GALILEO: Oh yes. We all orbit together. Also, if you could somehow observe from high above, and envision it in three dimensions, or, or better yet, in *four*, you would see, furthermore, that it is all expanding ever outwards! As though, in the beginning, the universe mixed itself together in a small space, like . . . like some sort of . . . (*Giving up.*) Ah. Metaphor is the province of the artist.

MENOCCHIO (*desperately*): *Please leave me alone.* They cannot see me with you.

GALILEO: Ah. You're on your way out.

MENOCCHIO: And I must remain silent.

GALILEO: I did not ask you to speak. Yet. Only to look. At one time, we embraced ignorance in exchange for residence in Paradise. But there is no Garden for the peasants of Italy. Why, then, is this forbidden?

MENOCCHIO: Do you have a daughter, Signore?

GALILEO: In fact, I do.

MENOCCHIO: Then understand: I cannot risk heresy.

GALILEO: The word no longer has meaning. The millennium of *faith* is ended. This is the millennium of *doubt*.

(GALILEO *offers the telescope again.* MENOCCHIO *takes it.*)

MENOCCHIO: Oh!

GALILEO: What do you see?

MENOCCHIO: The moon!

GALILEO: And what is on her face?

MENOCCHIO: Mountains! Craters!

GALILEO: Yes!

MENOCCHIO: It looks almost like an enormous wedge of bright green cheese.

GALILEO: I believe you are the first man ever to make that observation.

(MENOCCHIO *returns the telescope*.)

MENOCCHIO: It's wonderful. But the lenses hurt my eyes.

GALILEO: I'll have to work on that.

(*Beat*.)

MENOCCHIO: You know, I have a theory of my own. Would you like to hear it?

GALILEO: I thought you were to remain silent.

MENOCCHIO: As I feared, one glimpse through your lens has made it impossible. What matter instruments of horrific torture, in the face of *this*?

GALILEO: I . . . Horrific instruments?

MENOCCHIO: So: In the beginning—

GALILEO: When you say torture . . . exactly what . . . sort of . . . ?

MENOCCHIO: Oh, all sorts! But, my friend, listen:

ORACLE: From *The Cheese and the Worms*: "And the Inquisitor asked Menocchio: 'Are will and power the same thing in God?' And Menocchio replied: 'They are distinct, as they are in us. A carpenter may wish to make a bench, but without tools, his will is useless. Without will, his tools are.' "

(*Fade out on* GALILEO *and* MENOCCHIO.)

(RIVNINE *goes to his window. His shadow is huge against the wall, as though cast by a raging fire. Distant crowds chant.* LOMAX *appears, facing the audience.*)

LOMAX: The chaos that night was inexcusable. And, while the committee was able to conclude its business and to leave the campus unmolested, the protests continued, and, with no one at all in control, matters escalated. No one, thankfully, was harmed by the skirmishes, or arson, or projectile dairy products, and funds can be diverted from nonessential programs to pay for the damage caused by the riots.

ORACLE: From *The Brecht–Bentley Correspondence* by Eric Bentley: "Dear Brecht: you are right that it is too easy, especially for historians like myself, to assume that our own age is merely an age of transition, while some others are ages of fulfillment. Every age must seem transitional to those in it."

LOMAX: We did, however, incur one loss that night which cannot be replaced. It was always our intention to keep the reasons for his departure private. But the personal revelations were, it seems, too much for him to bear.

(THE VOICE *enters* RIVNINE's *office, with his briefcase. During the following,* RIVNINE *ascends to the level of his windowsill, and steps out onto the ledge.*)

ORACLE: From *Conversations with Brecht*, by Walter Benjamin: "I dreamt I was climbing in a labyrinth of stairs, and arrived at a summit. A wide view opened before me, and I saw others standing on other peaks. One was seized by dizziness, and fell. The dizziness spread, and others were now falling into the depths below. When I too became dizzy I woke up."

LOMAX: But there is one piece of glad news. The Parker estate has agreed to name this gift in honor of Daniel Rivnine. After all, it is in support of the field to which he dedicated his life. And so the wonderful things we'll teach the next generation of scholars can be taught, appropriately, in his name. Unless there are any objections. (*Pause.*) Anyone?

(STEVEN *appears, facing the audience.*)

ORACLE: The last line of Benjamin's notebook reads: "A Brechtian maxim: Don't start from the good old things, but the bad new ones."

(*The* ORACLE *fades away.* THE VOICE *approaches* RIVNINE, *opening his briefcase. He hands over the pages.*)

VOICE: New final scene. Andrea, and a young boy. At the border. This time, you will have to be Andrea.
RIVNINE: I can play either part.

(THE VOICE *fades back into the darkness.* RIVNINE *looks at* STEVEN, *and reads.*)

RIVNINE: "Young man, I must cross the border in a moment. But first, I can lift you to the window, so you can know for sure. What do you see? *What do you see with your own eyes!*"

(RIVNINE *and* LOMAX *begin to fade away.* RIVNINE *drops the apple to* STEVEN *as he disappears.* STEVEN, *alone, catches the apple. A silence. Expectant.*)

STEVEN: My name is Steven. I'm a student of the humanities. My
   thesis is called: *Outrage*. Here goes:

(STEVEN *bites into the apple.*)

(*Blackout.*)

ACKNOWLEDGMENTS

The publication of this odd volume, which collects three full-length plays of mine that were not written consecutively and then arranges them in reverse chronological order,* gives me an opportunity to reach back with thanks all the way to the beginning of my professional career, and beyond.

Outrage began as my actual senior thesis in college under the guidance of my adviser John Rogers, who was the first and for that matter the only person to suggest that I turn an essay on Socrates, Menocchio, and Brecht, and the relationship between martyrdom and theater, into a play in its own right, for which terribly misguided suggestion I am forever in his debt. He and my other essay adviser, David Quint—who were thankfully nothing like either of the essay advisers depicted in the play—along with various other mentors and friends, in and out of school, introduced me to the many philosophers, martyrs, and madmen who populate the world of the play, especially Norma Thompson, Owen McLeod, Gordon Farrell, and Tess Taylor,† who led me to Walter Benjamin, the final piece of the puzzle. My father, Gavriel Moses, provided additional indispensable insight into the world of academia.

Michelle Tattenbaum directed the very first reading of *Outrage*. This reading was attended by Emily Morse, then working, in part,

*In other words, in order to shelve my work properly, please place this book upside down after first inserting into it a copy of the Faber and Faber edition of *Bach at Leipzig* at page 169 and of *The Four of Us* at page 79.

†These are examples of friends and mentors, not of martyrs and madmen.

as a literary scout in New York for Portland Center Stage in Oregon. Emily sent the play to Chris Coleman, the artistic director of Portland Center Stage, who went on to invite the play to his theater's development workshop, JAW/West, and then to produce and direct its world premiere. Chris, along with Rose Riordan and Mead Hunter and the rest of the staff, gave me my first true professional artistic home, before almost anybody else was even paying attention. (Almost anybody else: a non-Equity production of an earlier version of the play at the Bloomington Playwrights Project in Indiana, directed by Rick Fonte under the artistic direction of Richard Ford and with an extremely game cast, helped very much to shape it, as did a workshop with Moisés Kaufman and the Tectonic Theater Project.) It was then Doug Wright who, in addition to providing his own helpful notes on the play, first introduced it to Blanka Zizka and Jiri Zizka at the Wilma Theater in Philadelphia, where Jiri then directed the play's East Coast premiere, further refining it. Both the Portland and the Philadelphia productions of *Outrage* were blessed with delightful casts whose work significantly improved the script. Those casts were also very large, and so I will let the production credits pages stand as a testament to their collective contribution, which was truly massive.

Celebrity Row began when I read the unbelievable facts at its heart: the existence of ADX Florence, the truth about who was housed there, and in what proximity to one another. It is my recollection that I read this in a *Newsweek* article about the delay of Timothy McVeigh's execution, but I have since then been unable to track down the article in question. In any case, I am indebted to the author of that article, and to the many other authors whose books and articles provided me with useful background and, in some cases, foreground information about the prison and the men inside it, including, but probably not limited to, *American Terrorist* by Lou Michel and Dan Herbeck; *The New Jackals* by Simon Reeve;

Harvard and the Unabomber by Alston Chase; *My Bloody Life* and *Once a King, Always a King* by Reymundo Sanchez; and *Afghanistan—the Bear Trap* by Mohammad Yousaf and Mark Adkin. Ian Ellwood, who has been explaining math to me since the eighth grade, explained Kaczynski's work on boundary functions well enough for me to make use of it. Martin Epstein of the Graduate Dramatic Writing Program at NYU encouraged my early experiments with the play. The city of Wilmington, North Carolina, where I was living for a summer when I began the play in earnest, inevitably became a character in its own right, and I am grateful to those lovely environs and to all the people I met there. It was then Chris Coleman who, exhibiting the only truly meaningful kind of commitment there is, which is to say "ongoing," first developed and produced and directed the play at Portland Center Stage.* With lessons learned from that production, the play was then radically overhauled, with developmental support from Oskar Eustis at the Public Theater and from Jim Nicola and Linda Chapman at New York Theatre Workshop, and with the help of the many terrific actors and directors who contributed their time and energy to the several readings and workshops at both those theaters, and also from Jillian Cutler, who spent an hour on the phone with me explaining how someone might fail at suing the federal government on behalf of prison inmates and then mailed me a book that explained in English what she had been trying to tell me on the phone. PJ Paperelli then produced the play in its new form at the American Theater Company in Chicago, where David Cromer, an all-around theater animal, directed it with a ruthless precision and intelligence. And both the Portland and the Chicago productions of *Celebrity Row* benefited from the questions, insights, and inspiration of their stellar ensembles.

*The reasons for my having dedicated this book to Chris are now perhaps becoming somewhat clearer.

Back Back Back began when I watched the first round of congressional hearings about steroids in baseball, a subject that I knew immediately I wanted to explore, and also one I knew I didn't know enough about. My due diligence in this case included, but again was likely not limited to, *Game of Shadows* by Mark Fainaru-Wada and Lance Williams; *Juicing the Game* by Howard Bryant; and, of course, *Juiced* by Jose Canseco. I wrote the play's first draft as a commission for Lisa Timmel and Tim Sanford at Playwrights Horizons, and it was then developed by Andrew Polk at the Cape Cod Theatre Project in a terrific workshop directed by Pam Mackinnon and starring Darren Pettie, Joaquin Torres, and Justin Hagan ("Yippie-yie-no-wi-fi . . ."). Darko Tresnjak, Lou Spisto, and the Old Globe Theater in San Diego gave the play its first full production, under the direction of Davis McCallum, a director as talented as he is tall, and starring Brendan Griffin, Joaquin Perez-Campbell, and Nick Mills, who are also as talented as Davis McCallum is tall. Lynne Meadow, Daniel Sullivan, Barry Grove, Mandy Greenfield, Lisa McNulty, and everyone at the Manhattan Theater Club gave the play a home in New York, in a production directed by Daniel Aukin, whom I'm lucky to have as a collaborator and proud to call a friend, and in which Jeremy Davidson, James Martinez, and Michael Mosley are, even as I type out these acknowledgments, still giving eight electrifying performances a week. And the great Jerry Patch, who brings new meaning to the word "champion,"* somehow managed to be involved in shepherding the play through those West and East Coast premieres both.

Thanks are also due—finally, overall, and throughout—to Mark Subias, my agent, the best advocate a playwright could hope for, and to Denise Oswald, my editor on what I hope is not our final

---

*I don't have a witticism here but I feel like I should.

collaboration, for at long last giving me a book big enough to rest my head on and to hit people with.

It is both a cliché and the truth that writing something like this invariably involves accidentally leaving out some deserving names, or at least including them only implicitly via compression.* And so, if you flipped directly to these acknowledgments to see whether or not I had done this to you and discovered to your total lack of surprise that I had, comfort yourself with the knowledge that not only do I regret it already but that, even worse, I also probably left in several undeserving names, which I will likely regret even more, and for much longer.†

ITAMAR MOSES
Brooklyn, New York
December 2008

---

*As in "many terrific actors." Or: "Portland and Chicago." Or: "Jesse J. Perez."

†Oh, and thank you, Nick Frankfurt, for suggesting that I assuage my guilt by including the paragraph to which this footnote is appended. Good idea.